URBAN ZONING
AND
LAND-USE THEORY

Urban Zoning
and
Land-Use Theory

Sidney M. Willhelm

THE FREE PRESS OF GLENCOE

Library of Congress Catalog Card Number: 62–15355

To My Parents

PREFACE

Mere observation by a concerned layman confirms the necessity for zoning land utilization within American cities. Nonetheless, a concerned scholar cannot locate a sociological analysis that examines the impact of zoning upon the placement of social activities or that sets forth how zoning decisions are reached; a concerned city planner possesses a limited theoretical understanding of the social values attributed to the physical setting within our highly developed industrial society. I can only express a desire that the case study of the zoning process contained in this volume will furnish a useful approach for the fulfillment of these needs.

The theoretical perspective of this study is designed not only to encompass land-use change as affected by zoning but also to initiate at least the embryo of a general social action theory capable of dealing with the dynamics of social change taking place within various cultures. The theory offered here, however, remains to be fully developed and tested by application to empirical and cross-cultural data.

Through the years invested in the collection of data and devoted to the construction of a specific social action theory for presentation in this monograph, I had the assistance and encouragement of several individuals. To Gideon Sjoberg I owe considerable personal appreciation for allowing me the opportunity most graduate students seek: the chance to develop one's own perspective. The ecological approach of this study required the atmosphere of tolerance that Professor Sjoberg permitted as director of the dissertation upon which this work is based. I should also like to express my gratitude to Richard Colvard and Ronald J. Silvers for the careful reading of certain chapters; I wish to acknowledge the ever-present encouragement given by Herbert Blumer, Leonard Cain, Jr., Truett and Leone Marshall, and James Clark during the preparation of this work for publication. And, finally, I owe much to the many members of the Planning Commission, City Council, and personnel of the Planning Department of the city of Austin, Texas, who generously and courteously provided me with the information so essential to the writing and analysis of a zoning process.

Sidney M. Willhelm

CONTENTS

ix

URBAN ZONING
AND
LAND-USE THEORY

Chapter One

INTRODUCTION

With the rise of a metropolitan America we find intense attention being given by scholars, city planners, government officials, and laymen to the nature of urban land use. More than ever before in the history of our society, deliberate efforts are being made to direct the pattern of development within our cities. It is no exaggeration, barring complete destruction, to claim that the future of American cities rests upon those activities connected with land utilization; the well-being and destiny of life within our cities will depend very much upon the course of land use. Yet the planners and theorists who endeavor to design our cities of tomorrow proceed without an adequate understanding of the manner in which man relates himself to his environment. Social scientists, in particular, rely upon theoretical approaches that do not treat our cities as the product of man's own activities. Rather, contemporary land-use theorists inquire into metropolitan life as though urban existence were but a physical phenomenon. As a result, the dynamics of the city as a way of life have been overlooked by many writers interested in land-use development.

[Zoning activities offer an excellent opportunity to evaluate contemporary land-use theory. For not only is zoning apparently characteristic of almost all major urban communities within our society,[1] but it is also quite obvious that zoning as an effort to exert control over the distribution of land use is an integral part of urban master planning] Consequently, we shall undertake, as the purpose of this study, an analysis of a zoning process so as to achieve an understanding of just how land utilization occurs.

The zoning process within the city of Austin, Texas, has been selected to test the various hypotheses for constructing a theory of land use. The data taken from the zoning proceedings of this city will clearly support the view that existing sociological theories cannot account for land utilization and that an alternative approach will have to be developed in order to incorporate a wide range of land-use phenomena. The framework that is to be formulated in this study will be designated as a "cultural" approach.

This study is not to be organized, however, so that it describes all the facets of a zoning process as it occurred within one city; instead, only those data are used that relate to the hypotheses to be set forth below. The principle that one's theory and hypotheses cause a selective process in the collection and organization of empirical data is a well-accepted postulate within the social sciences.[2]

Hypotheses to Be Tested

Sociological examinations of land use, up to the present time, may be divided into two basic frames of reference: (1) a school of thought that calls for an analysis of certain forces that lie beyond man's active control—an orientation we shall describe, in Chapter 2, as "materialistic"; and (2) an opposing school of thought that relies upon human volition as its key variable—a perspective we shall represent, in

Chapter 3, as "voluntaristic." The cultural approach—the framework we seek to establish as our orientation—falls under the voluntaristic heading, since it is a theoretical justification for the necessity of volition for analyzing not only zoning activities but also all social phenomena concerned with man's utilization of space.

Speaking more precisely, the concern with land-use development is essentially within the domain of those sociologists called "ecologists." For the study of land use is—to be formally correct—an ecological inquiry. From this point onward, then, we shall interpret our interest in a zoning process and our evaluation of land-use theories as an ecological pursuit. Consequently, we shall assert the zoning process to be ecological in nature, our examination of land-use theories to be actually a critique of the contemporary ecological thoughts espoused by sociologists, and the cultural approach presented by this writer to be an alternative voluntaristic ecological orientation.[3]

Very briefly, the cultural approach, to be elaborated in Chapter 3, holds to the proposition that man locates over space through the social activities he performs; ecology is the study of those social activities that orient man to space. The cultural ecologist approaches his subject matter by applying a theory for analyzing ecological phenomena. The theoretical formulation presented for this study is a *specific* social action theory that calls for (1) the establishment of the goal within the social activity that orients man to space; and (2) an explanation of how the selection from certain alternatives that constitute the means for attaining a goal takes place. Two hypotheses we are to test in light of the empirical zoning data collected by the writer state this particular social action orientation to ecology:

HYPOTHESIS I: There is an effort to locate social activities over space for the attainment of a given goal through the selection, in accordance with certain social conditions, of a norm from the alternative norms that constitute the means.

HYPOTHESIS II: Ecological phenomena must be examined by discovering and analyzing the interpretative significance given to

3

the goal, means, social conditions, and cognitive data by actors resorting to value systems.[4]

The third hypothesis places within our social action framework the theoretical writings of those ecologists espousing a materialistic orientation:

HYPOTHESIS III: The theoretical perspective of ecological materialism is a *value system* that prevails in the American culture and, therefore, cannot be considered "value-free."

The fourth and final hypothesis argues that competition is a social process affecting ecological phenomena rather than a subsocial force as claimed by materialistic ecologists:

HYPOTHESIS IV: The competition that affects ecological phenomena is a social process rather than a subsocial force.

The factual data to be used for evaluating each of these hypotheses were collected by this writer from personal observations and official records of zoning activities as performed by various decision-making bodies in the city of Austin, Texas. Before explaining the procedure the writer followed to gather the empirical zoning data, however, a brief orientation of Austin as a metropolitan community must be presented.

The Community Setting

Census statistics reveal that Austin experienced a continuous population growth of 11,000 in 1880 to 22,000 in 1900, and from 35,000 in 1920 to 89,000 in 1940; the population for 1960 is 186,-000. In 1959 Austin had a labor force of about 73,000 persons. As the location for the state capital of Texas, 20 per cent of the employed were engaged in the state government; 10 per cent were federal or city employees. The absence of a population engaged in industry is also characteristic of the economy of this metropolitan community; there is only a handful of business pursuits in such fields as chemicals, agriculture, and mining. Austin, in brief, is an urban community with a service labor market as revealed by the concentration of state offices and medical and professional endeavors as well as the presence of the University of Texas with an enrollment of approximately 20,000 students.

Through the years Austin's city limits consistently expanded to the present area of about 55.3 square miles. The Colorado River, once the focal point for community affairs as well as the economic core of the city, meanders through the southern part of the city. Its waters no longer flood the immediate area since the construction of federal and city dams.

Austin has a city-manager form of government wherein the City Council, composed of five members elected from the community at large every two years, appoints a city manager to direct and supervise governmental responsibilities. The city manager, however, is involved in the zoning process only indirectly—by appointing the planning director charged with the affairs of the city's Planning Department. On the other hand, the City Council is the ultimate decision-making body with regard to zoning applications.

The Formal Organization of Zoning

Austin's Zoning Ordinance requires a zoning procedure to process requests for changes of zoning classifications upon land so as to expand or reduce a range in land usages. The initial agency designated for the purpose is an advisory group of citizens called the City Planning Commission. The nine persons composing this body are Austin residents appointed by the City Council. Each person serves for one year under his first appointment; each successive appointment extends for two years. There are no formal restrictions upon the number of reappointments.

Four alternative methods for initiating applications for zoning changes are prescribed by the Zoning Ordinance: (1) an individual property owner or his representative may apply for a zoning change; (2) a zoning change may be recommended by the Planning Commission; (3) the planning director may submit a request for a zoning change; or (4) a person may submit a petition signed by 50 per cent of the property owners within 200 feet of the property proposed for rezoning. Formal applications for rezoning property are made to the Planning Department to provide such factual information as ownership, area, present and proposed uses, and present and proposed zoning classifications. Upon receipt of a change-in-zoning application, the Planning Department must send notices of the proposed change to all property owners within a 300-foot radius of the property in question.

Three open hearings are conducted to consider all applications. The first is held by a subcommittee of the Planning Commission called the Zoning Committee—a group of five composed of members from the Planning Commission. The committee holds open and public meetings for the opportunity of hearing arguments for and against requests to rezone property so that recommendations may be forwarded to the Planning Commission for action. Prior to each session most members, individually or collectively with the planning director, inspect the land in question.

A Zoning Committee hearing begins with the planning director presenting factual data referring to: existing and requested zoning classifications for the property in question; topography of the area under consideration; proposed and existing land uses for the property covered by the application; land uses in the general vicinity; right-of-way widths of surrounding streets; "car" counts on bordering streets; size of the area being considered for rezoning; past zoning history of the land in question; and city needs in the way of utilities, parks, streets, and so on. Near the end of the research period for this study, the planning director began to offer departmental recommendations as part of his official report.

6

Following the planning director's presentation, members of the Zoning Committee have the opportunity to question the director on matters related to his presentation of facts. The applicant (or his representative) and any person favoring the request then present arguments explaining the reasons for seeking a zoning change and, sometimes, describing the specific nature of the proposed use. Afterward, the opposition, if there is such, expresses cause for not granting the proposed zoning change. After all persons have been heard who oppose the request, the applicant and his supporters return for a rebuttal; no further argument is heard from the opposition except as impromptu outbursts in the formal procedure. The Zoning Committee votes to "close the hearing" in order to bring the public arguments on a particular case to an end.

It should also be mentioned that the Zoning Committee—as well as the Planning Commission—receives legal advice throughout its sessions from a representative of the city attorney's office. In addition, a secretary attends each meeting for the purpose of taking minutes; only occasionally will she comment upon applications.

After all evidence has been heard on each application to be acted upon, the Zoning Committee enters into a public decision-making period during which every case is discussed. Further questions may be directed to either the planning director or the legal adviser, or, occasionally, the applicant or persons in opposition. Members also rely upon maps and data sheets related to each application that all commissioners receive prior to the formal meetings. Requests are acted upon one at a time by a vote of the committee.

When a motion is offered to deny or grant a recommendation, the committee member making the motion is expected to state reasons for doing so. A second to the motion follows. Any recommendation by the committee to the full Planning Commission requires a majority vote; a tie vote is defined as "No recommendation." In addition, a motion can be passed stating that the Zoning Committee makes no recommendation concerning an application or recommends that an applicant's request to withdraw an application be accepted by the Planning Commission. The Zoning Committee undertakes no duties other than to submit recommendations upon applications and to recommend zoning changes it deems necessary.

A second hearing on zoning applications is conducted in a formal proceeding before the Planning Commission. However, this body permits the admittance of additional evidence from either the proponents or the opponents only by a vote of the entire commission. While its sessions are open to the public, the introduction of further evidence from an audience seldom takes place. It should be noted that the Planning Commission's duties extend beyond strictly zoning action: the Planning Commission acts upon subdivision applications; passes upon various types of proposals such as the city's Capital Improvement Program; recommends changes in the Zoning Ordinance; and fulfills several other obligations.

With respect to zoning applications, the Planning Commission acts upon the recommendations submitted by its Zoning Committee. After the chairman of the Zoning Committee reads the recommendation of the Zoning Committee, the motion to accept is made and usually seconded. A general discussion may follow among Planning Commission members, the planning director, the legal adviser, and, with the commission's permission, persons from the audience. The planning director again extends a formal recommendation. A majority vote by members in attendance is required for recommendations to approve or deny zoning changes. In a tie vote, the request is submitted as a denial to the City Council. In addition, motions can be made to postpone action or to issue a "No recommendation" to the City Council. No zoning action by the Planning Commission is final; the application must be acted upon by the City Council—with one exception. Under one type of zoning application—to be explained more fully in another chapter—known as the "Special Permit," the decision of the Planning Commission is final except upon appeal before the City Council by the applicant or an opponent. It is uncertain as of this time whether the planning director may legally appeal the

8

action taken by the Planning Commission on Special Permits before the City Council.

Three weeks after action by the Planning Commission, the zoning applications are submitted to the City Council. Prior to the eleven o'clock meeting held on Thursday mornings, the city clerk mails notices of the public hearing to property owners within 300 feet of the property in question. The city government must also publish "in a daily newspaper of general circulation," fifteen days before the hearing by the City Council, a listing of property for which zoning applications have been made.

The third and final formal open hearing takes place before the City Council where arguments for and against zoning applications are expressed. Several days before a session, each member of the City Council receives minutes of the Planning Commission meeting, a map of the property covered by the request and of the immediate area, and a factual data sheet. Usually the mayor calls for the applicant to present his case, and the opposition's contentions follow. The planning director contributes very little during the hearing; he seldom states his recommendations unless specifically asked to do so by a member of the City Council. The city attorney, very active in many zoning hearings, offers legal counsel. If there is no opposition, the City Council usually votes upon a motion to grant, deny, or withdraw an application. When there is opposition, the City Council usually postpones final disposition of a case for the purpose of making a personal inspection of the property, since, unlike the Planning Commission, it seldom conducts a survey prior to the hearing. Of course, action can be postponed indefinitely for a variety of reasons.

Formal approval of a zoning change requires that the City Council instruct the city attorney to "draw up" a change in the Zoning Ordinance covering the land area in question. Alteration of the Zoning Ordinance involves only a reclassification of the area involved as shown on the "Use District Map" contained within the Zoning Ordinance. Three public readings of an amendment to the Zoning Ordinance make the zoning change official.

Collection of the Data

The empirical data employed in this study are drawn from various sources. Most of the information was collected by the writer through attendance at the regular monthly meetings held by Austin's City Planning Commission and this commission's own Zoning Committee over a four-and-one-half-year period: January, March, April, November, and December, 1956; February–April, 1957; March–May and August–December, 1958; January–May, 1960. Extensive notes were also gathered through attendance, from September, 1958, to June, 1960, at the weekly session of Austin's City Council.

Other information was obtained through conducting extended interviews with: (1) thirteen of the sixteen individuals serving on the Planning Commission between the years 1956 to 1960; (2) six of the seven persons serving on the City Council for the two terms 1957 through 1961; (3) administrative officials such as the Director of City Planning; and (4) persons who appeared at the zoning hearings to voice either approval of or objection to a zoning change. Finally, data were obtained from official files, publications, and legal documents of various city government departments and through personal inspection of the property involved in certain zoning applications.

During the time span devoted to data collection, this writer established strong rapport with some of the decision-makers composing the Planning Commission and City Council. The full cooperation given by most decision-makers enabled this researcher to become a quasi-participant, and exposed him to many facets of the zoning process. Having won the confidence and assurance of the decision-makers, the researcher sought to maximize his knowledge of the zoning process as it took place in the city of Austin, Texas. Frequent, informal conversations, in addition to the several formal interviews, were held by the writer with virtually all persons serving on the Planning Commission during the years 1956–1960; fewer contacts, though in some instances with considerable depth, were made with council members.

This research relationship over a relatively long period made it

10

possible for the writer to formulate and test various hypotheses in the field. However, as the field work continued, some hypotheses were rejected in the light of new or contradictory data. The hypotheses finally selected for testing in this study, then, are the result of analysis during the period of observation. But not content to seek validation only by examining the formal aspects of the zoning process, the researcher sought also to collect data for testing these hypotheses through informal and formal questioning of decision-makers and other individuals contributing to the zoning process; the researcher constantly endeavored to elicit data contrary to his viewpoints and to reformulate the hypotheses in terms of these materials.

In treating the stated hypotheses, certain meanings have been assigned to particular terms. The term "decision-maker" refers to a member of the Zoning Committee, Planning Commission, or City Council; the proper, formal titles will be used to refer to city personnel; and the term "participant" refers to any person (other than decision-makers and city personnel) appearing at the public sessions of the Zoning Committee, Planning Commission, and/or City Council. Thus, an individual is to be identified hereafter only as he belongs to one of these three categories: decision-maker, city personnel, or participant. In addition, persons of the same category who engage in conversation within an illustration will be identified by numbers— such as "Commission Member 1." The number is not constant for any one person throughout this investigation; the numbering is consistent only within any one illustration. Thus, where "Commission Member 1" is quoted several times within a particular example, this refers to a single individual. However, "Commission Member 1" does not refer to the same person for all illustrations.

The primary objective of this study, then, is to present not only an analysis of what appear to be dominant features of a zoning process but also a critique of contemporary ecological theory, and, in light of this critical evaluation, to offer the cultural approach as a more adequate framework for examining zoning, as well as other social phenomena, from an ecological perspective. The chapters that follow have been designed to forward an investigation of zoning data for testing the four hypotheses set forth in this introductory chapter. We shall begin our inquiry, in Chapter Two, with a survey of the traditional and contemporary ecological thought that stresses physical and biological factors in analyzing ecological phenomena. Those ecological orientations emphasizing the importance of volition (that is, ideational) concepts in examining ecological data, along with the theoretical position assumed by this writer, are presented in Chapter Three. In Chapters Four, Five, and Six the theoretical approach of this study is tested; Chapter Seven places materialistic ecological theory within the cultural framework; a conclusion is offered in Chapter Eight.

Chapter Two

MATERIALISTIC APPROACHES TO ECOLOGY

Certain ecologists seek explanation for ecological developments in "nonsocial" conditions. They reason that specific forces determine ecological phenomena apart from man's efforts to intervene through the imposition of social choice. In arguing their case, materialists implicitly or specifically deny the relevance of social values and/or culture; they rely instead upon biotic or physical premises. We shall assign the label "traditional materialism" to the ecological viewpoint espousing biotic determinism, and give the label "neoclassical materialism" to those materialists advocating physical determinism in ecological thought.[1]

Traditional Materialism

This ecological approach stems from the founders of ecology, located for the most part at the University of Chicago. Foremost

13

among the first to contribute, as sociologists, to the development of human ecology were Robert E. Park, Ernest W. Burgess, and Roderick D. McKenzie. Later, other sociologists modified and expanded the viewpoint of these founders to establish the framework of biotic determinism.

Traditional materialists interpret ecology as the investigation of the impersonal competition that determines man's symbiotic adaptation to space. We find Park defining ecology as a science that seeks to explain the competitive forces that trend to bring "an orderly and typical grouping" of human populations and institutions into "symbiotic rather than societal" relationships.[2] McKenzie states that ecologists examine "the relations of man to man" in order to determine the "nexus of sustenance" and spatial location. Competition, according to McKenzie, accounts for the "function of order" as human beings struggle for positions in a "communal organism."[3] C. A. Dawson perceives ecology as the distribution of human beings and their institutions over space and time.[4] He views ecology as a study that seeks to account for the "functional" integration between positions in competition and symbiotic relations. J. W. Bews interprets ecology as the interaction between man and environment wherein man influences the environment, and in turn is affected by the environment.[5] Although Bews fails to elaborate upon what he refers to as "psychological" factors, that is, man's mental processes, he nonetheless contends that man's adaptation to space includes the "psychological element." And, finally, James A. Quinn thinks of ecology as "the study of relations between man and environment."[6]

These materialists perceive a set of biotic conditions underlying and supposedly prescribing the content and form of man's social activities. They maintain that there is an ecological order resulting from biotic processes that affects man's cultural life: "ecological or economic forces are naturally basic to the play of cultural forces."[7] As Dawson explains:

> Ecological position is of sociological importance because of its bearing on social contacts and social interaction. The ecological pattern of

14

distribution marks out physical distances between units and determines the direction of social contacts. *It is the framework on which the social order is woven.*[8]

According to traditional materialism, man, in his struggle for existence, competes with man while adapting to space:

> . . . spatial relationships of human beings are the products of competition and selection. . . . Human institutions and human nature itself become accommodated to certain spatial relationships of human beings.[9]

However, it is possible for several persons to cooperate so as to enhance their chances for survival in a particular environment:

> . . . manifestations of a living, changing, but persistent order among competing organisms—organisms embodying "conflicting yet correlated interests"—seem to be the basis for the conception of a social order transcending the individual species, and of a society based on a biotic rather than a cultural basis. . . .[10]

Subsequently, a structure develops that traditional materialists term the "community." The community structure is composed of a human population territorially organized and bound "in the soil it occupies" as individual units engage in symbiotic activities in accordance with the so-called "process of competitive cooperation."[11]

A specific concern of traditional materialists centers upon the competitive results they refer to as "dominance." Traditionalists insist that the competitive economic strength—dominance—of each endeavor prescribes the location of man and his activities. Land values, in particular, reflect this process, since "the area of dominance in any community is usually the area of highest land values."[12] As a result, the central core of a city is the business district that sets the pattern for development throughout the community. Activities unable to compete economically with more profitable pursuits must either relocate or desist their operations.[13]

As an increase in population is experienced, there is a heightening of competitive cooperation which initiates changes in the community structure to "bring about a new, more minute and, at the same time, territorially extensive division of labor."[14] As a result:

15

Under the influence of an intensified competition, and the increased activity which competition involves, every individual and every species, each for itself, tends to discover the particular niche in the physical and living environment where it can survive and flourish with the greatest possible expansiveness consistent with its necessary dependence upon its neighbors.

It is this way that a territorial organization and a biological division of labor, within the communal habitat, is established and maintained.[15]

Owing to competitive cooperation, man and his activities locate in functional relationship so as to maximize efficiency over a territorial expanse. In this adaptive effort toward efficiency, man utilizes technology. His inventions, particularly those related to transportation, further the realization of the efficiency demanded by the biotic competitive order. There is, therefore, instability in man's adjustment to space. The conditions bringing about such change are: (1) shifts in forms and routes of transportation facilities; (2) "obsolescence"; (3) erection of dominant structures such as office buildings; (4) new industries; (5) changes in a prevailing system of economic distribution; and (6) types of real-estate promotion.[16] All these factors operate so as to place "every individual and every race into the particular niche where it will meet the least competition and contribute most to the life of the community."[17]

Traditional materialists do not entirely deny the relevance of culture in their presentations. For instance, Park claims that "competition and the freedom of the individual is [sic] limited on every level above the biotic by custom and consensus"[18] and "the cultural superstructure imposes itself as an instrument of direction and control upon the biotic substructure."[19] Still, Park definitely qualifies his position with respect to culture by stating:

The incidence of this more or less arbitrary control which custom and consensus [that is, culture] imposes upon the natural social order complicates the social process *but does not fundamentally alter it*—or, if it does, the effects of biotic competition *will still be manifest* in the succeeding social order and the subsequent course of events.[20]

McKenzie reaffirms Park in holding that while human ecology differs from plant ecology *only* because of man's ability to exert greater

16

control over and selection of his habitat, nonetheless "the total effect of individual action is neither designed nor anticipated."[21] And, finally, A. B. Hollingshead, a person who first spoke as a materialist only to shift later to the voluntarist position, once argued:

> The competitive process operating through the human mechanism of economic organization acts as an impersonal agency which distributes individuals *territorially* into the different parts of the community and *socially* into the several classes such as the elite, the upper class. . . .[22]

Thus, although traditional ecological materialists admit the existence of cultural factors in their writings, they eventually perceive man's spatial distribution as an *inevitable* consequence *preordained* by the biotic, competitive cooperation which they claim underlies the social order. Being impersonal, ecological processes take place regardless of man's desires to control them through the development of a social organization. Traditional materialists insist that ecological phenomena evolve as a "natural" course unmolested by human endeavor. As Robert Faris maintains:

> The coherence of the ecological order is based on relations of a symbiotic character, similar to the symbiosis that produces the elaborate and interdependent communities of animals and plants, in that it arises *automatically and unintentionally* out of the struggle for survival. The component elements cooperate without knowing it, or at least without having to know it.[23]

So it is that, regardless of the differences in opinion found among these writers, each holds to biotic determinism in offering ecological explanations. All of them share the notion that the ecologist studies the biotic, subsocial, competitive processes that prescribe man's location within an environment, while rejecting the significance of social values and/or culture for ecological theory.

Neoclassical Materialism

The popularity of biotic materialism in ecological theory appears to have faded for the present. This is not to say, however, that imper-

17

sonal notions no longer persist. For there are still efforts, in the tradition of Park, Burgess, and McKenzie, to separate ecology from sociological research.[24] Moreover, a very vocal group of ecologists is presently endeavoring to define a subject matter peculiar to ecology within an impersonal materialistic framework. The contemporary ecologists who write from a physical rather than from a biotic perspective view ecology simply as the study of impersonal functional relationships they contend exist between the social activities connected with man's sustenance efforts within a physical habitat. The continuation of impersonality notions in ecological theory by such writers as Amos Hawley, Otis Duncan, Leo Schnore, Jack Gibbs, and Walter Martin, among others, justifies the choice of the label "neoclassical materialists" to refer to the group of recent ecologists holding to a materialistic viewpoint.

Amos Hawley, the most outspoken neoclassical materialist, defines ecology as the study of man's adaptation to physical space through the "morphology of collective life" that he conceptualizes as the "community."[25] Otis Duncan and Leo Schnore interpret ecology as a field of investigation encompassing the interrelationships prevailing among environment, technology, population, and social organization as these factors bear directly upon the "morphology of collective life."[26] Jack Gibbs and Walter Martin continue in the course set by Duncan and Schnore in arguing that ecologists should investigate only sustenance activities in a cultural setting "independently of cultural values and the individual motives of men."[27]

There is the general tendency among neoclassical materialists, as seen from their definitions of ecology, to retreat from the traditional ecological studies of spatial distributions of human populations. Instead, there is the inclination to deal with ecology as a field concerned primarily with sustenance and/or social organization.[28] Thus, we find Duncan calling for the examination of what he labels the "ecological complex." This complex consists of population, social organization, environment, and technology. Ecology, according to Duncan, seeks to investigate "the ways in which populations are or become organized to

18

cope with problems afforded by their environment"[29] through an analysis of population composition, organization, technological developments, and the nature of the physical habitat. He writes:

> An ecological account of social change is attempted by referring to such instigating factors as environmental change (whether caused by man or by other agencies), changes in size and composition of population, introduction of new techniques, and shifts in the spatial disposition of organization of competing populations. The interdependence of factors in the adaptation of a population implies that change in any of them will set up ramifying changes in the other.[30]

Very closely associated with the position advanced by Duncan— as well as with the viewpoint voiced by Duncan and Schnore[31]—is the stance assumed by Gibbs and Martin.[32] The latter pair of writers insists that ecology is concerned only with the investigation of sustenance activity, not with the spatial aspects of social activity. Gibbs and Martin claim:

> That man survives through collective organization is fundamental to both sociology and human ecology. It is obvious, however, that not all populations organize themselves for the exploitation of natural resources in exactly the same manner. To the contrary, a wide variety of organizational forms are to be observed. It is in this variability in the characteristics of sustenance organization among populations that human ecology finds its fundamental problem. This subject matter—the nature of the sustenance organization of human populations—is largely ignored by contemporary ecology.[33]

According to Gibbs and Martin, the ecologist seeks explanations for sustenance activities by examining "purely" demographic characteristics of human populations, geographical characteristics, "purely" technological facets of man's culture, and forms of sustenance organization. These four factors, assert Gibbs and Martin, integrate so as to accord with the impersonal "mechanism" of selective survival that governs all organic matter regardless of cultural context. Because the mechanism of selective survival "operates independently of cultural values and the individual motives of men," all forms of sustenance activity must comply with the demands of the four "external" fac-

19

tors.[34] The physical determinism of their viewpoint is distinctly revealed in Gibbs and Martin's conclusions to a study in which they apply their particular ecological approach:

> It has been shown that the conception of cities as a particular type of organization for sustenance leads to a theory of the dispersion of objects of consumption *as a possible explanation* of differences between countries in the extent of urbanization and metropolitanization. . . . [A] measure was used to test two propositions derived from the theory: (1) the degree of urbanization of a country varies directly with the extent of the dispersion of its objects of consumption; (2) the magnitude of the relationship by countries between a measure of the dispersion of objects of consumption and the proportion of the population living in cities increases directly with the size of the cities.[35]

Amos Hawley's neoclassical view portrays ecology as a study of the functional relationships among individuals resulting from man's attempts to adapt to space with a minimum of effort. According to Hawley, "all human behavior manifests a tendency toward economy of effort through the dovetailing of activities and the development of division of labor."[36] As a result, Hawley sees ecology as the study of how the "structural features of functional organization" change with shifts in "external conditions."[37] Population and the physical environment constitute the "external conditions" that generate change:

> The inevitable crowding of organisms upon limited resources produces a complex interaction of organism with organism and of organism with environment in the course of which individuals adjust to one another *in ways conducive to a more effective utilization* of the habitat. In consequence there arises among the organisms occupying a given habitat an equilibrium of relationships which approximates a closed system; that is, the aggregate assumes the characteristics of an organic unit as each type of life accommodates its behavior to that of every other. The community, as the ecologist is wont to call the pattern of symbiotic and commensalistic relations that develops in a population, is in the nature of a collective response to the habitat; it constitutes the adjustment of organism to environment.[38]

Functional relationships between organisms develop as an "inevitable" consequence, therefore, in response to (1) population growth and (2) the nature of space. The first is the "principal controlling factor"

20

determining functional differences—for increase in size brings differentiation within a population. The second affects population distribution because "the distribution of interrelated activities over the area comprised in the community is controlled *in the main* by the friction of space and the character of competition, the effects of the latter expressing themselves in rental charges for land."[39] Human activities are distributed over space, then, on the basis of their competitive strength:

Activities, or rather the units in which they are embodied, least able to contend against the friction of space, by virtue of their specialization and hence need for maximum accessibility and also their adaptability to intensive land use, seek central location.[40]

Thus, for Hawley, ecologists investigate the competitive order which is unrestrained by social factors. The competitive process is generated by the physical properties of: (1) an increased population, which results in a shortage of favorable locations for both human collectivities and social activities, and (2) the friction inherent in space, which in turn hinders maximization of the conjoining social activities that are essentially "functionally" interdependent.

And, finally, Ernest Fisher and Robert Fisher, who hold to competition as the determinant of land-use change, also view the causes for land-use development as completely free from human values. They contend that shifts take place as the result of: "(1) changes in the size and [demographic] composition of the urban population; (2) changes in the level and distribution of income; (3) changes in technology; and (4) consequent changes in the social and economic organization of urban communities."[41]

This survey of the writings of neoclassical materialists reveals the assumption that ecological phenomena must be explained by impersonal physical determinants. The neoclassical materialist argues, for the most part, that man's sustenance activities and/or social organizations as affected by certain conditioning forces independent of both culture and social values form the subject matter for ecology. Neoclassical materialists perceive social values and culture as psychological, internal states:

> . . . ecology focuses attention on the functional aspect of organization rather than on the psychological mechanism of learning stressed by culturological interpretations of organization as an aspect of the social heritage. Functionally, human social organization bears many significant analogies to organization at all levels of life . . . irrespective of the phychological mechanisms that may be involved in organized activity.[42]

The neoclassical materialists' desire to seek ecological analysis within physical conditions justifies the elimination of culture and values in this fashion. Even though Hawley states in the preface to his main work that ecological theory "leads to the investigation of a fundamentally yet long neglected sociological problem,"[43] he nonetheless denies the relevancy of values for ecology—in striking contrast to the significance given to values in most sociological theory.

Limitations

We find both traditional and neoclassical materialists relying upon nonsocial conditions in offering ecological theories. Man—regardless of his culture and desires—and his social activities—irrespective of volition—must comply with impersonal biological and/or physical conditions to be ecologically relevant from a materialistic perspective. A methodological evaluation of the arguments, however, reveals fundamental errors that arise from the slavish attention ecological materialists give to false analytical premises.

First, neoclassical materialists resort to tautological reasoning in conforming to their notion that "ecology lays claim to the status of a scientific discipline on the basis of its formulation of a problem and the heuristic principles employed in attacking that problem."[44] They initiate this error when they "lay claim" to the "ecological complex" in formulating "a problem" for investigation. According to neoclassical materialists, ecologists should investigate "the precise technological, demographic, and environmental conditions under which various urban forms of organization may be expected to appear."[45] They specifically recognize the cogency of values and culture with the factors they consider ecologically significant, but then choose to reject values and culture as ecologically valid variables. We find Hawley writing:

Sustenance activities and relationships [as the subject matter for ecology] are *inextricably interwoven* with sentiments, value systems, and other ideational constructs. Human ecology is restricted in scope, then, not by any real or assumed qualitive differences in behavior but simply by the manner in which its problem is stated.[46]

Gibbs and Martin exclaim:

Sustenance organization *is* social and *is* cultural; but this does not mean that it is concerned with values, attitudes, or other variables of a psychological nature.[47]

Hawley, Duncan, Schnore, Gibbs, Martin, among others, insist, then, that they seek to investigate only the interrelationships between the variables constituting the ecological complex with particular emphasis upon sustenance and/or social organization. To quote from Duncan once again:

For the ecologist, the significant assumptions about organization are that it arises from sustenance-producing activities, is a property of the population aggregate, is indispensable to the maintenance of collective life, and must be adapted to the conditions confronting a population—including the character of the environment, the size and composition of the population itself, and the repertory of techniques at its command.[48]

As a result of such analytical exertions, the neoclassical approach becomes tautological: after deducing data relevant only to the "ecological complex" as "analytically distinguishable elements,"[49] neoclassical materialists then seek to explain their ecological data by the identical "ecological complex." In brief, the neoclassical materialist relies upon the ecological complex to explain the ecological complex. Sustenance activities are defined as taking place in terms of social organization by a population adapting to the dictates of environment through technological devices: such is both the subject matter and the explanation for neoclassical materialists.

The second methodological error the neoclassical materialists commit also centers upon the ecological complex. For in this "complex" they advocate, the neoclassical ecologists indiscriminately blend the nonmaterial elements of social organization with the material components of technology,[50] geography, and population. From these parts constituting the ecological complex, the materialists set about positing whole systems of predetermined consequences to establish their "heuristic principles" in order to answer such far-reaching and "persistent" questions as: "How is human social life possible? What is the nature of the bond that holds men together?"[51] In their efforts, neoclassical materialists claim to be "interested in [only] the pattern of observable *physical* activity"[52] as a human population goes about adapting its sustenance organization within an environment by the application of technology.

But the patterns materialists tend to label "sustenance activities" or "social organizations" as a focal point of ecological concern are only analytical abstractions. Social organization—an element of the ecological complex—cannot exist as a "physical activity"; it refers only to a mental construct conceptualized by an observer. Yet, neoclassical materialists treat both the nonmaterial concept of social organization and the material items of population, environment, and technology, as noted in the above quotes, as both the cause and result of one another. In essence, materialists integrate a mental construct with material objects to form their dynamic "complex." Sorokin denies the feasibility of this type of orientation, and claims:

. . . these theories take the components of meanings and of vehicles from the *same system* and confront the factor of vehicles with the ideological meanings. However, they treat the vehicles, not as components of the same system, but as independent entities, existing by themselves. Having cut out the heart or a leg of an organism and assumed that it exists by itself as an independent variable, they dogmatically announce that this material vehicle definitely determines the rest of the system in its structure and its dynamic functions. Thus they derive the conclusion that the material variable . . . determines the immaterial variable. . . . In line with this logic, one could easily prove that any part of an organism (lungs,

24

gland, heart, or what not) determines, as an independent variable, the organism as a whole, including its functions and changes.[53]

And as Stuart Chase exclaims:

The scientific method demands that when facts are compared, they must be of the same order. Do not add cabbages to electrons and expect to get a total which means anything.[54]

Neoclassical materialists are guilty, then, of taking elements that they themselves admit, as evidenced in the quotations above, are inseparable from the cultural system and then treating such facts as something physically external to the entire cultural system. Their factors composing the ecological complex, as "objective" conditions, remain free from cultural restraints even though they are elements of a culture. Sorokin rejects this line of reasoning:

. . . a scientist cannot assume that black is white and that what is an inseparable and dependent part is an "independent" factor.[55]

In seeking to "develop a description of the morphology or form of collective life under varying external conditions,"[56] there are no sound methodological grounds for materialists to claim that "the ecologist seems to be contributing to the maintenance of a traditional *sociological interest* in explaining forms of organization and changes therein."[57] There can be no sociological significance in placing causal analyses for social phenomena within physical objects. As Sorokin notes on this point:

If investigators take the vehicles *externalistically*, without consideration of their meanings and human agents, the results are bound, in most cases, to be either insignificant or utterly absurd. If the vehicles are taken as purely physicochemical or biological phenomena, "externally and objectively" given, without consideration of their meanings, the *sociological study* of their relationships as physical objects is unnecessary, because the physicochemical and biological sciences furnish all that can be known of their relationships as physicochemical and biological variables.[58]

A third shortcoming contained in this position we are evaluating stems from the firm insistence on the part of neoclassical materialists that social values are psychological and therefore must be excluded

25

from an ecological inquiry. The justification for this neoclassical stance rests upon the contention that ecologists must assume a collective perspective rather than an individualistic framework supposedly intrinsic to the social value concept. Complete trust in external determinants, however, precludes the possibility of choice. Yet, there are many instances of choice situations within the very subjects presented by neoclassical materialists.

Otis Duncan, for example, deals with the smog situation in Los Angeles as though a population *automatically* reflects the changing physical setting through a social organization's implementation of technological devices in a *unidirectional* fashion, when in fact serious alternative responses have been and are now being discussed by governmental agencies as well as other social organizations.[59] Disputes involving *populations* with regard to establishing the form and/or content of *social organization* within Los Angeles for *technological* control of the *environmental* smog are taking place. But Duncan presents his analysis as though a social organization merely mirrors environmental alteration in a *rigor mortis* fashion.

Leo Schnore continually acknowledges the possibility of choice in dealing with social problems of underdeveloped countries from an ecological perspective—for example, the on-and-off-again birth-control policy in Communist China, the alternatives of capitalism and Marxism for industrialization, the possibility of choosing the "correct" course of action in contradistinction to "failure."[60] He goes so far as to claim: "The harsh truth is that there are *alternative* forms of government, and the main organizational question facing us is which of the various directions will be taken by the new nations of the world."[61]

The neoclassical ecologists simply do not introduce concepts in their framework to deal with choice situations. Instead, they perceive fixed relationships between the forces composing the ecological complex that operate outside any individual and that dictate the course of ecological development.[62]

The traditional materialists perform in the same erroneous fashion as do their neoclassical cohorts. By defining ecology as im-

26

personal competition and then taking impersonal competition as the cause of ecological phenomena, they are guilty of tautological reasoning. Furthermore, when the traditional materialists admit the influence of culture but "analytically" separate this essential component from consideration, they commit the second fault of the neoclassical materialists, namely, that of extracting parts from an inseparable whole. Finally, like the neoclassical ecologist, the traditional orientation allows for no decision-making process, since, apparently, no choice situations ever occur in biotic competition.

These methodological limitations underlying materialistic ecology cannot be resolved by continuing the study of ecological phenomena "as if" both the subject matter and explanation were one and the same and independent of values and culture. Because, as noted by the materialists themselves, ecological phenomena reside in a cultural setting and, as indicated by succeeding chapters of this study, volition cannot be ignored in seeking ecological explanations, it is imperative that an investigator acknowledge the significance of culture and the role of social values. To overcome these methodological shortcomings of materialistic ecology, a voluntaristic approach is offered in the following chapter as an alternative ecological framework.

Chapter Three

VOLUNTARISTIC APPROACHES TO ECOLOGY

With the appearance of Milla Aissa Alithan's critique of traditional materialism in her *Social Ecology* in 1938,[1] and Warner E. Gettys' significant article published two years later,[2] the voluntaristic approach to ecology was initiated. Unwilling to treat man as an animal meekly conforming to impersonal competition, these two writers called for the application of sociological principles in studying ecological phenomena. They vigorously attacked as unrealistic the biological premises of traditional materialism, and demanded instead that ecologists seek explanations in man's social organization. Nevertheless, it was the publication of Walter Firey's *Land Use in Central Boston,*[3] published in 1947, that offered the first systematic treatment of ecology from the perspective advocated by Alihan and Gettys.

In his ecological work, Firey defines ecology as a study that seeks to explain "the territorial arrangements that social activities assume" in man's adaptation to space.[4] To accomplish this task, Firey applies a cultural approach in which he specifically notes the importance of social values in influencing man's location over space.

28

Firey maintains that man's adaptation to space does not take place in compliance with biotic features in the form of geography and population for the purpose of minimizing cost. Instead, he perceives an interplay between what he refers to as social values—volitional adaptation as an end in itself—and interest—rational adaptation. Thus the patterning of activities over space will frequently develop in response to interests in conflict with social values. But regardless of which factor eventually exerts the greatest force, "the specific nature of spatial giveness and the specific form of compliance on the part of social systems are both manifestations of particular cultural systems."[5] Thus, Firey approaches ecology from the standpoint of "diseconomic" versus "economic" uses. Through his study of certain land usages in Boston, Firey counters the economic orientation of ecological materialism by demonstrating the importance of social values as symbols applied to sustain certain land uses.

Following the appearance of Firey's classic study stressing the importance of social values, A. B. Hollingshead rejected his former biotic perspective toward ecology to argue for a sociocultural framework.[6] He now admits that competition itself is not completely impersonal and subsocial in nature; rather, this process "occurs within the purview of a sociocultural matrix." He maintains that distribution of institutions and individuals results from competition between cultural usages and values; social forces within a society, contrary to the materialists' position, regulate and prescribe the conditions under which competition operates.

Another voluntarist, William Form, furthers the attack against ecological materialism by demanding complete abandonment of materialism in favor of a social structure approach.[7] Form claims that the subsocial order cannot possibly encompass the forces at work that account for shifts in land use. He sees the patterning of human activities forming what he calls four types of "social congeries" in regulating the land market in modern urban centers: real estate and building businesses; "larger" industries, businesses, and utilities; individual homeowners and "small" consumers of land; and local governmental agencies. He calls for the analysis of each grouping in terms of its functions, power, and internal organization. It is Form's contention that interrelationships between "social congeries" ultimately determine the course of land use.

Still other writers contribute to the advancement of voluntaristic ecology at the expense of materialism. We find Christen T. Jonassen's study of an ethnic group from a ecological perspective sustaining Firey's original thesis. Jonassen concludes that "men tend to distribute themselves within an area so as to achieve the greatest efficiency in realizing the values they hold most dear."[8] Also, Hiram Friedsam writes that "competition is to be conceived as one of the institutional arrangements characterizing this society [that is, the United States] and not as a biologistic universal which is actually determinative of things social."[9] Julian Steward, moreover, attacks the notion of impersonal competition by holding that competition "is always culturally determined." He states further that "culture, rather than *genetic potential* for adaptation, accommodation, and survival, explains the nature of human societies."[10] However, he ascribes to the environment a determinative role: ". . . the kinds and seasons of fish runs *will determine* the habits of riverine and coastal tribes."[11] He modifies his voluntaristic leaning to avoid the passive role normally assigned to geography by other voluntarists. And, finally, this writer and Gideon Sjoberg have contended, in a recent publication, that the materialistic notions actually reflect a particular value system individuals employ in orienting to space, and that, therefore, biotic competition and impersonal forces as defined by the materialists are not subsocial in nature.[12]

Although different viewpoints apparently exist in the writings by voluntaristic ecologists, there is still the common notion that volition must be taken into consideration in developing ecological theories. The recognition of social values as an essential component of ecological thought characterizes the voluntaristic approach to human ecology. Culture, therefore, is a paramount feature in voluntaristic writings. In brief, the voluntarist seeks to analyze cultural data with particular emphasis upon the role of volition. The impetus, voluntarists contend, for the arrangement of a human population over space comes from man's own creative efforts rather than from forces external to social organization or from factors having no social value orientation for man as surmised by the ecological materialists.

Each of these voluntarists contributes to the framework of this study not only by his criticisms of ecological materialism but also by his positive contributions. In the presentation to follow, the voluntaristic orientation dominates. However, it is the purpose here not only to argue from a voluntarist position but also to attempt an integration of the variety of insights and propositions advanced by various voluntaristic ecologists. The position assumed within this study will be referred to as the "cultural approach" to ecology, or simply "cultural ecology."

The Cultural Approach

Human ecology, from a sociological perspective, is the study of the social activities that are created and sustained to orient man in adapting to physical space. Ecology is not to be interpreted as the study of only functional relationships between "physical" factors as a population pursues sustenance activities, as most neoclassical materialists would claim. Nor is ecology concerned only with competition as an impersonal force that determines the distribution of man over a territorial expense, as traditional materialists hold.

Several reasons justify this definition assigned to ecology. First, the meaning avoids the materialists' framework, followed by traditional ecologists and such neoclassical ones as Hawley, Quinn, and Duncan, that limits human ecology to the treatment of man as an animal. Indeed, Hawley, and implicitly other materialists, subscribe to the notion that man differs from other animals in degree rather than in kind.[13] Consequently, it is to be expected that materialists would treat man from a physiobiological perspective and seek eco-

31

logical explanations in factors outside man's social organization and beyond man's control.

Voluntarists, on the other hand, seek the determinants for man's distribution over space in sufficient, not just necessary, conditions. The performance of social activities, from the voluntarist's perspective, requires not only a physical and biological capacity to perform— the necessary condition—but also the utilization of symbolic data— the sufficient condition. Thus, while man must have the biological capacity to perform within a territorial environment, he nonetheless performs in accordance with sufficient conditions on the symbolic level. Indeed, culture, in the words of Firey, "defines the very being and conditions of survival."[14]

Man's unique capacity to create and apply symbols enabling him to transcend immediate situations and give meaning to the world about him becomes the distinctive feature that separates him from all other living organisms. No other creature has this potential.[15] Man has, as a consequence, created and sustained an order of data that is neither physical nor biological and, therefore, does not belong to the natural sphere.[16] An ecological analysis from a sociological perspective must, then, be at least on the level of human, not animal, capacity.

The level of data created and sustained by man is commonly referred to as the "cultural order." More specifically, the concept "culture" refers to a system of symbolic ideas shared by at least several individuals[17] to give interpretative significance to human behavior or to objects.

Culture becomes the intervening variable between man and his physiobiological setting that determines man's location over space. Man's biological requirements for survival within a habitat impose only *physical limitations* and define only the *nonpermissive* range of *physical, not social, action* within a given setting. As C. Daryll Forde writes:

Neither the world distribution of the various economies, nor their development and relative importance among particular peoples, can be regarded as simply functions of physical conditions and natural resources.

32

Between the physical environment and human activity there is always a middle term, a collection of specific objectives and values, a body of knowledge and belief: in other words, a cultural pattern. That the culture itself is not static, that it is adaptable and modifiable in relation to physical conditions, must not be allowed to obscure the fact that adaptation proceeds by discoveries and inventions which are themselves in no sense inevitable and which are, in any individual community, nearly all of them acquisitions or impositions from without. The people of whole continents have failed to make discoveries that might at first blush seem obvious. Equally important are the restrictions placed by social patterns and religious concepts on the utilization of certain resources or on adaptations to physical conditions.[18]

The physical and biological systems stressed by ecological materialists remain *outside* the subject matter for investigation by ecologists *except as these components are made relevant by man's culture.* As Forde claims:

The habitat at one and the same time circumscribes and affords scope for cultural development *in relation to the pre-existing equipment and tendency of a particular society,* and to any new concepts and equipment that may reach it from without.[19]

And Forde also states:

Physical conditions enter intimately into every cultural development and pattern, not excluding the most abstract and non-material; they enter not as determinants, however, *but as one category of the raw material of cultural elaboration.* The study of the relations between cultural patterns and physical conditions is of the greatest importance for an understanding of human society, but it cannot be undertaken in terms of simple geographic controls alleged to be identifiable on sight.[20]

Thus, the range of nonpermissive *physical action* imposed by man's biological makeup and his environment is an outcome of man's *cultural* development.

A second justification for the definition of ecology presented here lies in the contention that man adapts to space through the social activities he seeks to perform. This has important implications for numerous studies purporting to be ecological in nature. For many of the inquiries that deal with the so-called "ecological distributions" of mental illnesses, crime rates, social disorganization, divorces, and so

33

forth,[21] are not considered ecological according to our definition of ecology. While all activities take place over space, man does not necessarily relate all his activities to space itself. To plot mental disorders or divorces upon a map in delineated districts or areas and speak of the results as ecological departs very significantly from the scope of human ecology. Such studies are simply areal distributions of a purely factual sort; it is not essential that individuals orient their activities to space simply because they are divorcees, criminals, mentally ill, and so forth. If, however, it can be shown that people assume a spatial location *because of* their mental illnesses and *because they are* criminals or divorcees, then such characteristics become ecologically relevant; these social factors would then have to be taken into account in an ecological study dealing with these items.

Ecology, therefore, can claim no special analytical sociological constructs as its distinguishing feature. The *raison d'être* of ecology is not to be established in a unique methodology nor in the materialists' analytical frameworks of an impersonal competitive order or the ecological complex. Instead, it lies in the subject matter ecologists examine: the patterning of social activities man performs for adaptation to a territorial expanse.

Because man's "universe of meanings" separates him from all other beings, his performances take place in terms of the notions he possesses, and he, in turn, is perceived and interpreted by the notions of individuals about him. Any act or object is made socially meaningful by the interpretations of the participants through shared ideas. Man directs his action toward others and is directed by the imposition of meanings insofar as his acts are social in nature. Thus, variations in socially conceived behavioral patterns result from variations in the applicable "universe of meanings."[22]

Ideas, however, do not exist in isolation; they are interrelated. Consequently, we speak of "systems of symbolic ideas" to convey the combination of several notions. The systems of ideas held in common establish the existence of culture.

The cultural approach to human ecology does not study the individual in psychological terms, as some ecological materialists

34

claim;[23] it avoids both the psychological reference[24] and the population perspective advocated by materialists as its units for investigation. The shared systems of symbolic ideas—the determinant to be investigated by ecologists to explain man's adaptation to space—may be implicit or explicit, conscious or unconscious,[25] latent or manifest. The cultural approach, moreover, interprets man as an active agent rather than as a passive animal conforming to physical and biological properties in the effort to accommodate within a habitat.

A number of writers perceive human behavior in its cultural form rather than in the psychological and strictly social frames of reference. One of the most vigorous exponents of the cultural framework is Leslie A. White. He insists that cultural traits must be treated and examined as very real things in that cultural data "constitute a distinct class of phenomena."[26] We also find Florian Znaniecki arguing not only that all data produced and sustained by man's conscious acts are the proper domain for investigation by social scientists but also that the social system belongs within cultural conceptualization.[27] Firey, a cultural ecologist, places the social system and values within a cultural framework: ". . . both the character of space and the make-up of social systems are of cultural origin."[28] Finally, speaking more broadly, Malcolm M. Willey explicitly declares that "the study of culture—the processes of its origin and its growth, its spread and perpetuation—constitutes the study of sociology."[29]

Following in the footsteps of these and other writers, the approach developed here as an alternative to materialism for the investigation of ecological phenomena places the social system within its framework. That is, our level of data is the cultural order; our theory for examining cultural data is to be a *specific* social action scheme. The elements composing social action theory remain, but their customary meanings have been modified in light of the empirical data taken from Austin's zoning process.[30] The following terms, therefore, represent the basic concepts of the *specific* social action theory that will be used in this study when organizing and analyzing empirical data presented in later chapters for the purpose of sustaining the stated hypotheses:

35

End: An anticipated future state of affairs to be realized through the actor's own efforts.[31]

Norm: A standard of expectation for social conduct to be approximated or actualized in performance.

Normative system: A set or arrangement of interrelated norms.

Means: The presence of *alternative* norms (or normative systems) for the accomplishment of a given end.

Social condition: A norm for accomplishing an end that excludes the presence of alternative considerations within a situation.

Value: A concept specifying what aspects of a situation are desirable, undesirable, or nondesirable; or appropriate, inappropriate, or nonappropriate.[32]

Value system: A set of interrelated values.

Cognitive data: Conceptualized criteria defining social and/or physical objects and their properties.

With respect to ecology, the cultural perspective holds that the distribution of man over space is not haphazard; rather, man locates within a habitat by the social activities he creates and sustains through culture. The social action theory specifies the interrelationships between the concepts given above for examining ecological data in the following manner:

> In locating over space, individuals seek to attain a certain end. To accomplish the goal, a specific norm must be selected from the means in accordance with social conditions that prescribe the course social action is to take.[33] Furthermore, such performance requires cognition on the part of actors concerning the properties—actual or potential—of the circumstances in a situation. But because the goal, means, normative conditions, and cognitive data must be given specificity to arrive at concrete decisions and conclusions or to voice opinions and viewpoints, actors must develop and employ evaluative standards, that is, value systems.

36

This social action framework is meaningful to analyze the zoning process in the city of Austin as an ecological phenomenon. The data presented in the following chapters appear to substantiate the argument that the decision-makers taking part in Austin's zoning process have as their goal the regulation of land use in an orderly fashion so as to promote and sustain the public peace, healthy, safety, morals, and general welfare. To accomplish this purpose, individuals conceive zoning classifications as the means. But in seeking to realize this goal—through zoning classifications as the means—individuals abide by certain social conditions. Foremost among the normative conditions relevant to zoning are the legal order, rules established by the planning bodies, and ethical standards to which conformity is expected.

In Austin's zoning process, moreover, decision-makers rely upon cognitive data; they share certain objectified knowledge without necessarily expressing approval or disapproval of these data. For instance, they recognize the number of cars traveling upon particular streets, current property usages, topography of land, and so forth. Such relevant data, independent of the evaluative aspect in the form of social values, constitute cognitive data.

Finally, to give meaningful specificity to the stated goal, to select from the means, and to evaluate the cognitive data and social conditions when arriving at concrete zoning decisions, the decision-makers develop and employ a variety of social value systems. For these individuals rely upon value systems to give interpretative significance to the goal, means, social conditions, and cognitive standards. Otherwise, such items would be hollow, void of meaning, and hence not amenable to concrete interpretation. Only by an analysis of the values that prevail in the zoning process can an adequate explanation of zoning as an ecological phenomenon be presented.

In the following two chapters we shall set forth and examine the several value systems prevailing in Austin's zoning process and the consequences these have for zoning and for ecology. The empirical data will demonstrate that while the decision-makers in Austin's zoning process accept a certain goal to be attained through zoning of land, nonetheless, differences do exist among them due to their dissimilar value systems. Since there is agreement with respect to both the end that is sought and the means of achieving the given goal, and, furthermore, because there is disagreement between the several value systems to be employed in interpreting the goal, the zoning process is competitive rather than characterized by conflict or "pure" cooperation.

The cultural approach, although seeking the determinant elements in systems of ideas, still belongs within the voluntaristic perspective. For the essential ingredient of choice remains: individuals may choose from alternative normative courses of action (that is, the means) to bring about a development which, in the absence of their efforts, would not otherwise have resulted. Volition prevails in the sense that persons can attain a certain end even in the face of social conditions designed to restrict social action.

The general theory of such writers as Sorokin, Parsons, Durkheim, Firey, Znaniecki, and Taylor offer methodological support for the cultural approach to ecology;[34] these writers recognize the importance of conceptualization in analyzing social action. In particular, Sorokin, in the first two chapters of his book *Sociocultural Causality Space, Time,* deals with the fallacy of extracting data as materialists continue to do in defining the field of inquiry for ecological analysis.

Sorokin begins by asserting that the study of sociocultural phenomena cannot proceed along the lines followed by the physical and biological scientists owing to the existence of what he refers to as the "component of meanings" man imputes to matter. Because of this imposition on the part of man, social meanings remain undetected in the application of physiobiological techniques. Physical matter simply serves as a "vehicle" that "materializes, externalizes, or objectifies" internal feeling states possessed by the agent. And man, as the agent, operates vehicles in terms of his imposition of meanings upon matter conceived as vehicles. Social meanings are not components of matter;

38

rather, they are independent of physical objects, and must therefore be located in man's social organization. As Sorokin writes:

Thus, somewhat unexpectedly for many, we come to the conclusion that the *location of meanings in the universe of meanings consists in an adequate classification of the main systems of meanings with the super-system as a further step toward a convenient universal, cosmopolitan, referential principle for the determination of the relational positions of the meanings.*[35]

It is therefore the task of the social scientist, according to Sorokin, to discover and define the system of meanings operating in the sociocultural situation as data for investigation. An explanation of social action requires an examination to seek, describe, and explain the interrelationships between meanings.

To accomplish this task outlined by Sorokin, the cultural approach involves the application of the analytical method[36] to analyze the *entire system* of relevant meanings in order to discover data explaining man's adaptation over space. Through this stance, the cultural approach escapes the methodological limitations contained in materialistic ecological thought. First, the cultural perspective avoids the error of using identical factors as both the subject and the explanation for ecology: by working only within the cultural order of data, we shall seek to investigate the social activities that orient man to space by testing the specific social action theory presented above. The conceptual framework among the end, means, social conditions, values, and cognitive data as developed for this study serves as a possible theory for examining ecological phenomena.

The cultural perspective, furthermore, refuses to commit the second methodological shortcoming characteristic of materialistic ecology, namely, to separate inseparable parts. Culture encompasses the *entire system* of meanings by which man orients to a geographical surrounding. There is no extraction from physiobiological data; there is only demarcation of distinguishable ideas. Because of the divergent meaningful content that ideas contain, we can justify the introduction of a social action theory that relies upon such concepts as values,

39

social conditions, goals, cognitive data, and means to analyze cultural data. The interrelationship among these conceptions, as presented above,[37] constitutes the specific theory developed in this study of zoning as an ecological phenomena.

Two specific conceptualizations that have preoccupied ecologists since the founding of human ecology are notions dealing with space and time; the writings by ecological theorists reflect a long-standing interest in the role of space and/or time as possible explanatory factors accounting for ecological phenomena. The cultural approach as presented in this study does not disrupt this continuous interest. But because materialistic ecologists fail to perceive the social meanings of and certain social relationships between space and time—so essential to the interpretation of the empirical zoning data—it is now necessary to devote careful and considerate attention to the place of space and time in the cultural orientation.

SPACE AND TIME CONCEPTIONS

Space, according to the cultural approach, is what people make of it. So is time. Both have meaning for ecology, not as physical phenomena, but rather as social conceptualizations that orient man within an environment. Even physiomathematical and biological notions toward space and time do not escape from sociocultural circumstances. As Sorokin states concerning spatial conceptions:

. . . geometric or physical space, supposed to be quite objective and scientific, is but a variety of sociocultural space conditioned in its characteristics by the sociocultural milieu.[38]

And Sorokin exerts an identical contention toward time:

. . . mathematical time itself is in a conspicuous degree a variety of sociocultural time and has come into existence through a play of sociocultural circumstances enlarging the net of interaction of a society.[39]

Living within a physical environment as a social creature, man must conceptualize and give meaning to the world about him. As

40

Mircea Eliade declares: *"If the world is to be lived in,* it must be *founded*—and no world can come to birth in the chaos of the homogeneity and relativity of profane space."[40] And man "finds" his world by establishing fixed points for reference within a territory through the social activities he pursues. For as Emile Durkheim claims:

. . . space is not the vague and indetermined medium which Kant imagined; if purely and absolutely homogeneous, it would be of no use, and could not be grasped by the mind. Spatial representation consists essentially in primary coordination of the data of sensuous experience. But this co-ordination would be impossible if the parts of space were qualitatively equivalent and if they were really interchangeable. . . . But whence come these divisions which are so essential? . . . All these distinctions evidently come from the fact that different sympathetic values have been attributed to various regions. Since all the men of a single civilization represent space in the same way, it is clearly necessary that these sympathetic values, and the distinctions which depend upon them should be equally universal, and that almost necessarily implies that they be of social origin.[41]

Without culturally created indicators for delineation of what would otherwise be homogeneous vastness, no orientation to space would be possible for man. Consequently, man locates in space by creating a social organization which gives peculiar significance to the habitat in which he resides; it is through conceptions that man attaches symbolic meanings to his physical settings. A proper study of ecology, therefore, must be accomplished, not by examining space in the geometric and topographical sense, as do the materialistic ecologists, but rather by exploring and determining the social meanings man applies when locating within a territory.

Individuals perceive space, from an ecological perspective, in terms of utility in much the same manner that Erich Zimmermann, in his classic writing, depicts the meaning of resources.[42] For man interprets space in terms of what it (does) (will) or (does not) (will not) provide: either what is or (will) (will not) be taking place upon land, or what is or (will) (will not) be extracted from land. Individuals conceptualize physical attributes of space as either assisting, complementing, or resisting their social activities. One lo-

41

cation is an area of residence, another an area of businesses, still another an area of ceremonial processions. There is, furthermore, the social conceptualization of "vacant" property applicable when certain anticipated activities do not take place upon a designated location. Territorial vastness, for instance, is perceptible because of the absence of social activities or socially designated physical indices—as in the case of "wide open spaces." "Vacant" space is simply one type of social conception orienting man to space. Indeed, vacancy appears to be a residual category in man's social scheme for viewing space.

Space, then, is defined here as the physical location of events and/or social activities demarcated by social conceptualizations. Space is the "place where" event and/or social activities occur shorn of "scientific" fixation (physiomathematical notations—which, in fact, are social conceptualizations). Man expresses his orientation to and within an area through the social activities he seeks to perform and the social events that develop.

One of the most fundamental notions accounting for the arrangement of ecological phenomena over space is the sacred-secular conceptualization toward property. Sacred-secular notions toward space affect the range of social activities allowable upon land. A society whose members treat their territorial expanses in a secular manner permits a greater range of activity upon space than does a society espousing sacred notions toward locations. A sacred society not only eliminates more alternative land usages in comparison to the secular; it is also unwilling to allow a rapid rate of land-use change relative to secular notions toward space. Eliade maintains:

> Revelation of a sacred space makes it possible to obtain a fixed point and hence to acquire orientation in the chaos of homogeneity. . . . The profane . . . maintains the homogeneity and hence the relativity of space. No *true* orientation is now possible, for the fixed point no longer enjoys a unique ontological status; it appears and disappears in accordance with the needs of the day.[43]

Because religions, for instance, in American society generally attribute a sacred quality only to the activity within a church or upon

42

church grounds rather than to religious buildings or to the space upon which churches stand, there is a greater likelihood for relocation. If the land itself were made sacred by the very location of a church upon it, there would be the imposition of severe restrictions—that is, social conditions—upon land use thereby to prevent considerations of alternative uses.

Time conceptualizations also loom large in any explanation of ecological phenomena. Although time is sometimes incorporated into the very definition given to human ecology, the meaning assigned to ecology in this paper omits the time element entirely. Justification for this lies in the fact that if time were included in the subject matter, time could not become part of the explanation accounting for man's distribution over space. Yet, as the empirical zoning data substantiate, time conceptualization can be an explanatory factor in ecological thought.

Time, from an ecological perspective, becomes relevant only as man applies *conceptualized* time in orienting his activities to space. As Sorokin and Merton write: "the calendrical reference itself becomes significant only when it is transformed into social action."[44] The same holds true for all physiomathematical time conceptions. For while activity takes place over a period of time designated by physiomathematical time conceptions, physiomathematical time as such is not a determinant of social action. It possesses no intrinsic quality to which social action must comply irrespective of human volition.[45] Instead, it must be demonstrated that time interpretations account for various patternings of social action over space before time becomes an explanatory factor in ecological writings. In brief, only to the extent that time conceptions become referents for social action orienting man to space do notions of time become ecologically relevant.

Individuals view time as either secular or sacred. Time is secular whenever actors conceptualize it as homogeneous—in the sense that time is a regularity that makes it absolute, everlasting, and inevitable. On the other hand, time is conceptualized as sacred when (1) actors accord respect and reverence to time in the sense that the mere passage of time becomes significant for the *perpetuation* of social activities and/or events; or whenever (2) actors conceive of time as if it were recoverable or reversible. We shall label the first type of sacred time "traditional"—time made sacred because persons conceive of it as circumscribing events and/or activities to which acknowledgment must be accorded; we shall label the second form of sacred time "ritualistic"—time made sacred because individuals conceive of it as recoverable through ritualistic behavior.

Rituals "reverse" time.[46] Through ritualistic notions of time, individuals perform so as to *preserve* in the present and for the future what is believed to have taken place in the past. Rituals enable the accomplishment of this feat by establishing time continuity: events of the past are "indefinitely repeatable" in the immediate world of reality through ritualistic behavior. Rituals "recapture" time so that significant events that have already occurred can be memorialized and sustained in the present and for time yet to come.

These two vehicles for imparting sacredness to time—tradition and ritual—become involved with events and/or social activities that man pursues to create and sustain sacred values toward land itself. It appears that one or the other of these two media is required before space can be symbolized as sacred. It is postulated here that if events and/or activities, in their relationships to space, were stripped of social conceptualization of sacred time, then expressions of sacredness toward physical locales and other objectified data could not exist.

In his study of sentiment as an ecological variable, Firey noted that the very ground in Boston upon which certain cemeteries are located was sacred.[47] The awe toward Boston's three colonial burial grounds persists to this day not only because of due regard for human remains but also because of tradition. If the duration expressed by tradition were not combined with sacred values toward the dead, then it would be most improbable that importance would be given to the physical space devoted for use as cemeteries in Boston. But honor for the dead is now intrinsic in the very land as granted by the impetus of sacred time.

44

The element of time is even essential for the perpetuation of Beacon Hill, which Firey also discusses. He treats not only the symbolic importance of this exclusive residential area located in downtown Boston but also the historical impact of the area. Firey notes certain expressions toward Beacon Hill—"architectural landmarks," "former glory," "historical quarter," and "these dear crooked lanes traced in ancestral mud"—which clearly indicate the historical tie necessary for attributing sacred qualities to Beacon Hill residences. However, as Firey comments, the reverence toward Beacon Hill as a physical object is attributed to the presence of social activities. In particular, there is a reverence toward residences in which people believe prominent events took place. For instance, he quotes one person as saying, "I like living here for I like to think that a great deal of historical interest has happened here in this room." This expression distinctly reflects the sacred quality attributed to land-use *activity* rather than to the land upon which the activity occurs. There is no sacred value toward space itself in this case. Indeed, it would be reasonable to suppose that if the esteemed activity Firey describes as taking place upon Beacon Hill were removed, the land itself would be treated as secular territory.

When sites or social activities become sacred through either traditional or ritualistic time notions, there will be strong resistance to suggestions of change in land use. The social power necessary to overcome opposition to efforts designed to bring change in land use must be perceived as overwhelming to assure success. And once the new use is established, it is most devastating to the sacred social values formerly responsible for sustaining sacredness. This is so because, as Durkheim notes, man's value orientations toward space do not perpetuate for long in the absence of external objects that symbolize the sacred meaning attached to sites.[48]

These voluntaristic generalizations from a cultural approach concerning the nature of space and time are not acceptable to ecological materialists. For materialists refuse to include social conceptualizations toward space within their theories. Rather, they employ notions such as "ecological distance" and "natural areas." Traditional ecological materialists, for the most part, perceive space as a physical attribute demanding outlays of energy by a population as it moves over space. McKenzie, for example, claims:

> Ecological distance is a measure of fluidity. It is a time-cost concept rather than a unit of space. It is measured by minutes and cents rather than a unit of space.[49]

According to some neoclassical materialists, the competitive strength of each activity explains the arrangement ecological phenomena assume. Hawley, for instance, succinctly writes that "the territorial pattern of collective life is largely a result of the friction of space as manifested in time-cost distance."[50] Because each function requires peculiar demands and services, it must locate in such a position as to be accessible to other functions supplying its needs. "The outcome," exclaims Hawley, "is a distribution in which the most intensive uses of space occupy the most accessible locations."[51] Even "routes of travel *must be* bent and shaped to the lines of least [topographical] resistance."[52]

Firey aptly summarizes the materialistic viewpoint toward space as follows:

> Systematization of ecological theory has thus far proceeded on two main premises regarding the character of space and the nature of locational activities. The first premise postulates that the sole relation of space to locational activities is an impeditive and cost-imposing one. The second premise assumes that locational activities are primarily economizing, "fiscal" agents. On the basis of these two premises the only possible relationship that locational activities may bear to space is an economic one.[53]

Since Firey's concise summary of the materialists' interpretation of space, the neoclassical materialists have come to argue that space is an element of the "ecological complex"—consisting of population, environment, technology, and social organization—that affects ecological phenomena. Space is perceived as the physical environment that imposes requirements upon man's sustenance activities. Space,

46

therefore, is studied only as an "external" conditioning force that supposedly affects and determines the organization of sustenance activities. That is to say, neoclassical materialists exclude the notion of "permissiveness" in dealing with space; social values and attitudes have no ecological role for these materialists to explain the significance of space.

Volitional ecologists explicitly reject the premises of the materialistic approach toward space. For voluntarists maintain that space has only sociocultural meaning as expressed in the social activities man pursues. Firey states:

> Spatiality . . . is not only an impediment but may be a symbol as well. This symbolic quality is referable only to a system of social values through which space may become invested with certain meaningful [social] properties. More than this, the very impeditiveness of space itself does not reside in it as a physical phenomenon but rather in the costfulness which it imposes upon social systems which must deal with it. This constitution of social systems is itself the product of a particular value system which defines the very being and conditions of survival for those social systems. Thus both the character of space and the make-up of social systems are of cultural origin.[54]

The viewpoint taken in this study toward the interpretation to be given to space by ecologists is essentially the same as Firey's. That is, man's mobility over space is not entirely explained by his ability to spend the energy required to locate himself or his social activities over space. To be sure, the expenditure of energy is a necessary requirement. But it is not a sufficient condition: energy outlays become ecologically significant only when energy expenditures reflect socially prescribed patterning unexplainable by an examination of physical data. Efficiency in terms of the traditional materialists' time-cost postulate is simply a value that bears no ecological relationship to the nature of physical terrain; rationality is not a matter of geography. Moreover, individuals perform cultural activities that at times apparently run counter to an ultimate "adaptability to intensive land use."[55]

Materialistic ecologists deal with time in much the same manner that they consider space except that there is a tendency to ignore time. Hawley is the most outspoken of the few materialists concerned with time. He maintains, in his theoretical perspective, that time is simply a cost factor that, in reality, cannot be separated from space since "space and time are different aspects of the same thing such that it is difficult to experience one without reference to the other."[56] The "thing" to which Hawley refers is the cost factor that he claims lies outside cultural conceptualization; it is another "external" condition to which man *must* adapt regardless of culture. According to Hawley, man accommodates to nonsocial forces operating in his environment to reduce the friction of space that, in turn, lowers cost. Consequently, "space and time are separable from one another only in abstraction."[57]

On the other hand, we find voluntarists also overlooking the importance of time in presenting ecological explanations; there is even a paucity of material on time by voluntarists in general action theory. Indeed, Sorokin appears to be the only voluntarist of note to treat time in a systematic manner.[58] Christen Jonassen, a voluntarist ecologist, considered time in tracing the movement of an ethnic group over space.[59] But he accomplished this by examining a *period of time* during which a certain ethnic group migrated, rather than presenting time as a *social conceptualization* orienting man to space.

It is the contention of this writer, however, that time and space are ecologically relevant only as social conceptions that orient man for settlement in a habitat. It will be demonstrated in a subsequent chapter that the materialists' view of space and time as cost items— requiring passive conformity by man in the social activities he pursues —is only a value orientation within a particular culture. Indeed, only a circular interpretation of time and space enables Hawley to sustain his statement that time and space are "inseparable": time is costly, distance over space is costly and, hence, Hawley could conclude, there is an "abstracted distinction only."

Of course, materialists could retort that time and space are ecological variables only insofar as the two are cost factors; when time

48

and space are not cost items, they are no longer ecologically significant. This is certainly the treatment materialists accord social values. But in the performance materialists would have to commit themselves to tautological thinking: ecological data would be defined and explained by the cost factor. Thus, if materialistic ecologists continue to call all contradictions within their theories nonecological, they will do so, of necessity, in a most methodologically unsound and unrewarding fashion.

Chapter Four

THE MEANS AND END
IN THE ZONING PROCESS

The first hypothesis of this study for which supporting data are provided deals with the establishment of a goal, the means by which the objective is to be accomplished, and the normative systems directing decision-makers in the attainment of the desired goal in the zoning process. The formal statement of this hypothesis is:

HYPOTHESIS I: There is an effort to locate social activities over space for the attainment of a given goal through the selection, in accordance with certain social conditions, of a norm from the alternative norms that constitute the means.

To test Hypothesis I, four problems must be analyzed. First, it will be necessary to present empirical data taken from the zoning process as performed in the city of Austin, Texas, demonstrating that individuals locate over space in terms of the social activities they pursue; second, the goal in the zoning process must be established; third, the means and social conditions directing decision-makers in accomplishing the goal must be ascertained; and, fourth, the effects of zoning upon land use must be determined.

Spatial Distribution

The analysis of the first of these four problems involves a test of the definition of ecology as offered in this study. For we have defined ecology as an investigation of the social activities that orient man's adaptation to space. Do the zoning data in this study comply with this definition of ecology?

The empirical data indicate that individuals do in fact perceive space as the location necessary for the performance of certain social activities. That is, persons interpret space in terms of utility: the location for what has been, is, or will be taking place. The following instances taken from data obtained from zoning hearings held by Austin's Zoning Committee, Planning Commission, and City Council support this contention:

INSTANCE 1: An applicant sought a "DL" zoning classification to permit the expansion of an existing light-industrial use to manufacture electrical fixtures. A member of the City Council inquired of an opponent to the zoning change: "Did you buy after the original zoning request [was made for the property in 1957]?" The opponent replied, "Yes sir. But I bought [a house near this property] thinking it [the property in question] was 'C' Commercial, not industrial. If I knew it would be industrial, I would not have bought here."

INSTANCE 2: Here the applicant requested a "C" classification to allow him to locate a used-car lot upon the land in question.

Applicant: No one would build another home to live here. This [the zoning request] has been up four or five times [before the City Council] and why it hasn't been given approval, I don't know. The person next door objects. He took a business risk and should not complain [after erecting a duplex for rent income].

51

Council Member 1: What do you want to do with it [the property in question]?

Applicant: I want to use it for a used car lot.

Opponent 2 [*owner of the duplex*]*:* I don't have any objection to a use that is nice and quiet. I wouldn't have any objection to a used car lot if it does not look like a junk yard.

Council Member 2: But the land has been vacant for a long time. There's "C" Commercial all down the street.

Opponent 2: We [who live in the area] own our houses and we keep them up as best we can. But we can't move. A man this morning told me he tried to buy this property for a home and a man wanted it for a church. We can visualize it as something better than a used car lot.

INSTANCE 3: The owner of an existing vacant drugstore requested a change in zoning from "C" to "C-2" to convert his former drugstore into a package store. An objector made this statement related to utility:

At the time I bought my property ten years ago, I was living alone with my youngest son. We drove all over town before buying here. We looked for good and holy and fine people. We did not want to live with people who would touch liquor. Have any of these businesses [now located in the area] ever caused any trouble in our area? No! People go to these stores to get the necessities they need.

INSTANCE 4: In opposing a change in zoning to permit businesses to locate upon the property in question, a person declared:

A city is not altogether a business area, super stores and expressways. As much as we value Sixth Street [as a major business corner], none of us would want to live there.

INSTANCE 5: An applicant argued in favor of his case by saying:

The neighbors are very happy that the land is being utilized. It was a sore with weeds and trash. . . . Eventually the whole area will become commercial.

INSTANCE 6: Several persons vigorously protested a proposed zoning classification change:

52

Council Member: How far are you set back now? [That is, what are the set-back requirements for the land we are considering?]

Opponent 1: I don't know. [But the] twenty-five feet [that will be required by this zoning change] will kill that corner [I own]. On the corner of Riverside Drive and Barton Springs Road, the set-back will kill that corner. Now I don't know what I will do. I bought this property thirty years ago when it was just a hole. I filled in with thousands of [dirt] loads. It's been a tremendous expense. With a 25-foot set-back, it means throwing away valuable property. The 25-foot set-back will be out of line with the present property [improvements].

Opponent 2: We feel that the property is essentially business property because of the heavy traffic going by. The Council should take measures to encourage business rather than do harm. This is truly a business area.

INSTANCE 7: In making a motion to deny a request for a zoning change from "D" to "C-1" for the sale of beer within an existing drive-in hamburger stand, a member of the Planning Commission maintained:

I move that we deny this request. I would like to help the people [the applicants] as much as I can. But this piece of land is barely suitable for its present use. There is not enough ground to accommodate the requested use.

Each of these seven instances demonstrates the perception of space in terms of use; each person conceptualized space by considering how land might be utilized through the performance of certain social activities. As an opponent to the proposed car lot in "Instance 2" exclaimed, "We can visualize it [the land in question] as something better than a used car lot." This "visualization" of space involved the conception of how man should adapt in his habitat. In each instance, individuals oriented to space through conceptualized social activities. When a councilman, discussing the application under "Instance 2," perceived land as having been "vacant for a long time," he interpreted space as the absence of "significant" social activities. Thus, even the notion of "vacant" space requires reliance upon conceptualization in the form of the residual category of "vacant" property.

53

On the basis of our empirical data, then, we maintain that in zoning activities individuals do in fact orient themselves to space through creating or sustaining social activities. The very definition given to ecology in this study is, therefore, supported by the available evidence; no data that would serve to disprove this orientation were uncovered. An analysis, however, of the variety of space orientations remains to be offered.

The Objective in the Zoning Process

A further facet to be considered in testing Hypothesis I is the necessity to show the presence of an end, that is, a goal, as an essential element within the zoning process. The term has already been defined as an anticipated state of affairs to be realized by the actor's own efforts. It is now our intention to offer an explicit statement of the goal in the zoning process.

The present Zoning Ordinance governing Austin's zoning procedure states the goal decision-makers endeavor to accomplish: land use must be regulated in an orderly fashion so as to promote and sustain the public peace, health, safety, morals, and general welfare. The zoning data reveal that decision-makers direct their efforts to accomplishing this end as stated in the Zoning Ordinance.

INSTANCE 1: On April 20, 1960, the City Council met in regular session.

At the beginning of the meeting, a group of seventh-graders entered the council room to observe the city government in operation as part of its civics course assignment. During the question period that took place between the students and the City Council members, one student asked for an explanation regarding the purpose of zoning. A councilman replied that "zoning can be said to be the regulation of the use of land." Then the city attorney offered his viewpoint and

54

read from Austin's original zoning ordinance of 1931 in stating the objective in zoning land:

Section 1: That the zoning regulations and districts as herein adopted and established have been made in accordance with a comprehensive plan, for the purpose of promoting the health, safety, morals and general welfare of the community of the City of Austin. They have been designed to lessen congestion in the streets; to secure safety from fire, panic and other danger; to provide adequate light and air; to prevent the over-crowding of land; to avoid undue concentration of population; and to facilitate the adequate provision of transportation, water, sewage, schools, parks and other public requirements. They have been made with reasonable consideration, among other things, to the character of the district, and its peculiar suitability for the particular uses; and with a view of conserving the value of buildings and encouraging the most appropriate private use of land throughout the community.[1]

INSTANCE 2: In conducting interviews with various decision-makers, this question was asked: "Why does the city government make an effort to plan through the use of its zoning powers?" Each of the following comments represents the viewpoint of a specific decision-maker:

Council Member 1: I think planning is necessary for a city. It is necessary to have an over-all master plan to live by and work toward in order to have an orderly growth of the city. I was instrumental in bringing about the master plan [for Austin].

Council Member 2: Austin has always been a planned city. I think that any city ought to work toward a plan. We have got to recognize that a plan for a city is like a plan for a home: it always requires remodeling. A plan must be used as a guide and not a hard set of rules. . . . You have the old justification for zoning: it's to have an orderly development taking into consideration the traffic, safety, and welfare of its people.

Council Member 3: I feel that the basic purpose of zoning is to bring about a sensible growth of the city. Also, zoning gives a certain amount of protection to all property owners. Without zoning, a man who builds a $100,000 mansion may someday find a pig pen or a stock yard across the street.

Commission Member 1: To restrict usage to certain zones, to afford subdivision areas protection, [and to afford] industry and commercial uses protection. . . . [Zoning also provides] for a program of orderliness and

55

maintains the standards of the neighborhoods and the city—keeping commercial encroachment from entering into residential neighborhoods and all those policies that tend to make for bad environments for children to grow up. And, [finally] to plan for the over-all planning of the city.

Commission Member 2: The fundamental purpose of it all [i.e., zoning regulations] is to have the land and areas of the cities so that they are properly arranged and developed for the benefit of the public and for the people who have to live in them [that is, the cities].

INSTANCE 3: A third technique to obtain sustaining data showing the existence of the end set forth above is reliance upon the comments of the decision-makers. The following statements are oral expressions made during open hearings:

Council Member 1: We're looking at this [zoning application] from the aspect of the people's safety.

Commission Member 2: Planning [through zoning] is the orderly growth of the city and it also takes into consideration the convenience of living in a city.

Commission Member 3: I move that we deny this request. It is a detriment to the health, welfare, and safety of the community.

These remarks indicate the presence of an end in zoning such that men seek to promote orderly development in land use in order to forward the health, safety, morals, and general welfare of the community. Although the goal in the zoning process is legally prescribed, volition remains. Accomplishment of the end requires deliberate effort; actors must still seek to create and sustain those social activities necessary to attain this end.

The Means in the Zoning Process

To achieve the goal in the zoning process, Austin's decision-makers must utilize certain specified means. Although the goal of public welfare obtains in a legally established form, a course of conduct whereby the end may eventually be attained must be selected by the decision-makers. Indeed, the very term "decision-makers" implies the

56

presence of an array of alternatives that makes for a choice situation. What, then, are the alternatives facing the decision-makers as they go about selecting from the means for the accomplishment of the zoning objective?

Analysis of the zoning data from our means-end schema approach[2] reveals several choices facing decision-makers: the very zoning classifications specifying the utilization that can be made of space within the political bounds of the city become the means in the zoning process. For what is "decided upon" by individuals to achieve an objective becomes a means to achieve an end. And it is empirically verifiable that Austin's decision-makers select a zoning classification from alternatives so as to forward the public-welfare objective.

Again, the Zoning Ordinance of the City of Austin contains the means, that is, the zoning classifications, from which actors choose.[3] Because of the complexity and elaborate nature of this classificatory system prescribed within the Zoning Ordinance, it will be necessary to omit some of the categories as well as many permissive uses set forth under any one category and to consider only the more significant aspects:

"A" Residence District: One and two-family dwellings; churches; schools; private clubs.

"BB" Residence District: Apartment houses; boarding and lodging houses.

"O" Office District: Hotels; professional offices; art, dance, and other types of studios; gift, seamstress, and tailor shops; organizational headquarters.

"LR" Local Retail District: Bakery; bank; cafe; cleaning shop; drug store; service station; meat market; variety store; washateria; wearing apparel shop.

"GR" General Retail District: Auto repair garage, outdoor billboard; department, electrical, plumbing, and hardware stores; motion picture theatre; used-car lot.

"C" Commercial District: All uses permitted under the above classifications and all other types except those under the following classifications.

57

"C-1" Commercial District: Sale of beer and wine for off-premise consumption and for consumption incidental to the sale of food within a restaurant or cafe.

"C-2" Commercial District: Sale of liquors for off or on-premise consumption.

Three of the remaining four classifications denote industrial use. The final category—"Special Permit"—is an involved zoning classification that exerts strict control not only of the specific use but also of the design and structuring of all improvements, operating hours, parking facilities, signs, lighting arrangement, pavement, drainage, or any other features considered essential to "secure and protect public health, safety, morals, and general welfare."[4] A special permit is to allow for certain uses under an existing zoning classification not prescribed in that district use. For instance, service stations normally require at least an "LR" zoning classification for operation. But it is possible to secure a Special Permit to place this use under an existing "O" zoning. Furthermore, unlike any other, this zoning classification automatically reverts to the prior classification if the proposed uses under the conditions set forth by the Planning Commission are not met within two years after its issuance. In addition to this expiration specification, the Special Permit may be withdrawn through the proper official at any time in the event of violation of the conditions prescribed by the Planning Commission.

The various zoning classifications contained in Austin's Zoning Ordinance are alternative normative standards from which decision-makers choose one in preference to all others in exercising control over land-use development in order to achieve the public welfare objective. In acting upon any specific zoning application, the decision-makers either choose to sustain the prevailing zoning classification as one choice from among these listed alternatives, or select a classification other than the one existing upon a piece of property at the time a zoning change is requested. These various alternatives—or means—that prevail are in actuality norms, as this term has been defined for use in this study, in that the zoning classifications prescribe standards of expectations that are to be met in the utilization of space on the

58

part of individuals. The combination of (1) the presence of alternative courses of social action and (2) the fact that such alternatives consist of norms complies with the definition assigned to "means" in Chapter 3 of this study.

The empirical zoning data support the statement that normative alternatives in the form of zoning classifications constitute the means in the zoning process. That is, the actual performance by the decision-makers with regard to the means takes place by selecting from the zoning classifications. However, because, as in the case of ends, means are an abstraction, some of the following instances only implicitly substantiate zoning classifications as the means. The contextual meaning the decision-makers give to zoning in the following illustrations is that zoning refers to the act of specifying a particular classification from the alternative categories listed above for a socially specified physical space.

INSTANCE 1: A City Council member made the following statement concerning a particular application:

It was understood that "LR" [zoning] will give him [the applicant] what he wants and at the same time we will have control. It [the "LR" classification] will give us the necessary control; I will not vote for "C" [as requested by the applicant] because it will not give the necessary control.

INSTANCE 2: A commission member commented in voting to deny a request seeking a zoning change from "O" to "Special Permit" to allow for the construction of a service station:

I think one of the purposes *of zoning* is the welfare of the people. [Emphasis supplied.]

INSTANCE 3: In response to an interview question as to the purpose of the zoning process, a City Council member replied:

I feel that planning *through zoning* is a control to keep from hurting an area. . . . It is a control to hold a certain development in a certain area. [Emphasis supplied.]

INSTANCE 4: A commission member voted against approval of a zoning change. He apparently considered as proper the prevailing zoning classification for the property under consideration rather than other zoning categories, one of which, as his own words indicate, could have been chosen:

I voted against it [the zoning application] not because I thought it [the land in question] was improper for residential use, but it [the land in question] isn't quite ready for commercial use.

INSTANCE 5: A member of the Planning Commission rejected a "GR" zoning recommended by the Zoning Committee for the property under consideration and instead favored a "C" classification:

This is a logical extension of "C" zoning to grant this request, not "GR." I make a substitute motion to grant "C" for tract 1.

While these several instances contain evidence of a normative choice situation confronting decision-makers, not all norms relevant to the zoning process are to be perceived as constituting the means. For in reaching zoning decisions, the individuals comply with certain social conditions. That is, the decision-makers recognize certain standards of expectations that eliminate the possibility of alternative courses of action as they endeavor to arrive at zoning decisions. Indeed, not only do normative requirements prevail in Austin's Zoning Ordinance but also Texas state laws, sustained by decisions of the United States Supreme Court, impose restraints upon zoning efforts as an external factor in the zoning process.[5]

The following instances demonstrate the impact of the state and city governments' legal normative systems as social conditions that face decision-makers in the zoning process:

INSTANCE 1: Spot zoning is prohibited by state law; to the Planning Commissioners it is a normative facet over which no control can be exerted. An applicant requested a change in zoning from "A" to "B" to permit the placement of a beauty shop in her residence. The Planning Commission rejected this request on the grounds that it involves spot zoning:

Commission Member 1: I hate to see this spot zoning in a well-developed residential area.

Commission Member 2: I zone [land] for the "B" [Classification] and not for the beauty shop. I move that this request be denied on the

60

grounds that this is spot zoning in a very fine residential-A neighborhood and because there is no parking area provided [by the applicant].

Commission Member 3:   I am going to vote for this motion to deny. It represents a kind of difficult problem. In some cases it doesn't do damage to the neighborhood, but in this case it does. I can't vote for it [the application] when it goes against the state law that it is illegal to grant spot zoning.

INSTANCE 2:   State control also prevents regulation of certain uses by city governments through the latter's power to zone property:

Planning Director: The Supreme Court [of the State of Texas] has struck down all rulings forbidding a church in "A" residential [areas].

INSTANCE 3:   The impact of the normative system as a social condition is remarkably demonstrated in cases involving applications requesting zoning classifications for the purpose of selling intoxicants. Although almost all members of the City Council and Planning Commission insist that this authority should be taken out of their control and placed in a governmental licensing agency, nonetheless these bodies continue to zone such usages as required by state laws. As one commissioner commented:

There is another issue involved that you [the applicant] didn't touch upon. The request is for a "C-1" [to permit the sale of beer for off-premise consumption]. We on the Planning Commission feel that we should not pass on "C-1" or a "C-2" unless it is in a well-developed "C" area. Beer, whiskey, and wine should be restricted to commercial areas well developed with business.

INSTANCE 4:   A lawyer arguing against a zoning change asked if it would be legal to permit the proposed use under a Special Permit if the land is now zoned "A":

Council Member: Can this be done?

City Attorney: No. It's not legally possible [under the City's Zoning Ordinance].

INSTANCE 5:   Members of the City Council acknowledge the legal normative system as a condition, as indicated in this comment made by a member of the council:

I am not voting my opinion, but according to our [City] Ordinance [in denying this request]. We are dealing with things that are not vested

61

rights. . . . Until it is proven to me that there is anything against the law of our city or the state, I will be the first to vote no.

These illustrations indicate that city and state laws become dominant social conditions affecting the entire zoning process. They obtain as conditions inasmuch as these decision-makers have no direct control for altering the legal normative system when acting upon concrete zoning applications. That is, laws as *conditions* to social action in the zoning process eliminate the presence of certain alternatives for accomplishing the public welfare goal.

In addition to the legal normative system setting forth certain social conditions, the several bodies acting upon requests have created other conditions for arriving at decisions. The Planning Commission has been the most active group in this respect; it has formulated certain policies tending to direct the course of its own decisions without the presence of choice. The City Council appears to have hesitated in this regard to rely instead upon *ad hoc* formulations.

One of the most important social conditions formulated by members of the Planning Commission has to do with the issuance of zoning classifications governing the sale of intoxicants—the "C-1" and "C-2" categories. This ruling specifies that an area must be developed with commercial establishments before a zoning classification for the sale of intoxicants can be approved. On the basis of this social condition, the Planning Commission has acted upon various applications.

INSTANCE 1

Commission Member: I move that this "C-2" classification be granted. It [the area in question] conforms to our general rules of a well-developed "C" area and does not conflict with state laws or city ordinances.

INSTANCE 2

Commission Member: In view of the fact that the zoning [classification upon the land in question] is a "GR" and is across the street from a "C-1" classification and is in a well-developed commercial area, I move approval. . . .

Another conditional norm followed by the Planning Commission to realize the public welfare objective is the requirement that an appli-

62

cant be willing to dedicate land in the event that widening of a street upon which the applicant's property borders becomes necessary. Although the legality of this social condition has not been contested in the courts, it is nonetheless prescribed by the Planning Commission:

Planning Director: In matters where wider streets are needed, the Commission should deny the request. This will put the burden on the applicant in order to meet one of the conditions for granting the request. Lawyers are saying that the [dedication] letters are [legally] meaningless. They have said: "Tell me what to say and I'll write it down." They [the lawyers] claim it [the letter dedicating a right-of-way] is not enforceable.

Commission Member 1: We as a Commission must back our staff. We cannot let the staff require one thing and then we narrow it down.

Commission Member 2: Will we get a letter or an actual dedication?

Legal Counsel: It is an actual dedication.

(The Commission then voted unanimously to grant the application under consideration provided the applicant submitted a letter dedicating the necessary right-of-way in the event of widening of the street that abuts his property.)

Commission Member 4: It will be the responsibility of the staff [that is, members of the Planning Department] to notify the applicant that he must be willing to widen the street.

Planning Director: That's right.

Commission Member 5: All the staff will have to do is to tell the applicant that it is the policy of the Commission not to approve a request without a dedication. If the applicant refuses, we can deny the [zoning] change.

At one time certain Planning Commission members attempted to establish the normative condition of presenting a united vote to the City Council. Several members wanted to do this to strengthen the influence of the Planning Commission's decisions upon members of the council, and it was felt that members of the City Council desired unanimous votes in order to defend the council's decision on zoning. But after a brief trial period, the policy collapsed. Nonetheless, the effort is demonstrated in the following instances:

INSTANCE 1: The Planning Commission voted four to three to grant a change from "A" to "B" for establishment of a beauty shop in an existing single-family residence. The commission members then discussed this split vote:

Commission Member 1: Let's don't send any more [split votes] to the City Council.

Commission Member 2: They [the members of the City Council] complained to me about this.

Commission Member 1: I had two of them [the council members] on me. They want us to decide one way or the other—it doesn't matter which way.

Commission Member 3: They [the council members] don't like to make original decisions.

INSTANCE 2: For a particular request, the Planning Commission voted three to four against a motion to grant an application for a zoning change. Then a general discussion took place among commission members concerning the unanimity condition:

Commission Member 1: We made an agreement not to submit a split vote to the Council. Is anyone weak?

Commission Member 2: We granted the right to sell beer right across the street.

Commission Member 3: This property is right across the street from industrial uses.

(A second vote was taken upon the motion to grant the request, and resulted in a five-to-two approval of the zoning application.)

Zoning and Land Use

[To be ecologically relevant in accordance with the definition of ecology advanced in this study, zoning must have a demonstrable impact upon the development of land.] That is, zoning itself must be a causal factor in directing the course of land usage if it is to be considered of interest from an ecological perspective.]

To show that zoning creates and sustains a patterning of land

64

use, it is necessary to investigate whether or not land-use change actually takes place following action upon zoning applications by the City Council. To be ecologically significant, the empirical data to be examined must reflect the impact of zoning upon the social activities oriented to a territorial location.

In August, 1959, the writer made a personal inspection of property covered by various zoning applications to accomplish this task. Almost all applications heard by the Planning Commission and City Council for the years 1956, 1957, and 1958 were included for a total of 378 cases.[6] Regardless of the action taken by the Planning Commission and City Council, an attempt was made to locate each piece of property in order to determine if any change in land use had taken place. Table I reveals the results of this investigation.

Table I is divided into two major sections to separate those zoning applications granted or denied by the City Council, since the council's action is final and subject only to review by the courts. Zoning applications that were withdrawn or postponed before final action by the City Council have been treated as denials in the computations presented in Table I inasmuch as no legal approval was given to such cases. The term "unchanged" refers to land use remaining the same as the usage prior to the filing of a zoning application; "change" means that a shift in land use has taken place following action upon the zoning application by the City Council; and "undetermined" indicates an inability to specify if a change in land usage has or has not occurred. The "undetermined" column contains instances where: (1) the actual location could not be ascertained by this researcher; (2) there was incomplete information in zoning reports prepared by the Planning Department; or (3) applications were denied in one of these three years but granted at a later date.

The researcher, by comparing the land use described in the zoning report prepared by Austin's Planning Department at the time of application with the use taking place at the time this researcher made a personal inspection of the property, listed the property under one of the columns. A shift in land usage is said to have taken place when the use *at the time of inspection* was not permitted by the zoning

65

classification for the property *at the time of application* for a zoning reclassification. Land use is considered to be unchanged when the use *at the time of inspection* accorded with the uses permitted by the zoning classification for the property *at the time a change in zoning was sought* by an applicant.

TABLE 1

Land-Use Survey of Zoning Cases for the Years 1956, 1957, and 1958[a]

YEAR	ZONING APPLICATIONS GRANTED			ZONING APPLICATIONS DENIED[b]			TOTALS
	Land Use Unchanged	Land Use Changed	Land Use Undetermined	Land Use Unchanged	Land Use Changed	Land Use Undetermined	
1956	23	57	16	12	0	5	113
	(20.4%)	(50.5%)	(14.1%)	(10.6%)	(0.0%)	(4.4%)	(100%)
1957	25	59	10	24	0	9	127
	(19.7%)	(46.5%)	(7.8%)	(18.9%)	(0.0%)	(7.1%)	(100%)
1958	46	57	10	18	0	7	138
	(33.3%)	(41.3%)	(7.3%)	(13.0%)	(0.0%)	(5.1%)	(100%)
Totals	94	173	36	54	0	21	378
	(24.8%)	(45.8%)	(9.5%)	(14.3%)	(0.0%)	(5.6%)	(100%)

[a] "Special Permit" zoning applications and so-called "areal studies" have been omitted.
[b] This category also includes requests given incomplete action by the City Council or withdrawn by the applicant.

The first outstanding generalization to be drawn from Table I is the obvious fact that the granting of a zoning change does not automatically bring about a change in land use. For we find that 20.4 per cent of the zoning requests granted in 1956 resulted in no change in land use; almost 20 per cent of the properties in question remained unchanged for 1957; and a third remained constant in 1958. It is therefore to be concluded that shifts in zoning classifications do not compel shifts in land-use activity.

On the other hand, Table I also indicates that many changes actually took place that accord with the zoning reclassification granted by the City Council. For the year 1956 we find that there were new uses upon lands for 50.5 per cent of the applications inspected; in 1957, there were 46.5 per cent; and 1958, 41.3 per cent.

But the direct impact of zoning upon land use is most apparent

66

when zoning applications are finally denied or postponed by the City Council or withdrawn by the applicant. For it is clearly seen from Table I, under the heading of "Zoning Applications Denied," that in every case inspected there had been no change in the land-use activity. While the percentages of denials are rather small for these three years, nonetheless all such cases reflect a continuation of the earlier land uses. For 1956, 10.6 per cent of all inspected cases remained unchanged following disapproval, postponement, or withdrawal of the application for a zoning change; in 1957, the percentage was 18.9; and for 1958, 13.0 per cent. It is a reasonable assumption that we could expect at least some alteration in land use if all cases under denial had in fact received approval by the City Council. For certainly some of the persons seeking a zoning change would have actually employed the land differently had the requested zoning changes been approved rather than denied by the City Council. The *actual* potency of zoning as an independent causal factor, therefore, takes place only to the extent to which decision-makers allow zoning to affect the land usage that would apparently have taken place in the absence of zoning restrictions.

[The impact of zoning as a negative force that prevents the development of an alternative patterning of land use—that is, zoning as a social condition—cannot be properly measured, however, simply by examining the council's formal action upon zoning applications. For there is no way fully to evaluate the inhibiting strength zoning regulations have in discouraging individuals to even apply for zoning changes for property. There was evidence that some individuals refrained from filing applications for zoning changes simply because they were certain their applications would not receive the council's approval. Thus, the probability of failure in obtaining zoning changes hinders land-use change, and in this manner zoning regulations affect land-use development without the direct involvement of the decision-makers acting upon zoning applications]

These observations based upon the data presented in Table I support the social action theory advocated in this study. First, the "changed" and "unchanged" cases noted in Table I are possible alternatives facing the individual applicant following action upon a zoning application by the City Council. For upon the council's approval of a zoning change, the applicant may choose to alter the contemporary use upon a piece of property or simply refrain from initiating any change in land use. In such cases, zoning classifications serve to facilitate means even for an applicant. Second, the denied cases represent a social condition for applicants: individuals either conform to the zoning decisions, and thereby the land use remains constant, or they refuse to conform to the requirements of the sustained zoning classification and thereby violate zoning as a normative condition. The data in Table I indicate that property owners elected to abide by the zoning classifications of the applications that were denied, thus revealing the most direct impact of zoning upon land use. But regardless of whether zoning classifications become means or conditions, applicants implicitly or explicitly rely upon social values to: (1) select a specific use from alternatives when zoning classifications are a means; and (2) conform or violate when zoning classifications are social conditions. Volition, consequently, must be at least implicitly exercised by individuals, thereby sustaining the contention by voluntaristic ecologists that social values must be included in any complete and correct accounting of ecological phenomena. However, the concept and role of social values will be considered in the two following chapters.

Chapter Five

VALUE ORIENTATIONS
AND ZONING DATA

The second hypothesis to be tested deals with what has been referred to in Chapter 3 as "value systems." A value system is a set of inter-related concepts individuals utilize to decide what is to be desired, negated, nondesired or what is to be considered appropriate, inappropriate, nonappropriate. Hypothesis II relates the value system to the zoning data. A formal statement of this hypothesis is:

HYPOTHESIS II: Ecological phenomena must be examined by discovering and analyzing the interpretative significance given to
the goal, means, social conditions, and cognitive data by actors
resorting to value systems.

There would be no need to present Hypothesis II if normative systems—incorporating both means and social conditions—completely accounted for the manner in which individuals realized an objective. Essentially, Hypothesis I states a normative argument: The mere existence of norms and recognition of them by actors result in so-

69

cial action automatically complying to normative systems. An exclusive concern, however, with normative systems as the determining feature of social action ignores several other problems. First, norms cannot account for the selection from the means; second, norms cannot account for conformity or nonconformity to social conditions. For these reasons, the normative emphasis contained in Hypothesis I does not encompass the concepts necessary for comprehending the zoning data collected for this ecological study of a zoning process.

But a recognition of these shortcomings of the normative approach in Hypothesis I does not require a reliance upon a positivistic ecological perspective on the part of an investigator. The positivist approach argues, according to Parsons, that norms simply manifest "the real forces governing action" and, therefore, have "no causal significance at all."[1] On the basis of this reasoning, positivists also reject subjective feelings as possible components in social action. Therefore, because of their insistence on analyzing only "external" forces, without regard for socially shared internal feeling states, ecological materialists adhere to a positivistic orientation. Materialistic ecologists maintain that social organization is a result of such physical forces as environment, population, and technology. Zoning data, however, refute the positivists' contentions.

Because of the incompleteness noted above in Hypothesis I and because of the emphasis upon physical conditions and repudiation of social values by those holding to positivism, Hypothesis II will be treated as a possible alternative for analyzing zoning data. It should be remembered, however, that Hypothesis I is not invalidate; it simply omits certain essential aspects necessary for an explanation of Austin's zoning process from an ecological perspective. In brief, then, Hypothesis II complements Hypothesis I.

To treat Hypothesis II, we shall consider first the relevancy of normative systems for analyzing zoning data; second, the applicability of positivism for investigating zoning data; and third, the place of value systems in the zoning process.

70

Normative Systems and Zoning Data

Two concepts involving the normative system have been dealt with in this study: (1) means—the presence of alternative norms for accomplishing a given end; and (2) social conditions—norms prohibiting various alternative considerations for the attainment of a given end.[2] In applying these normative concepts to the zoning data, it was found that the decision-makers sought to realize their public welfare objective by selecting from alternative zoning classifications—the means—as set forth within Austin's Zoning Ordinance. In no instance was a zoning classification employed that was not to be found in the Zoning Ordinance. However, compliance with social conditions was not always forthcoming on the part of Austin's decision-makers. For there were instances when the decision-makers purposefully ignored normative legal requirements in selecting a particular norm from the means when making a zoning decision:

INSTANCE 1: One of the legal strictures on zoning is the provision that zoning applications cannot be granted if approval results in spot zones. Although the decision-makers are fully aware of this legal social condition, their decisions, nonetheless, do not always reflect this stipulation.

Case A: A person asked for a change in zoning from "B" to "O" to permit the erection of a decorating shop. In discussing this application, the decision-makers fully appreciated the possibility of spot zoning. Yet, the request was approved:

Commission Member 1: That's [the zoning classification under consideration] a spot zone.

Commission Member 2: There's a doctor's office across the street.

Commission Member 3: It is zoned ["O"] on the west of this property [we are considering for rezoning].

Commission Member 1: I think the area is in transition to offices, but it [the zoning classification under consideration] is a spot zone.

Planning Director: Yes, it is. It's a spot zone.

71

Commission Member 1: That's [the spot zoning] against the law.

Commission Member 4: It is an area in transition; there are apartment houses in the area.

Commission Member 1: That's why I think other property should be included [in the application]. I'd vote for it [the zoning change] if they [the applicants] had an area with the legal area.

(The Planning Commission then voted eight to one recommending that the zoning request be granted.)

Case B: This application involved a request for a "B" zoning to allow for a beauty shop in an existing residence. Again, although the commission members recognized the fact of spot zoning, certain members still voted in favor of the request—in direct violation of the legal norms:

Commission Member 1: I move that this application be granted.

Commission Member 2: I second that motion.

(The motion lost by a three-to-five vote; a countermotion to deny passed by a five-to-three vote.)

Commission Member 1: Within one-half of a block there is a house with a beauty shop.

Commission Member 3: I voted against that request.

Commission Member 4: I also voted against that request.

Commission Member 2: It's a spot zone. But if the Council has set up a policy to move in beauty shops [into single-family residences], we should follow it. I don't see any need in knocking our heads against a stone wall.

Commission Member 4: This [zoning request for beauty shops] is for areas with [existing] "B" zoning.

Commission Member 3: If the Council is going to set all the rules, then we should just let the Council do our job.

In the last illustration we find that a normative condition set up by the City Council is not acceptable to a majority of the Planning Commission members. Yet, one commission member (Commission Member 2) recognized that the zoning would result in a spot classification, but chose to abide by the normative condition established by

72

the council rather than to dismiss this social condition as did the majority.

INSTANCE 2: It was noted in discussing the normative system under Hypothesis I that the Planning Commission formulated the normative condition requiring an area to be fully developed with commercial business as a requisite for "C-1" or "C-2" zoning. Still, we find deviations from this standard by commission members:

Case A

Commission Member 1: I move that this request be granted.

Commission Member 2: I think the request is logical; the sale of beer in cartons is no more harmful than the sale of other drinks for off-premise consumption.

Commission Member 3: I think we ought to restrict our comments to zoning. The restrictions to cartons are not zoning.

Commission Member 4: I think I shall have to vote against it [the application] in view of the Commission's rule that we grant this [type of request] only in a well-developed area. There is no commercial development [in the immediate vicinity].

(The commission voted four to four on the motion to grant.)

Commission Member 5: The fact is that it [the area surrounding the property in question] lends itself to commercial development. Anderson Lane will become a thoroughfare.

Commission Member 3: Your reasoning is sound; if we depart from the [commission's] rule [governing our action on "C-1" classifications], we should change the rule.

Commission Member 2: There is something wrong with the zoning system which gives a "C-1" for a grocery store that at the same time will allow for honky-tonks, filling stations, etc.

Commission Member 7: It would be bad for the people if ——— [the name of a chain store] were to move out [of Austin]. It would be good if we could grant an "LR-1."

Commission Member 3: But this would be illegal.

Commission Member 5: We don't know if they [the applicants] have a contract [to purchase the land upon receiving the zoning change] or not.

73

Commission Member 4: The motion loses. It [the application] passes [to the City Council] without a recommendation.

In this example we find certain members voting to grant the application aware of the fact that the evidence did not warrant approval on the basis of the social condition set forth by the commission for acting upon "C-1" and "C-2" classifications. On the other hand, half of the commission complied with the normative requirement, and argued from the position that if members departed from the commission's own prescription, then the normative standard should be eliminated. But departure from this norm continued:

Case B

Planning Director: I would like to see a subdivision [constructed on this property in question].

Commission Member 1: I have some reservations on this [application]. It's not good planning to do something like this [to permit the erection of a drive-in grocery store in an undeveloped area as proposed in the zoning request].

Commission Member 2: I have seen a contract on this by——— [the name of the food store which will sell beer for off-premise consumption if this application is approved] with Mr. ——— [the applicant]. I got that information from Mr. ———.

Commission Member 3: It would be inconsistent for me to vote against this [request]. I don't see any difference in the sale of beer as coke.

Commission Member 2: I move that this [request] be granted for the reason that there are definite plans to sell the tract [of land].

(The motion to grant was approved by the Zoning Committee on a two-to-one vote.)

These illustrations offer empirical evidence that the decision-makers can depart from certain social conditions in reaching decisions. Consequently, a complete reliance upon the normative system for analyzing social action fails to give an adequate account of the zoning process. Before we consider a more acceptable alternative, however, the argument of the positivists deserves consideration.

74

Positivism and Zoning Data

While the normative concept requires conformity to standards of expectation, positivism in ecological thought stresses conformity to physical, external conditions prevailing in a situation. "External" forces are the only real elements that act upon man and, therefore, explain the nature even of ecological phenomena. The notion that ecological phenomena result from physical conditions makes the materialistic ecologist a positivist; those ecologists who deny the significance of social values and seek casual analysis instead in biological and physical determinants are, in reality, espousing the materialistic orientation of positivism. Action, according to the materialistic-positivistic ecologist, becomes an automatic accommodation on the part of individuals to prevailing physical circumstances.

The zoning data seem to offer a degree of support for the positivists' contention; there appears, at first glance, to be some evidence reinforcing the claim advocated by materialistic ecologists. Foremost are the factual data collected and presented by the Planning Department at public sessions before the Planning Commission. As one of its primary obligations, the Planning Department gathers data of the factual sort to assist decision-makers in reaching decisions on zoning applications. The results appear in the "Zoning Change Staff Report."

This report provides a description of the land, giving the location, nature of the topography, present land uses, size of the area being considered, count of automobiles on abutting streets, and uses in the area surrounding the property in question. The staff report also states the existing and proposed zoning classifications, past zoning classifications, proposed usage, as well as several other items related to the property in question. The importance of such factual material, in addition to other "external" data, is seen in the following instances. The examples will show that decision-makers "conform" to physical conditions in arriving at decisions upon zoning applications, apparently "confirming" the arguments of materialistic ecologists.

INSTANCE 1: A person applied for a zoning change from "A" to "B" to permit the establishment of apartment units. The zoning request was unanimously denied by the Planning Commission on the basis of "external" conditions:

Commission Member: I make the motion that this [application] be denied due to the fact that it is a spot zone and due to the fact that Marlton Drive is not wide enough to justify the change.

INSTANCE 2: An applicant requested a "C-1" zoning to permit the sale of intoxicants. The zoning request was unanimously rejected by the Planning Commission on the basis of certain cognitive data:

Commission Member: I move that this request be denied. It [the proposed zoning change] would not do the neighborhood or the community any good. Diza Street is a heavily congested area and for this reason I move denial—and also there is no provision for off-street parking.

INSTANCE 3: Most zoning cases are approved on the basis that the proposed request is similar or identical to the zoning classifications of surrounding property. Consequently, many decisions reflect this fact in the following manner:

Commission Member: I move that this application be approved. It is a logical extension of an existing zoning.

INSTANCE 4: The Planning Commission rejects some cases because the requested zoning classification fails to reflect the prevailing classification surrounding the property under consideration:

Commission Member: I move that we deny this request. This [zoning request] is a well-developed, large "A" residential area.

INSTANCE 5: The following illustration is perhaps the most vivid example showing the importance of physical data upon zoning decisions. The Zoning Committee unanimously voted to grant a change in zoning from "A" to "B" to allow the placement of a beauty shop in an existing single-family residence. It did so because the staff report erroneously listed certain land uses as existing in the area when

76

in fact these did not. In the following discussion among Planning Commission members, the error is corrected. There was then the unanimous vote by the Planning Commission to deny the request with all members who first approved the request at the Zoning Committee hearing reversing their votes:

Commission Member 1: I move that this application be granted.

Commission Member 2: We have established that the map [furnished by the Planning Department showing usages in the surrounding area of the land in question] is wrong and that this [land covered by the request] is not in a commercial area. The fire station [reported by the Staff Report as in the area] is not there, either.

Planning Director: The City Council zoned back the triangle there [located on the use-map] from commercial to "A."

Commission Member 3: What is the attitude of the neighbors?

Secretary: There aren't any replies [from the notices sent to the surrounding property owners by the Planning Department].

Commission Member 1: I move that we deny this request. It is not in a commercial area, and due to the fact that the commercial property in the area is being re-zoned to "C."

There are also instances of conformance to physical conditions by members of the City Council.

INSTANCE 1: A person appeared before this body asking for a zoning change from "A" to "O" for the purpose of using the property for a doctor's office. The council voted unanimously to grant the request even in the face of determined opposition:

Council Member: We heard the arguments [on the request] last week. Is there any new evidence?

Opponent: What considerations do you take into account in making your decisions?

Council Member: You are supposed to zone the land for the highest and best use. *If the character of the land is changing, the zoning must change.* All along the Interregional [Highway] was [once] residential and everyone knows that it is not [suitable] for residents now. Time has changed. [Emphasis supplied.]

77

The above sentence—"If the character of the land is changing, the zoning must change"—clearly reflects "compliance" with physical conditions. For if land use were stable in the area, the ecological materialist would contend, then the zoning would remain constant for the property. But as external conditions shift, so must zoning.

INSTANCE 2: An attorney for an applicant presented arguments before the City Council in favor of his client's request for a change in zoning from "A" to "O" in anticipation of a future location for a doctor's office. However, members of the council hesitated to grant the request on the grounds that this zoning would then permit the applicant to return and request a special permit for construction of a service station. Still, the council unanimously voted to grant the application. In doing so, the reflection of physical evidence was shown in the vote of one council member who stated:

I look at this piece of property as an extension of an [existing] "O" Office [classification]. This property is not suitable for a residence. We can handle any future change. The character of the neighborhood is for an "O" Office.

The empirical data presented thus far in this section would appear to substantiate the contention by positivists—hence ecological materialists—that social action reflects physical conditions apart from volition. It would seem, simply on the basis of the evidence thus far offered, that individuals automatically comply with the "demands" of factual data of the physical sort as conditions. According to the positivistic leanings of materialistic ecologists, technological developments, shifting land uses, traffic arteries, population distribution, and physical environment prescribe the pattern of land use; man's social organization meekly conforms to the edicts of these material substances.

By introducing further empirical data, however, we find that physical conditions and cognitive data are only some of the elements to be taken into consideration when presenting an analysis of zoning as an ecological phenomenon. There is considerable evidence that runs contrary to the arguments of the positivist and, hence, the ecological materialist. In many instances, decisions by members of the

City Council and Planning Commission failed to reflect the prevailing physical attributes that the positivists advocate as determinants of social action and ecological phenomena. Moreover, illustrations presented below demonstrate that, contrary to the positivist's view,[3] social action does not of necessity conform to physical forces. Instead, the zoning data reveal that the decision-makers impose interpretative significance upon physical conditions; social meanings in the form of conceptualization are ascribed to external data rather than vice versa as claimed by positivists. Consequently, identical physical matter and other factual data are susceptible to various meaningful interpretations by actors. And indeed the above illustrations that apparently sustain the positivist's orientation represent in reality only one type of social imputation that might be given to physical conditions by the decision-makers.

INSTANCE 1: A person applied for a "BB" classification to erect an apartment house. The staff report described the land uses in the vicinity as follows:

The area north of the site is developed with single-family dwellings and the following uses: a drama studio, church, office building, gift shop, florist, service station, washateria, plumbing shop, cleaners, and a boat shop. The area east, south, and west of the site is developed with single-family dwellings and a school.

Given these cognitive data concerning land development, members of the commission advanced several interpretations:

Commission Member 1: I move that this request be granted for the reason that even if this is a spot zone, it is an area which is losing some of its residential characteristics and is in a period of transition to a multi-unit area.

Planning Director: I, frankly, admit it is a spot zone. It can become otherwise by extending [the proposed classification to] the whole area. . . . It [the proposed zoning change] will over-intensify the development. The streets are only 40–50 feet in width. They will be two-way streets.

Commission Member 2: I am going to vote against it because it is spot zoning and that is illegal. I recognize that it is an area of transition but it is not in accord with the law. [Emphasis supplied.]

79

Commission Member 3: It is my opinion that when an area is in a period of transition, it is reasonable to approve a spot zone.

Commission Member 4: Are there enough off-street parking places for a nine-unit apartment?

Planning Director: There has to be because of the ordinance [requiring designation of proper parking facilities].

Commission Member 5: Do you [the applicant] have definite plans for the development in the immediate future?

Applicant: Yes. Within six months.

Commission Member 5: I am opposed to spot zoning. But since it is in an area of transition and there is no one in opposition [to the request], I am in favor of it.

(The commission voted seven to one to grant the request.)

INSTANCE 2: The applicant requested a change from "A" to "LR" for one tract of land to construct "certain retail services for the immediate neighborhood"; on an adjoining tract he requested a change from "A" to "C-1" in order to "operate [a] drive-in grocery with [the] right to sell beer for off-premise consumption. . . ." When the case was opened for discussion, the applicant's attorney filed a letter withdrawing the "C-1" request for the second tract.

In addition to the factual data given in the staff report, the discussion that follows indicates an awareness of the presence of heavy traffic upon streets in the vicinity of the area under consideration and the presence of a human population. Again, the interpretations given to each of these "physical" data should be noted in this illustration:

Commission Member 1: I move that this request be denied.

Commission Member 2: We have a letter from Mr. ———— [the applicant's attorney] in which the applicant asks for a withdrawal of the "C-1" request.

Commission Member 3: I move that we accept the withdrawal.

(The Commission unanimously voted to accept the applicant's withdrawal.)

Commission Member 3: I make the substitute motion that we grant an "LR." I checked pretty carefully on that area. One of the principal objections of the people was that it [the zoning change] would devaluate their land. But the fact that this is a natural area set apart from the other [land uses devoted to residences] by a natural barrier [that is, an eight-foot drainage ditch], this objection does not hold.

One of the other objections [stated by opponents to the proposed zoning change] was that it would create a traffic hazard. But it is the residences that create traffic; business just takes advantage of it.

This ["LR" zoning I propose] is a more restricted zone [than a "C" or "D" Industrial]. This land is not suitable for residential use. I believe that we must vote for the long-run advantages.

Commission Member 4: I feel the same way. Sooner or later we are going to have businesses [on this property]. Since this land is cut off by natural barriers, I believe it is suitable for business [use].

Commission Member 5: He [the applicant] left us with the lesser of two evils [by withdrawing the "C-1" zoning request].

Commission Member 2: I have a letter from the attorney representing the applicant. It [the letter] claims to have new evidence. I don't think so, but I'll read it to let you decide. [The commissioner reads the letter.] We'll be glad to hear from the opposition now.

Opponent 1: We have been up here three or four times on [that is, opposing] this application. They [the applicant and his attorney] admitted that the "C-1" [request] was premature. This means that they will come back for a "C-1" [at a later date]; no drive-in grocery can do business without beer. We'll come back if we have to [and oppose the request once again]. We are getting better organized all the time as we come back here [before the Planning Commission].

We bought our property in 1955. We were the first to buy within 200 feet of this property [being considered for rezoning]. At that time it was zoned "A" Residential. There was no whisper of anything else. We certainly feel that bringing in business will hurt us.

There is a 14-acre "LR" [tract] near us. We are not pleased with it [there]. But it's alright. We knew of it when we moved there [where we now live]. . . .

Opponent 2: That is very sound residential property [where we now live]. The creek [that is, drainage ditch] has been given [as a reason] for not making it residential. But our home borders on it [the drainage ditch]. If it [the speaker's property] were not suitable for homes, we would not have bought there.

Opponent 3: I am particularly concerned with children. We have enough commercial property [around us now]. The majority of the people were not in favor of it [the proposed zoning change].

Planning Director: I have checked the original subdivision plan. This street [which the land in question faces] is a subdivision street [and not a commercial street].

Commission Member 2: I am going to vote against this request. Although there is "LR" [zoning] across the street, it has not been fully developed. It doesn't appear to me to be a logical extension of an existing commercial area.

Commission Member 1: I would like to give an "LR" if it were in any way of benefit to the area.

Commission Member 6: It would be very unlikely that . . . [Mr.] ————'s tract [located near this area] will be retail.

Commission Member 2: We have no way of knowing.

Commission Member 7: If we zone this property "LR," it would be extremely illogical not to give . . . [Mr.] ————'s property [located in this area] "LR." For that reason, I think we should keep it [the area under consideration] "A" Residential.

(The Planning Commission voted six to two in favor of the motion to deny this request.)

INSTANCE 3: In certain cases commission members deny the relevancy of particular cognitive, that is, physical, data in making decisions; others insist upon the importance of the identical factual data. In the discussion below, the significance of soil composition is raised. The applicant sought a "BB" zoning coupled with a second height and area category to allow for more intensive development of the area than would be permitted under the existing first height and area. The first commission member to speak seeks to grant the "BB" zoning classification as requested by the applicant, but to deny the applicant's request for a second height and area:

Commission Member 1: I move that the applicant's request be denied and that we grant "BB" with first height and area.

Commission Member 2: I can't go along with this [zoning request]. No one has brought up the matter of foundation. The nature of the soil

82

is such that it will not support large buildings [that could be erected if a second height and area were approved].

Commission Member 1: We are not to consider this in making our decision.

Commission Member 2: It's just as important as anything else.

Commission Member 1: It [the area in question] is a large area and a vacant tract, and I don't think it will develop into single-family homes.

(The Zoning Committee rejected the motion to grant a "BB" zoning with first height and area.)

Commission Member 3: I move that the application be denied.

(The members of the Zoning Committee unanimously voted in favor of this motion to deny.)

INSTANCE 4: This illustration is composed of excerpts taken from two separate hearings before the City Council. A person applied for a change in zoning from "A" to "O" for the purpose of erecting a furniture store. The staff report described land usage in the area as:

The areas to the south and east of the site are developed predominantly with single-family dwellings. North of the site is the State Highway Department service yard. West and adjoining the site are the I. and G.N. Railroad and the Austin State School.

The same report stated that the car count on the street—West Thirty-fifth—upon which the property in question fronts was 5,850 per day.

Attorney for Applicant: . . . The area consists of several different types of uses: residences, a state school, and the State Highway Department's service yard. Thirty-fifth Street is in excess of 60 feet and the traffic count is over 5,000 cars per day.

Opponent: You can't use traffic as a reason for not building anything. Out on Bull Creek Road [a heavily traveled traffic artery in the city] they [certain individuals] are building brick homes as fast as they can.

Council Member 1: The character of 35th Street is changing. You wouldn't build a home there [upon the land we are considering for re zoning] now.

83

Opponent: No, I wouldn't. . . .

Council Member 2: . . . They [the Public Works Department of the city] are going to widen 35th Street.

Each of these four instances illustrates that social action does not conform to cognitive data in the form of physical conditions in an automatic fashion as materialistic ecologists contend. The decision-makers variously interpreted the cognitive data in the form of physical conditions, although they would all recognize these physical items as identical. If "external" conditions consistently force compliance, then social action should be identical when individuals confront identical physical conditions. But the above examples clearly reveal alternative interpretations of the same physical conditions. Moreover, even when there was unanimity, such agreement reflected social meanings held by the several decision-makers.

At this point, then, both the concept of normative system as social conditions and the condition-response of positivism fail to yield a satisfactory analysis of zoning data from an ecological perspective. Normative conditions, while relevant as a facet of social action, cannot fully account for social action in the zoning process; positivism is refuted because its advocates fail to recognize that physical conditions require not only social conceptualization but also social interpretation through the imposition of socially conceived values. Inasmuch as ecological phenomena must therefore be explained through an analysis of social meanings rather than through physical conditions and/or cognitive data, positivism within ecological thought is untenable. To offer a more complete approach, therefore, we now turn to the concept of social values.

Social Values and Zoning Data

The term "value" refers to a concept specifying what aspects of a situation are desirable, undesirable, or nondesirable; "value system" refers to a set of interrelated values. Through the implementation of so-

84

cial values, or social value systems, actors (1) give interpretative significance to the stated goal, social conditions, and cognitive data involved in the zoning process; and (2) select a norm from among the several possible alternatives that constitute the means for accomplishing an objective.

If social value systems were entirely absent as an element of social action—as positivists and ecological materialists contend—then there could be no social organization. Conceptualization in terms of ends, means, social conditions, and cognitive data would not only be eliminated as elements to social action, but these same items would be hollow and void of meaning were social values nonexistent for ecological analysis. The goal of promoting the public welfare in the zoning process is meaningless unless specificity is assigned to it through a social value system. Because this end is open to several interpretations as to what constitutes a desirable or undesirable public welfare, actors have no choice other than to rely upon notions of desirability or undesirability. The same is certainly true for cognitive data: the possibility of alternative meanings that might be ascribed to external data requires the application of differing value systems. And finally, because of the presence of value systems, social action does not always conform to the social conditions prevailing within a social situation. Before proceeding with illustrations to demonstrate these generalizations, however, a comment concerning the connection between *social values* and the *end* is necessary.

Clyde Kluckhohn and others define a "value" as "a conception, explicit or implicit, distinctive of an individual or characteristic of a group, of the desirable which influences the selection from available modes, means, and ends of action."[4] Thus, according to Kluckhohn, individuals employ values to select one *end* in preference to another. However, the logic of this argument cannot be sustained. For if individuals are faced with a choice situation with regard to *ends,* as claimed by Kluckhohn,[5] then it must be assumed that individuals decide so as to achieve an objective. When selecting from among alternatives it is logically impossible to do so without a *singleness* of objective. The presence of normative alternatives, rather than the selection of a goal per se, indicates the existence of means to achieve a goal.

An end, *qua* end, therefore, cannot be selected; it is, instead, to be realized. Actors relate social values to a goal, not in terms of selectivity, as Kluckhohn maintains, but in order to give *specificity* to an end. Individuals utilize values so as to give concreteness to what would otherwise be a more or less amorphous goal.

The following examples have been selected from the zoning data to illustrate the necessity, for both participants and decision-makers, of interpreting the stated goal, social conditions, and cognitive data by resorting to social values.

INSTANCE 1: The applicant requested a special permit to allow for the conversion of an existing residence into a veterinary hospital. This illustration, drawn from both Zoning Committee and Planning Commission hearings, demonstrates the varying interpretations given to the goal in zoning:

Commission Member 1: How much ground [area] must there be for a [veterinary] hospital?

Planning Director: There is no requirement.

Commission Member 2: It [the area under consideration] is too small.

Applicant: This request conforms to page 41 of your Zoning Ordinance [in a section setting forth the requirements that must be met under a Special Permit zoning classification]. This area [the building] will be made soundproof so there will be no noise. A pet hospital will promote the welfare [of the people]. There will be no runs or odor. My son, Dr. ———, is here and will be glad to answer questions about sound keeping of the hospital.

Dr. ———: Your business must allow inspection by the owners [of the pets I will be treating]. The fence will be stucco. There will be no windows or openings on the yard. The ventilation will take care of that [that is, there is no need for windows, since air circulation will be accomplished through air conditioning].

Commission Member 1: How large is this lot?

86

Planning Director: 266 square feet.

Commission Member 1:   How many pets will you have [at any one time]?

Dr. ———:   Ten. I intend to operate a hospital and not a place to keep dogs and board them. There are advantages [if this request is granted]: (1) taxes from increased value of property and fees for licensing, and (2) prevention of diseases.

Proponent: I think it would be wise to allow this business. A business of this sort will do no harm to the area. We enjoy having business nearby rather than going out to shopping centers.

Opponent 1:   I challenge anyone to go to a [veterinary] hospital and see if there isn't an odor. It can't be avoided. There are no hospitals that are so soundproof that doesn't have the noise. We are in an "A" Residential area. It will certainly lower the value of our property.

(The Zoning Committee voted unanimously to grant the request. The remaining discussion is taken from the hearing held by the Planning Commission.)

Commission Member 1:   I feel that if the applicant has complied with all the requirements in the Zoning Ordinance, we will have to grant it [the request]. I move approval [of the application].

Commission Member 2:   I asked for a legal decision if it [the request] could be denied even if the applicant complies with the [city's] Zoning Ordinance.

Legal Counsel: *It is my reading* of the [Zoning] Ordinance that the applicant must show evidence that he has complied with the Zoning Ordinance. You [members of the commission] *must decide* this in terms of the health and general welfare. [Emphasis supplied.]

Commission Member 3:   Would it be legal to construe that if this [property under consideration] is not the proper location for this [proposed] use, that this [reasoning] would come under the general welfare?

Legal Counsel: That can be done.

Opponent 1:   We object on the grounds of the Zoning Ordinance. First, there is the fire hazard. Second, there is the public health and welfare to consider. And third, it will be very noisy. This [area under consideration] is in a residential area. It is proposed to make an animal hospital around an old frame home with a stucco finish. The stucco will not prevent noise; it is not as effective as soundproofing. The stench is a

87

concomitant to the storing and keeping of animals. It is proposed to ventilate the building by taking it [air] from the inside outside to the neighborhood. This is not an area for an animal hospital. It is not the place for it in a quiet, residential neighborhood.

Opponent 2: I have in writing a protest by my wife and me. This day I talked to a gentleman who lives near a hospital similar to this proposal. He says that at the distance he lives, when the doors [to the veterinary hospital] are opened, the noise comes out and flies are attracted because of the odor. He said that if I lived across the alley from this I was "in a mess." We have made an investment in our homes. We believe that there are proper locations for this [use]. Milton Street is a narrow and strictly residential street. It is not conducive to heavy traffic. We do not believe that the sanitary conditions will be kept over a long period of time.

Commission Member 1: If this [request] is approved, they [the applicants] will not be able to change the [construction] plans as they have been submitted.

(The Planning Commission's vote resulted in a four-to-four tie. According to the legal norms, a tie vote on special permits is a denial of the application.)

This example illustrates a reliance upon social values by participants and Planning Commission members in an effort to interpret the goal, norms, and cognitive data. "Commission Member 1" maintained that by conforming to legal norms prescribed for special permits, the *fact* of compliance on the part of an applicant required approval of the application by the Planning Commission. Several members, as well as the legal counsel, rejected this value toward the factual datum by insisting that their desire to refuse approval would advance the public welfare. The applicant and his proponents maintained that the public welfare goal could best be served by approval of this request. On the other hand, opponents felt that the proposed use—a cognitive standard—would be undesirable and a detriment to their area. Consequently, we find actors expressing different values toward the identical goal, social conditions, and cognitive data in their efforts to give meaningful interpretation to these conceptions.

88

INSTANCE 2: A person applied for a zoning change to construct a residential building for housing university students. The uses in the immediate area consisted of several dormitories, a church, a church elementary school, several single-family residences, a drive-in bank, and a service station:

Commission Member 1: I move that this request be granted.

Commission Member 2: I still *feel* that this [request] is too dense development in the area. [Emphasis supplied.]

Commission Member 1: I went out and looked the situation over [on location]. Their [the applicant's] proposed construction will not *increase* the density hazard. The present elementary school there creates a traffic hazard. It [the proposed use] is a logical use of the land.

Commission Member 3: We are voting on zoning and not the use of the whole. There are narrow streets [throughout the area]. The zoning is appropriate, but the use should not be allowed.

Commission Member 1: Any use permitted in Commercial "C" as appropriate [has] got to be *appropriate* for the use of the land [in question]. The streets are there and we can't change them now. It's got to be used for this. [Emphasis supplied.]

Commission Member 4: A student motel will not cause more traffic than the school and the bank. There is nothing that causes more traffic than a school.

Commission Member 5: The fact that the bank and school are already there should be considered in refusing to extend this "C" property. The University neighborhood is getting too crowded. Even if the school does cause traffic, it's [the school] there. And so is the bank. This is the reason for *not* granting it [the request].

(The Planning Commission voted four to three in favor of the motion to grant the application.)

The importance of social values to give meaning to cognitive data is clearly shown in this illustration. Population density, presence of automobile traffic, and existence of prevailing land usages, such as the drive-in bank and the elementary school, are cognitive data that had different implications for the various members. Several commissioners considered these facts as enhancing a desirable use, and voted to grant

89

the application; other members strongly contended that the identical data made the request undesirable and, therefore, voted to reject the request.

INSTANCE 3: It has been noted that instances occur where the decision-makers do not conform to the normative system as a social condition. Here certain members reject a particular legal norm, while others accept the legal norm as binding.

Planning Director: This may not be a point that legally is binding for your decision. But Mr. ————, who was a subdivider of the property [in question], submitted a deed with the restriction to residential development.

Commission Member 1: They [the owners of property in the subdivision] will retain it [the deed restriction] only until 1960. We can't take [deed] restrictions into consideration [in reaching our decisions]. That is a [private] matter of the contracting parties. It [the enforcement of deed restrictions] can be attacked in the courts. . . .

In discussing another case, however, one member of the commission maintained that deed restrictions should be taken into account in acting upon applications. He considers this appropriate for the reason that he feels an obligation rests upon the owner of the property covered by an application to bear the expense of removing deed restrictions as a condition to filing a zoning change. This person once stated:

The deed restriction permits only residential development and I have voted consistently against granting a change in zoning that is contrary to the deed restriction.

It is seen, therefore, that at least one commission member considers certain social conditions desirable, while other decision-makers refuse to positively value deed restrictions as normative conditions. Because desirability is an essential element for expressing contentions to conform or not to conform to deed-restricting norms, it is possible for commission members to question the applicability of norms as social conditions. Thus, contrary to normative notions that social action complies with norms upon mere recognition of them by the actor, the

90

specific theory embraced in this study contends that recognition of normative systems as conditions does not necessitate conformity; rather actors must utilize a value system to determine whether they will abide by the requirements set forth in social conditions.

INSTANCE 4: A comment made by a commission member in discussing a request reveals the importance of social values in the zoning process:

I think the highest and best use is *one* reason [for granting or rejecting a zoning application]. I am in business and I guess I lean toward the idea of business development [when voting upon zoning cases]. I think one of the purposes of zoning is the welfare of the people. It [the purpose of public welfare] is set out in the law.

The commissioner who expressed this statement recognizes public welfare as an objective in zoning; his value judgment toward this goal is reflected in his statement that the highest and best use of property is an appropriate standard, among several, for approving or denying zoning classifications, and thus promotes the public welfare. This person applies his value judgment to validate his vote in a concrete instance.

INSTANCE 5: Members of the City Council also rely upon social values to interpret cognitive data. In the following example, Austin's council members compare the merits of factual data associated with two zoning applications covering several properties located near one another:

Council Member 1: I can't see any difference in the two pieces of property.

Council Member 2: One of them is surrounded by residences and a church, but the other has business improvements all around it.

Council Member 1: No—no it [that is, one area under consideration] doesn't.

Council Member 2: It doesn't make any difference to me; there is nothing personal about it.

Council Member 1: I can't see any difference in both pieces of property.

Council Member 2: Well, let's turn both of them down. You have some nice little well-kept houses [near one of the areas in question]. Then you drop down the street and there is a home used for commercial purposes. There is no reason to put a business in a well-developed residential area. There is no need to infuriate the people there.

Council Member 3: The only difference is that on one [tract] there is [the proposed] Springdale Road where it isn't there on the other.

Council Member 1: You can argue like that when Springdale Road comes through. But it isn't there now.

Council Member 2: . . . With the house and church there [near one area being considered for rezoning], there is no excuse for business. The other one [application] has been used for business for God knows how long.

(A straw vote to grant is then taken on one of the applications:)

Council Member 1: No.

Council Member 3: Yes.

Council Member 4: I abstain; I haven't seen the property yet.

Council Member 5: Yes.

Council Member 2: Yes.

(The council postponed final action to allow Council Member 4 to inspect the property. However, at a later meeting the council unanimously granted approval of one request, and a motion to deny was made on the second application discussed in the above conversation:)

Council Member 2: This [denial of the second application] is a matter of justice; the other one is debatable.

(The motion to deny carried unanimously.)

"Instance 5" indicates that council members, like members of the Planning Commission, thoroughly disagree on the relevancy of certain objectified cognitive data. A member desired to defend his vote to grant one application by recognizing a proposed street that he thought would cause the property to be unsuitable for residential use; another member refused to accept this cognitive fact, and argued for denial. The variety of value systems existing among council members, to be presented in the following chapter, account for this dissension.

Each of the above five instances reveals social activity as not always conforming to social conditions, nor do Austin's decision-makers share common values toward physical cognitive data when acting upon zoning applications. Instead, actors employ a variety of value systems in order to give interpretative significance to the stated goal, social conditions, and cognitive data in the zoning process.

A second application of value systems in social action occurs when individuals select from two or more normative alternatives in order to accomplish the public welfare goal. This is the situation facing decision-makers with regard to means; in selecting from alternative zoning classifications—the means in the zoning process—the decision-makers utilize social values. The social value systems that Austin's decision-makers employ to select from the means are to be discussed and examined in the following chapter.

Chapter Six

VALUE ORIENTATIONS
IN THE ZONING PROCESS

Expressions by decision-makers indicate the presence of numerous values. However, only three social "value-sets" appear to be basic for the decision-makers to arrive at zoning decisions. Each of these social value sets will be referred to as a "value orientation."[1] The three value sets to be presented in this chapter are: (1) the economic-protective value orientation; (2) the individual-collective value orientation; and (3) the present-future time value orientation.

The Economic-Protective Value Orientation

Of the three value sets to be discussed, the economic-protective value orientation is the most significant one for the decision-makers. This value set dominates the zoning process as decision-makers use it to select a specific zoning classification from the means and to interpret the end, social conditions, and cognitive data. For certain decision-

94

makers espouse economic values while others resort to protective values. Still others proclaim a combination of economic and protective values. If we let *E* stand for economic values and *P* for protective values, each value permutation within the economic-protective value orientation can be symbolized as: *E, EP, PE,* and *P.* To present this value orientation, we shall, first of all, explain these four possibilities. Examples will then be drawn from the zoning data that are representative of the *E, EP, PE,* and *P* values.

E VALUES

Decision-makers holding to this social value approach toward zoning argue that land use must be *dictated* by the prevailing market situation on the basis of supply and demand so as to allow for the operation of "natural" forces that set the market price for property. They maintain that the best use for property is realized under conditions that promote the highest investment returns. By contending, furthermore, that land usages involve competition, these decision-makers reason that the profit motive can be maximized only as a contemplated land usage *conforms* to the (1) economic pursuits of existing or anticipated land usages upon the area surrounding the land in question, and (2) geographical conditions considered suitable or essential for sustaining the contemplated land use. When a proposed use is deemed supportable because of existing or contemplated circumstances, then a zoning application deserves approval; conversely, if economically oriented decision-makers perceive that conditions do not warrant support of the proposed use, a zoning request must be denied. Economically oriented decision-makers insist that a designated space must be given a zoning classification in keeping with the conditions of existing or anticipated land uses and topography. Zoning classifications are expected to *reflect* economically relevant cognitive data because such data *inevitably determine* the pattern of land-use development.

The most important existing and anticipated uses that prescribe the desirability of a proposed land use in terms of the profit motive are: highways, street patterns, railroads, traffic counts, business and residential structures, land uses on property owned by the state government, and so on. Topography is also relevant as it enhances property values; the very nature of terrain is evaluated by economically oriented decision-makers inasmuch as it is thought to affect the profit motive. The presence or absence of creeks, hills, certain soil compositions, bluffs, and so on, supposedly affect the cost of utilizing land, thereby diminishing or increasing the economic returns.

In brief, the economically oriented decision-makers contend that zoning must mirror land valuations instead of prescribing land valuations. Such individuals treat zoning as a dependent rather than as an independent variable.

P VALUES

Two predominant values characterize the protective orientation toward zoning of property. First, the decision-makers holding to protective notions desire to control land usage so as to preserve and create cognitive data for residential utility of space. Protectionists perceive residential use as the most appropriate utilization of land. However, they do not deny the use of land for commercial development. For a second concern of protectionists is commercialization—they believe that utilization of land for other than residential development is to be regulated so as fully to protect and forward residential needs. That is, commercial development must accommodate to neighborhood requirements so as not to place residential use in jeopardy.

In espousing these values, protectionists deny the notion of competing land use as a value for determining zoning decisions; land development, they contend, is not necessarily a reflection of the conditions advanced by the economic approach. Consequently, the protectionists insist that zoning *must not necessarily* mirror land valuations in terms of the cognitive data promoted under E values. They interpret zoning to be an independent variable that *induces* land valuation; they tend to negate the idea that the profit-motive zeal should

96

dominate zoning. Accordingly, land values should be no greater than the economic returns *permitted* through the land usages set forth by the zoning classifications placed upon property. Moreover, in denying the validity of the profit motive as the basis for zoning, those advocating this viewpoint tolerate shifts in land usage only as *undesirable* cognitive notions considered unfavorable to residential utility develop.

In brief, the desire to protect certain existing cognitive data (that is, residential utilization), regardless of the effect upon the profit motive, accounts for land development from a protectionist's value perspective. In seeking to preserve or create residential land-use developments and needs, the protectionists act upon zoning applications so that zoning determines—rather than reflects—land-use development.

EP VALUES

This is one of two possibilities between the *E* and *P* extremes. While this combination contains elements of both orientations, the economic viewpoint dominates over protective considerations. According to this value concept, land usage must be economically productive in compliance with the prescribed conditions set forth under *E* values, but simultaneously the protective argument is acknowledged. Decision-makers holding to this position recognize that in yielding to the profit motive certain desirable protective cognitive data in the surrounding area are challenged in granting zoning changes, and, therefore, zoning requires preventive measures to preserve those desirable traits noted under *P* values. This viewpoint differs from *E* by the fact that it tolerates—as a matter of value orientation—the protectionists' position; but it differs from *P* by recognizing the legitimacy of the profit motive as though "intrinsic" under certain prevailing conditions. In brief, the decision-makers composing the *EP* bloc view land usage in competition with other uses; when economic yields exceed that of the protective, the former takes precedence over the latter. But, as we shall see, these decision-makers grant zoning changes to preserve certain cognitive standards associated with protective values.

PE VALUES

This is the second of the two possibilities between the *E* and *P* extremes; it contains elements of both arguments. However, unlike the *EP* combination, the *PE* value orientation designates the protective contention over and above the economic. The foremost concern is with the preservation of residential utility and needs. Decision-makers espousing the *PE* value combination differ from those advocating *P* values in that the former recognize land-usage competition from an economic perspective but refuse to designate this feature as the dominant component for land-use patterning. According to this approach, desirable land usage on the basis of preservation remains dominant in action upon zoning requests, but, nonetheless, recognition is accorded to *E* ideas. Failing to perceive any challenge to certain protective cognitive data under *P,* those decision-makers holding to this position yield to the economic values under *E* and, when it is considered necessary, require that protective devices be constituted in order to perpetuate existing cognitive data supporting residential utility and needs. In brief, this viewpoint holds to both elements, giving emphasis to the protective value orientation while relying upon the economic approach only as a second alternative.

Having explained and analyzed each value perspective within the economic-protective value orientation, we shall now turn to the data in the zoning process that demonstrate the existence of each.

INSTANCES OF *E* VALUES

The most outspoken expression of this value toward regulating land use through zoning is the statement "The highest and best use of the property under consideration." Since the economic value orientation "reflects" existing and anticipated land uses in accordance with topographical circumstances that prevail upon the area surrounding the property in question, this comment means: approval or denial of zoning applications so as to permit the possibility of property utilization

98

that realizes economic returns compatible with the conditional data. The decision-makers upholding the economic value orientation consider undesirable an existing zoning classification that fails to permit utilization in accordance with investment returns possible under the interpreted economic conditions. They discern an inevitable pattern in land-use development resulting from economic conditions. And processes taking place in land use, they contend, must be reflected in the zoning of property. This value orientation is seen in the following quotations taken from the zoning hearings held before Austin's City Council and Planning Commission.

INSTANCE 1:

Commission Member: It [the land in question] is fronting on what is slated to be a thoroughfare. It is a point for conjunction of three streets. It [the proposed use] is its [the property's] highest and best use.

INSTANCE 2:

Commission Member 1: I am generally for expansion of "GR" areas because it tends to prevent strip zoning. To me this [the application] is not a spot zone for it extends an existing "GR" zoning. I admit that it is hodge-podge zoning. But this is the way it is [at the present time].

Planning Director: Where are we going to start?

Commission Member 1: We have to take it like it is and work forward with it.

Commission Member 2: Due to your dollar situation there [in the area under consideration], there isn't any heavy residential [use] to go in there in blocks. We have to do the best we can [under the financial situation we face in zoning land]. [Emphasis supplied.]

INSTANCE 3:

Commission Member: When the City Council voted [funds] for a thoroughfare [in the vicinity of the area under consideration], it [the thoroughfare] destroyed whatever residential value it [the area covered by the application] might have had.

INSTANCE 4:

Commission Member: There is a railroad on the west [side to the property in question] which makes it [the property in question] unsuitable for residential development.

99

INSTANCE 5:

Commission Member: I recommend that we throw this [application] open to discussion. We all agree that it is difficult to determine its [the land in question] highest and best use. But we also must agree that it is not suitable for residential [development]. All the homes on Funston Street back up to what we hope will be the Missouri-Pacific Highway.

The present usage—regardless of its proposed use—[located on the site] across the street and the high traffic count destroy its residential utility.

INSTANCE 6:

Commission Member: I move that the application be approved for the following reasons: (1) the existing situation [of land uses in the area] lends itself to this [proposed] use and (2) the [automobile] count in front of the . . . [property] is 15,000. . . .

INSTANCE 7: If existing conditions such as street widths do not prevail, then commissioners holding to the economic value perspective advocate a self-fulfilling prophecy: they create the needed conditions required to justify their economic value orientation. The most general technique for accomplishing this has been to require the applicant to grant "his proportionate share" of land to the city in the event that the traffic artery upon which his property borders is widened:

Commission Member: This person has filed a letter granting the land for widening [of the abutting street]. I move that it [the application] be granted. This is a junction point for two thoroughfares, there are schools which are public uses, and, therefore, it [the land covered by the application] is not proper for residences.

INSTANCE 8: The following quotation reveals the notion of land-use inevitability that the economic orientation claims "flows out" of determining conditions:

Commission Member: That triangle [the area in question] is in transition [with respect to land use *because of* its proximity to two major thoroughfares. *Eventually*, all of it will be used for multi-family dwellings or business or both. [Emphasis supplied.]

INSTANCE 9: The impact of the economic argument is clearly demonstrated by these comments:

100

Commission Member: I would like to say that good planning takes into full consideration economic aspects of the situation. Planning and economics go hand-in-glove.

Commission Member: You City boys [employees of the City of Austin] and [the City] departments are overworked, underpaid, and understaffed. These people [zoning applicants] come in with $4,000,000 cash, and it speaks for itself.

INSTANCE 10: The economic interpretation given to land use by one group of persons also reflects the topographical setting. Topography—as do street widths, care counts, railroads—becomes a determining force to which land use must comply and which, therefore, zoning must reflect:

Case A

Commission Member: I move that this application be approved. The nature of the terrain does not lend itself to residential development.

Case B

Commission Member: I make the substitute motion that we grant an "LR" [zoning for the property in question]. I checked pretty carefully on that area. One of the principal objections of the people [in opposition to the zoning change] was that it would devaluate their land. But the fact that this [area in question] is a natural area set apart from the other [surrounding areas] *by a natural barrier* [a creek], this objection does not hold. [Emphasis supplied.]

INSTANCE 11: The importance of vehicular traffic for justifying the economic perspective is the automobile count upon streets within the city:

Case A

Commission Member: . . . it is the residences that create traffic; business just takes advantage of it.

Case B

Commission Member: With an 1,800 traffic count, it [the land bordering upon a street under consideration] is not suitable—I mean desirable—for residences.

INSTANCE 12: The economic value orientation calls for zoning to reflect investment. The following quotes of several decision-makers reveal that those who uphold the economic perspective inject even homeownership as an ongoing economically profitable venture:

Case A

Commission Member: I move that the application be denied. The houses [in the area of the request] are reasonably moderate homes and [are] in good repair; it [the granting of the request] would down-grade the area.

Case B

Commission Member: This [request] is spot zoning all right. But they [the applicant and people living in the area] know that the area has outgrown its use. They don't take care of it [the homes upon the properties in question] because of this reason.

Case C

Commission Member: I voted against that [application] not only because it was in a well-developed residential area, but also because there is no transitional trend, and many persons oppose it.

Certain council members hold to economic determinism for explaining shifts in land use as the utilization of property complies with the demands of the profit motive. Expressions by these decision-makers disclose the notion that zoning cannot interfere with the potential investment returns as set forth by economically-determining conditions; zoning must reflect conditions to promote the realization of land use that is "inevitably" in accordance with conditions considered economically relevant.

INSTANCE 1:

Opponent: Since 1931, those corners [in the area under consideration] have been [zoned] "C." This Council is not responsible for this. But you will be responsible for setting up a chain reaction that will make the entire block business if this change is granted.

Council Member: The *only thing* that will determine a chain reaction *will be the economics.* The character of 24th Street has changed over the years. If you had a lot there [on 24th Street], you wouldn't build a home on there now. [Emphasis supplied.]

102

INSTANCE 2:

Council member: A lot of those uses [listed under the "GR" classi-fication] are a little frightening [but these uses could not develop because of the economics].

INSTANCE 3: The economic orientation followed by certain members on the council also takes into consideration the presence of prevailing land uses. The following remarks by several council mem-bers illustrate the impact of conditions upon the value system of this approach:

Case A

Council Member: Most all of you [of the opposition to the zoning request] will agree that the property on the highway is commercial for its highest and best use. We have to zone property for its highest and best use. The new shopping center [just constructed in the area] has changed the [nature of] the area [under consideration].

Case B

Council Member: All the property along Interregional [Highway] is commercial. It is going to be commercial. He [the applicant] paid a good price for the land and he cannot afford to place houses on the land.

Case C

Council Member: You are supposed to zone the land for the high-est and best use. If the character of the land is changing, the zoning must change. All along the Interregional [Highway] was residential and every-one knows that it is not [suitable] for residents now. Time has changed.

Case D

Council Member: Don't you [the opponent] think the road is in-creasing in traffic and changing the nature of [the land use in] the area?

Case E

Council Member: The street is too narrow [for commercial de-velopment]. I am going to vote against it [the application].

Case F

Council Member: I think the entire area is suitable to commercial development. The lots are large; it [the area in question] has easy access to the immediate highways. It will definitely be an improvement and an

103

[economic] asset to your property. It will increase the value of your property.

Case G

Council Member: Ben White Boulevard has changed the nature [of the land use] in the area.

From the foregoing numerous illustrations taken from hearings before the Planning Commission and City Council, we find certain decision-makers maintaining that zoning must reflect market investments of land use as determined by conditioning features. Contemporary and predictable land uses and topography become *determining forces* that inevitably create and sustain "intrinsic" utilization. Zoning itself is not to interfere with the "natural" trend that would otherwise result in the absence of zoning; zoning intervenes only to promote those uses that reflect the "highest and best use" as dictated by determining economic conditions.

INSTANCES OF *P* VALUES

Protectionists interpret desirability in zoning land, not in the sense set forth by the economic value orientation of deterministic conditions, but rather as a matter of land use complying with certain prescribed requirements to encourage residential development. They rank residential use as the most desirable utility for land, while remaining uses are seen as serving residential needs. As several protectionists commented in reply to the interviewer's questions:

INSTANCE 1:

Commission Member: I am interested in maintaining stable neighborhoods. . . . I take into consideration the needs in the area. It is the total neighborhood that's affected, not tax considerations.

INSTANCE 2:

Commission member: If someone is making for economic growth, I always tend to favor that *if* it [the economic growth] doesn't harm a neighborhood. I am especially concerned with the needs of the people. . . . [Emphasis supplied.]

104

As existing cognitive data fail to promote residential land use, then residential areas must give way to another zoning classification. But protectionists do not see the fading of residential use as an inevitable process complying with economic conditions. Instead, zoning serves to control what would otherwise be a "natural" development. Protectionists, consequently, maintain that the "conditioning" forces recognized as deterministic in the economic value orientation are to be manipulated to facilitate residential development. It is not necessary for land to comply with the notion of "highest and best use" in accordance with the determining cognitive data of the economic perspective. The protectionists do not automatically adapt to circumstances that could support investments for realizing greater economic gains if a shift in zoning occurred. They advocate volitional control in such a manner so as to inhibit the "natural" trend that the economic value orientation contends takes place. The following comments made by several protective proponents indicate perception of certain cognitive data such as traffic, density of land use, street widths, and so on, as items that must be controlled rather than demanding adaptation:

INSTANCE 1:

Commission Member: [I object to the proposed use because] there is a traffic problem around all schools.

INSTANCE 2:

Commission Member: I make the substitute motion that we deny it [the application] for the reason that 51st Street is too narrow.

INSTANCE 3:

Commission Member: This [proposed use] is too high a density [to allow the proposed classification].

INSTANCE 4:

Commission Member: . . . to my mind, this [proposed] use is rather extensive. A "BB" [zoning classification] with first height and area would reduce the number of units to 25 [from the proposed 30]. This would be the best use.

Other expressions by protective commission members illustrate the rejection of the profit motive as a value standard for acting upon

105

zoning applications as revealed in the following discussion that took place between the commission members:

Protective Commission Member: This is one case where zoning will affect a lot of residential areas.

Protective-Economic Commission Member 1: Since she [the applicant] doesn't know what she wants to do with it [the area covered by the application], I move that it [the request] be denied.

Protective-Economic Commission Member 2: If she [the applicant] doesn't have any [proposed] use, she is zoning for profit.

Economic Commission Member: It [the application] is speculative zoning.

Protective Commission Member: That [the speculation for profits] doesn't affect me [in my decision]. Commercial use is rather [permissively] extensive [in the area]; any more restrictive zoning other than "C" would do.

Although this example would appear to indicate that both the economically oriented and protectively oriented commission members deny the relevance of profit making, in actuality this is not the case. However, a more complete explanation requires the introduction of another vital conceptualization in zoning which remains to be presented in the analysis, namely, time as a social value. Only by considering time as a value orientation within this identical illustration can we demonstrate that the profit motive underlies the arguments of the economically oriented commissioner in the above account. At this point, therefore, it is necessary only to recognize that the protective commission member rejects the profit motive. A treatment of this very example under the time orientation will reveal the profit motive underlying the statements made by the economically oriented members of the commission.

Further comments by protectionists relate the general value orientation they espouse as they seek to regulate land use through zoning so as to promote the general welfare in terms of residential utilization and need:

106

INSTANCE 1:

Commission Member: I move that we grant this request. It [the proposed use] is a more compatible use for the surrounding [residential] area than the existing "LR."

INSTANCE 2:

Commission Member: I move that this request be denied for the following reasons: (1) the property [in question] is in a well-developed residential area and it [the request zoning] is incompatible with the development in the area; and (2) there is no indicated need for commercial development in the area.

INSTANCE 3:

Commission Member: I move that the application be denied. This [proposed zoning] is a spot zone in a residential area. It will definitely be a detriment to one of Austin's nicest residential areas.

INSTANCE 4:

Protective Commission Member: There's no need for "C-2" [zoning in this area]. There's enough "C-2" for their [the people residing in the area] needs for the next ten to fifteen years.

Economic Commission Member: That's no reason [for denial].

INSTANCE 5:

Commission Member: The tendency of development out there [in the general area under consideration] makes it [the actual land covered by the request] unfit for residences. I am in favor of making the change [in zoning]. But I think every consideration should be given to protect the people [living] out there.

INSTANCE 6:

Commission Member: We must consider certain needs of the neighborhood. This is an area where a small store is needed by the neighborhood. It is good planning because it provides the needs of the neighborhood.

INSTANCE 7:

Commission Member: I move that the request be denied. In this case the request will not serve the neighborhood.

From the above expressions we can infer that certain individuals on the Planning Commission subscribe to the protective value orientation in reaching zoning decisions. By rejecting the contention that economic competition between land usage is dependent upon the presence or absence of certain cognitive data, the protectionists rely upon zoning as an effort to control land use so as to protect existing land uses *in accordance with a preconceived preference listing.* Their primary interest is the maintenance of residences as the most desirable land-use activity. Any use other than residential should be allowed only to the extent that the needs of residents are fulfilled.

It should be noted in passing, however, that expressions of the protectionists' perspective were not drawn from hearings before the City Council. This is due to the fact that during the period of this study covering the meetings by the City Council—September, 1958, through May, 1960—no member of the council sustained the protective argument. Every council member utilized the profit motive as an integral aspect of his value system when acting upon zoning cases; the protective contention prevailed among several members on the City Council only in the form of the *EP* value combination.

INSTANCES OF *EP* VALUES

Several decision-makers combine aspects of both *E* and *P* values in their orientation to zoning land. Such persons contend that land uses compete with one another in terms of the profit motive and cost, but at the same time they recognize the desirability of preserving residential use and needs. Those decision-makers espousing this social value orientation maintain that when the price of property is so great that residential development would not yield a reasonable return with respect to the profit motive, then zoning must conform to this economic condition. Furthermore, if the proposed use will not yield an economic return in view of existing cognitive-data-considered determinants of economic consequences, then the zoning application is denied.

Still, there is a genuine desire to perpetuate residential areas from commercial encroachment. It is recognized that certain economic developments permitted by zoning changes are not conducive to residential utility and need. Consequently, when granting a zoning change for

108

a site that borders upon well-developed residential areas, special provisions will be required of the applicant so as to separate one zoning area from the other through "screening" or the creation of buffer zones.

The following quotations expressing the *EP* combination are the statements of two decision-makers each of whom expressed economic values during one zoning hearing and protective values during another zoning hearing:

COMMISSION MEMBER 1:

a. Expressions of Economic Values

1. This is a logical place for "C" zoning since it [the property in question] will be on three major highways. It [the area covered by the request] is more suitable for "C" than for any other zoning classification.

2. Any use permitted in "C" as appropriate has got to be appropriate for the use of the land. The streets are there and we can't change them now. It's got to be used for this [proposed commercial purpose].

3. If you [an opponent to a zoning change] made as much money off of the selling of this house [you now own] as you did for that house I sold for you [several years ago], you would want to sell.

b. Expressions of Protective Values

1. Planning is the orderly growth of the city and it also takes into consideration the convenience of living in a city.

2. I feel like this is one case I can very well turn down because it is so obvious it is not proper zoning for the neighborhood. It is a neighborhood that is fast becoming livable—or whatever you call it. . . . There is no commercial property in the neighborhood. I wouldn't want a warehouse [the proposed use under the proposed zoning application] next to me.

3. Knowing that we have reputable people to whom we are granting this [zoning change], I feel that it's to the best interests of the people in the area. In the near future it [the property in question] could be "C." If we grant "O" now, we can protect the neighborhood. I think it is in line for "O."

109

COMMISSION MEMBER 2:

a. Expressions of Economic Values

1. I think the highest and best use is *one* reason [for granting or denying a zoning application]. I am in business and I guess I lean toward the idea of business development [in considering zoning applications].

2. ——— [the applicant] paid too much for the land [in question] to be used for residences.

3. If it gives me justification for voting for it [the zoning change from residential to a commercial classification], it [the land in question] is within one block of commercial property. And it [the area covered by the request] is in a changing neighborhood and it might be part of a trend.

4. I can't get away from being influenced by business [economic] considerations. I think it is bad business to have apartments in the University area. If large apartments are built on the narrow streets with no parking spaces, they will not be rented.

b. Expressions of Protective Values

1. I believe that one of the issues faced in zoning is the safety issue.

2. I don't think the area is a good area for a service station from the standpoint of safety for the public. There is a hospital there and apartments. The streets are too narrow. We do have a good residential area to the west.

3. I am in an odd position. I am going to vote against it [the zoning application]. A Negro man is operating it [the existing café upon the property in question]. All around it is occupied by white people. The people objected to it at that time [when the zoning was granted to establish the existing café business]. But I didn't see any objection [when I voted for that zoning change]. We vote on the basis of health, welfare, and safety of the community. Because it will be operated by a Negro, I believe that the sale of beer will endanger the welfare of the residents.

Certain members on the City Council, while being aware of and sometimes supporting protective contentions, still perceive land use from an economic perspective. But it should be noted that *EP* council

110

members also show concern with planning so as to expand the city's tax base. In stating their economic arguments, they indicate a keen awareness of what they would consider a need to maximize the tax revenue received from commercial property. They reflect this additional economic value in their actual zoning decisions to grant or deny applications. The following remarks by several council members express the value toward taxes as well as the standard economic value orientations of the economic perspective:

COUNCIL MEMBER:

   a. Expressions of Economic Values

      1. We have many service men living there [in the general area under consideration]. I have received letters and calls from them. Now Bergstrom [Air Force Base] spends $30,000,000 a year out there [on air base improvements] and we don't want to lose it.

      2. Planning is a wonderful thing, but I wish they [the planners] would plan to get more dollars into the city.

      3. . . . now the Interregional [Highway] is there [in the general area in question] and it [the Interregional Highway] is changing the character of the area.

      4. If that house [now existing on the land covered by the request] has been there vacant for two years is now torn down and replaced by a nice commercial building, the fire rates will go down and it [the commercial building] will improve the appearance of the neighborhood.

      5. That land [covered by the request] has changed out there in value—[because of] the connection of East Avenue and Air port Boulevard. . . .

   b. Expressions of Protective Values

      1. I didn't pay much attention to the church's lawyer [who spoke as a representative in opposition to the zoning change] because they [the church] are way down the block. They are too far away to be considered. I have never seen a nicer house than the lady's across the street [from the property covered by the application]. It's a trailer house, but she [the owner of the trailer house] has it fixed up very nice. Whatever is nicest for the neighborhood and what meets approval of your needs is what I want to see.

2. In principle, I'm for a "DL" [zoning classification]. But I don't want it [the "DL" zoning classification] restricted to this extent. I don't want you to restrict residents from a "DL" classification. . . . A residence is the most desirable thing. It's the most sacred thing and should be allowed under any zoning.

3. We promised the people [in opposition to this zoning application] adequate protection.

4. Well, let's turn . . . [this application] down. You have some nice little well kept houses [in the area]. . . . There is no reason to put a business in a well-developed residential area.

5. I don't know why it is, but I suppose the public creates a demand for [grocery] drive-ins. The people want them at all hours and on Sundays. Twenty-fourth Street has spread into a big thoroughfare. I believe that it will be many years before the fine residences in the area will fade out. In my mind, unless the owners agree that there will be a barrier put up behind the store and adequate facilities are provided for the trash, and the tenants and the property owner agree to this, I will not go along with it [the zoning change].

These quotations taken from hearings before both the Planning Commission and the City Council indicate certain decision-makers tend to maintain an *EP* position. Economic returns from investments take precedence, yet residential utility and needs are considered when the profit motive is not jeopardized.

INSTANCES OF *PE* VALUES

The remaining group of decision-makers consists of those individuals who maintain that land uses compete with one another only after protective stipulations are met. These individuals maintain that one's decision must first consider protective contentions before yielding to the economic circumstances. Only as the *E* determining conditions do not interfere with *P* values does the economic factor enter into their value orientation. In brief, the protective-economic position consists of a recognition that there is a competitive aspect in land use that deserves consideration in zoning decisions—but it is secondary to protective values. The remarks by such decision-makers substantiate this generalization:

112

EXPRESSIONS OF PROTECTIVE VALUES

1. I don't think the neighborhood has to support the stupid private enterprise because somebody can make a profit.

2. It's [the general area in question] a nice neighborhood; they [the inhabitants] take care of their homes, they keep their yards clean, they paint their homes. This [zoning change] would do damage to their homes.

3. I think that [it] is a good idea [to grant a "GR" zoning for the property in question]. This will be a buffer zone [between the existing "A" and "C" zonings].

4. I move that this zoning application be granted. The series of new structures will be an asset to the neighborhood.

5. I move that we deny this request. This is spot zoning and it [the proposed use] is a detriment to the neighborhood. The residences are being kept well; the houses are being painted; and the lawns are well kept.

EXPRESSIONS OF ECONOMIC VALUES

1. We are here to protect the values of the residences. If it [the zoning change request] hurts the value of the homes, then they [the residents] could not get a FHA [Federal Housing Authority] loan.

2. The city will gain about $2,000 [by selling the land being zoned since the property in question is city-owned], but the people in the area will lose more [money].

3. If I thought an apartment house would go up in the area, that would add to it ["improve" the area in question]. But it [the construction of apartments] can't be done [the "economics" of the situation would prohibit the erection of apartments as an economic investment].

These numerous instances that have been presented to portray the empirical data reveal the various values of *E, EP, PE,* and *P* contained in the economic-protective social value orientation espoused by decision-makers in Austin's zoning process. Those individuals holding to the economic perspective maintain that (1) land uses compete with one another in a bid for economic returns from investments; and (2) the profit motive must be reflected in zoning in accordance with certain determining conditions that either prevail in the present or are anticipated at some future date. Zoning is not seen as an intervening factor that actually determines land valuations. Instead, if land is to be properly zoned according to the economic values, all zoning must

113

mirror the cost of utilizing land under prescribed conditioning factors of existing or contemplated land usages and topography.

The opposite extreme to the economic approach is the protective social value orientation. According to this approach, residential use is the most desirable use possible; all other land usages must be regulated so as to meet the needs of residential development and above all to maintain the tranquillity of residential living. Protectionists firmly deny the economic contention that land use must necessarily comply with the profit motive; instead, protectionists maintain that zoning becomes a determining force in setting land valuations.

The *EP* and *PE* combinations simply blend components of protective and economic notions: *EP* proponents insist upon economic values, yet endeavor to promote protective values when the latter do not interfere with the former; individuals espousing the *PE* orientation give greater emphasis to protectionism but simultaneously endeavor to recognize economic considerations when the latter do not interfere with the former.

Regardless of the value orientation decision-makers possess— zoning that simply reflects determining conditions or zoning that denies the profit motive—a social value perspective is essential to the zoning process. All members perceive certain cognitive data as subject to interpretation through the employment of a social value system from one of the four possibilities offered in the economic-protective value orientation. On the basis of *E, EP, PE,* and *P,* the decision-makers then elect to deny or grant zoning applications.

The Individual-Collective Value Orientation

Irrespective of the theoretical stance espoused by ecologists, there is one issue that remains unresolved—namely, that of individual interest versus collective welfare. It is a dilemma noted in general sociological and economic theory as well as in philosophical writings. So involved is this particular aspect of social life that materialistic ecologists tend

114

to either ignore the problem altogether or arbitrarily select a collective approach; ecological voluntarists generally overlook the problem or simply raise the question.

Several materialistic ecologists explicitly state that it is necessary to perceive ecological phenomena from a collective perspective. For instance, Amos Hawley maintains that man is distributed over space in accordance with collective requirements rather than in terms of individualistic aspirations:

> In the ecological view, however, life is not an individual but an aggregate phenomenon. Hence the underlying assumption of ecology is that adjustment to environment is a mutual, in fact a communal, function. The adjustment of a population to its physical world occurs not through the independent actions of many individuals but through the coordination and organization of individual actions to form a single functional unit.[2]

Hawley, in advocating collectivism, offers no theoretical justification for his position. His choice, however, conforms to his foremost desire to remain entirely free from the psychological aspects he implicitly associates with conceptualization.

Otis Duncan and Leo Schnore, as neoclassical materialists, also argue for the collective approach without offering theoretical justification. They contend:

> Ecological structure is conceived as an organization of functions—activities that are dependent upon other activities. Ecologists have usually bypassed the question of "contributions to the maintenance of the system," although this problem logically does not lie beyond their purview. However, they have deliberately avoided the blind alley of exploring "functions versus dysfunctions," recognizing that what is functional for one part of the total system is often dysfunctional for another. . . . Moreover, the ecologist makes no use of the distinction between latent and patent functions, since this rests with the individual's knowledge and judgment, and the individual's personal view of things is, as such, of no ecological interest. Parenthetically, it might be remarked that the ecologist . . . has come to recognize that what is obvious, intended, and anticipated by one person may be unknown, unanticipated, and unintended by another. Perhaps his acumen has been fortified by wrestling with what now appears to be an irrelevant distinction between "natural" and "planned" processes. At any rate, it is clear to the contemporary ecologist, though it was not to the classical, that the subject matter of human

115

ecology cannot be defined residually in terms of an unmanageable psychological distinction.[3]

It is clear from this quotation that while Duncan and Schnore recognize the possibility of divergent interests in the form of private versus collective welfare, nowhere do they analyze the theoretical and empirical implications of this issue for ecological thought. Yet, the empirical data of this study distinctly reveal the existence of a collective orientation concerned directly with this problem.

Voluntarists, unlike materialists, take note of the collective-individual set as a choice situation. In sociological theory we find Talcott Parsons dealing with this aspect of societal life, first as the "utilitarian dilemma"[4] and later as one dilemma within his pattern variable scheme.[5] However, voluntaristic ecologists either avoid the problem or merely pose the question. For instance, Christen Jonassen concludes that "men tend to distribute themselves within an area so as to achieve the greatest efficiency in realizing [their] values."[6] But in making this comment he fails to deal with individual choice versus collective edict: Is efficiency to be evaluated in terms of individual satisfaction or collective accomplishment? Walter Firey, another voluntaristic ecologist, presented this challenge to the ecological materialists but then proceeded to present his analysis apart from the question itself.[7]

The cultural approach, as advanced in this paper, focuses upon the analysis of the social values man employs in coping with the issue of individual versus collective welfare in adapting upon space. Because members of a society, implicitly or explicitly, face this problem in the allocation of space for the pursuance of social activities, the ecologist must establish just how individualism versus collectivism is socially resolved. The cultural approach deliberately seeks to discover the shared system of ideas man applies in coping with this problem in the process of orienting himself to space. Insofar as the empirical data reveal a collective effort in this regard, the cultural perspective is sustained.

In presenting the zoning data bearing upon this problem, we shall

116

address ourselves to this question: How do the decision-makers perceive the derivation of a collective welfare as they reach decisions on zoning applications? Basically, it is an orientation problem dealing with the question of "Zoning for whom?" As such, we shall analyze how Austin's decision-makers go about incorporating the desires of individual participants into a collective decision. This particular social orientation is to be referred to as the "individual-collective value orientation."

INDIVIDUALISTIC VALUES

Decision-makers voicing the strictly individual approach hold that land use must be dictated by the prevailing market situation on the basis of a supply and a demand that are free from restraints that interfere with the "natural" forces operating to set market developments. They maintain that the individual should have the opportunity to utilize his land so as to maximize his personal worth. For ownership of land carries with it the intrinsic right to exploit the environment so as to forward the individual's welfare; the best use for any piece of land is that use which serves the interests of an individual property holder.

The public welfare, according to the decision-makers holding to the individualistic social value perspective, is ultimately served as each individual forwards his own self-interests. For it is crucial to the individualistic notion that the summation of each private increment consequently yields the best results and is the welfare function that will best serve collective interests.

The most outstanding characteristic of this value orientation, therefore, is the notion of certain decision-makers that the individual is the agent for promoting land-use development. As a supposedly "rational" agent in a "free" marketplace, the individual's choice reflects the prevailing conditions of an impersonal market governed by the "law" of supply and demand. However, according to this perspective, the individual, being a rational agent, may enter into agree-

117

ments with other individuals in order to restrict the manner in which property may be utilized. Through such compacts, individualistic decision-makers contend, individuals continue to forward private ends.

The presence of a collective agent is seen as an "unnatural" condition by individualistic decision-makers. Because control over land use resides in personal ownership of property, *direct* interference through collective representation challenges private welfare notions and eventually destroys collective interests. Inhibitions above a minimum level eradicate individual initiative and eventually prove to be harmful to the entire collectivity.

The individualistic value approach—that is, what has also been referred to as the utilitarian doctrine in sociological literature[8]—is, then, *ex post facto* in the sense that the public welfare must evolve. That is, according to this viewpoint, an adequate and appropriate state of affairs beneficial to a collectivity *results* as each individual promotes his own private end.

COLLECTIVE VALUES

This value approach consists of the desire to create and sustain a "collective will" transcending individual interests. Decision-makers holding to this position advocate the existence of a normative system designed to promote the collective welfare apart from individual aspirations. The distinctive feature of the collective social value orientation toward zoning, then, is the notion that land usage must conform to the stipulations of a given collective welfare concept. Consequently, the collectively oriented decision-makers consider undesirable the proposition that as individuals seek to realize their own private aspirations the public welfare is thereby advanced. Zoning must, instead, accord with established planning standards that are thought to promote collective interests. While it is possible under this approach to permit individual owners to initiate zoning changes, nonetheless this value orientation specifies that the collective will must be considered above and beyond individual volition when zoning decisions are made.

118

Private interests are eventually served as individuals conform to group welfare standards.

Decision-makers holding to the collective value orientation treat zoning as a matter of exerting social control; zoning serves as a regulatory device to enforce group welfare standards toward land use. Collective welfare, therefore, is an "if-then" proposition: *if* individuals adhere to a preconceived normative system prescribing a desirable state of affairs, *then* an adequate and appropriate state of affairs becomes a reality.

This individual-collective value orientation poses a dilemma for members of a social system. The difficulty stems from the desire to allow for individual inclinations on the one hand, but then to achieve simultaneously some degree of prediction of human behavior on the other. That is, as Parsons notes, there must be a relationship between individual wants and prediction; however, one is attained at the expense of the other.[9] Under the utilitarian value orientation, individual maximization requires rational and "free" agents whose actions make a difference, but then "wants" cannot be predicted; under the collective orientation, "wants" may be clearly demarcated, but this denies freedom of action to the individual. Because actors are atomistic under the utilitarian system, ends become random and thereby preclude prediction by interacting individuals. Such a state of affairs can be overcome by establishing a collective welfare function to permit prediction whereby a normative system provides an orientation to social objects for performers. Yet, as wants become predictable, the freedom of action on the part of the individual is restrained. Individual wants, therefore, can be predicted only at the expense of individual volition, creating what Parsons calls the "utilitarian dilemma."[10]

Kenneth Arrow[11] also deals with the problem of moving from individual desires to a collective consensus under certain conditions. After a formal treatment of the subject, he concludes that there is no *consistent* general welfare function whereby individual wants can be transformed into a collective decision in accordance with the pre-

119

scribed rules he sets forth. Consequently, group decisions are, at times, arrived at on grounds other than the rational, ranked-preference listings of individuals. The conclusion to be drawn from Arrow's work, therefore, is identical with Parsons' utilitarian dilemma: individual aspirations preclude prediction; prediction prevents the actualization of individual aspiration.

The empirical data collected for this study strongly indicate the absence of a *consistent* collective-welfare function. While various notions of general welfare persist among decision-makers, no distinctive orientation exists that overcomes the dilemma noted by Parsons and Arrow. Nonetheless, decision-makers seek legitimacy for their decisions in notions of general welfare. Specific instances of individual and collective values will now be offered to focus attention upon the empirical data indicating the decision-makers' social orientations of a welfare function within Austin's zoning process.

INSTANCE OF AN INDIVIDUALISTIC
VALUE ORIENTATION

According to this view, the most desirable public welfare function is one that should allow states of affairs to "evolve" by permitting individuals to maximize private interests. Individuals should be left to their own resources, being permitted to enter "private" contracts without any compulsion from the collectivity or its representatives.

Throughout the period that the author studied the zoning process in Austin, only one decision-maker voiced this viewpoint. He maintained that the public's interest could best be served by each person pursuing his own self-interest:

> I think that the law of supply and demand can handle the situation. If a person wants to protect his home, let him enter into a deed restriction. If a person wants to have expensive homes with certain things, there will always be homes to meet his wants.

This same decision-maker continued to express his orientation by saying that if a person desires a home of a certain quality—for example,

120

sufficient electrical wiring to support anticipated household appliances or adequate street widths—then home builders will furnish these goods and services. So strong is this decision-maker's belief in the controlling nature of the "impersonal" law of supply and demand for yielding desirable consequences that he stated during a zoning hearing:

If the person [the applicant] is going to use it [the land in question] for a doctor's office, he will have to build a nice building to stay in business.

Thus, needs generate demands, which, in turn, generate the controls thought necessary to bring about a favorable community development. The interest of the community is fully served because each individual's needs are satisfied through "the law of supply and demand."

Nonetheless, this decision-maker must participate in the zoning process as a representative of the collective welfare as required by the legal normative system, or else he would face the very definite possibility of removal from his decision-making position. Law—a collective standard—and social control demand the individual's conformity to the zoning procedure. Moreover, his value of yielding to the collective expectations of the normative system—Austin's Zoning Ordinance—in preference to his own private desires causes this decision-maker to act in accordance with the stated goal of zoning.

The legitimacy for holding to an individualistic value orientation lies in the fear expressed by the aforementioned person that a collective value orientation results in imposition: compliance with collective standards means the loss of individual expression. He maintains further that the loss of individuality eventually proves detrimental to the public welfare. Consequently, we find in the zoning process a definite hesitancy to establish a collective agency for fear of the imposition resulting from a collective-welfare concept. As this decision-maker commented during an interview:

I don't know for sure in my own mind that zoning as one uses this term is actually legitimate. In other words, do we have a right to tell the property owner how to use his property—what he can do with it? That is,

121

that ownership of a property carries with it the basic right of doing whatever you [the property owners] want to do with it. So, as a result of being uncertain about whether it [the zoning] is actually legitimate, I have never made up my mind that it is right or the best thing for the city. For example, we can take Houston which is a very progressive city and has developed more rapidly than any other Texas city. It doesn't have any zoning laws.

This fear of violating one of the conditions set forth by Arrow[12]— namely, the requirement that the collective welfare function cannot be an imposition—legitimatizes this person's notions of utilitarianism. For he contends, as witnessed by the above quote, that as the individual's right to decide his own course of action is absolved, then zoning decisions become impositions.

But utilitarian thought of the sort expressed by this decision-maker can be realized only at the expense of accurate prediction. In the absence of a collective obligation, prior expectation cannot prevail as individuals engage in social interaction. Consequently, the decision-maker holding to this value perspective must accommodate to an orientation that rests upon the unknown, wherein—if full appreciation is given to the utilitarian doctrine—speculative risk becomes the determining feature in social action and, simultaneously, legitimizes the outcome, be it failure or success. The degree of speculation varies inversely to the application of a collective welfare concept by this decision-maker. However, because this aspect of the zoning process involves a time dimension, the problem of prediction will be analyzed in the following section of this chapter that deals with social value orientations of time.

INSTANCES OF COLLECTIVE VALUE ORIENTATION

A variety of collective value orientations exists in the zoning process. Recognizing that zoning itself involves collective representation, nonetheless the several decision-makers holding to the collective-value perspective vary in their viewpoints as to the manner in which the desires of those they represent should be incorporated in zoning decisions.

122

To begin with, the decision-makers are aware of the social values expressed by the individuals they represent in the zoning process as collective agents. Several illustrations point this fact out.

INSTANCE 1: A member of the Planning Commission suggested that land be zoned for its specific use rather than in terms of zoning classifications. Several members commented upon this suggestion:

Commission Member 1: It [the suggestion under consideration] would be a restriction on a man's use of his property. . . .

Commission Member 2: It's [the suggestion under consideration] too restrictive.

Commission Member 3: When a man comes in to ask for a zoning change on his property, you are not restricting [his use of that property] —you are expanding it [the use of his property].

Commission Member 2: You are [restricting the owner of the property] for the community as a whole.

INSTANCE 2: The following remark made by a Planning Commission member reveals the possibility of discrepancy between individual desires and collective standards:

There is bound to be a good compromise between what he [the applicant] wants and good planning.

INSTANCE 3: Members of the City Council are aware of the existence of a general welfare above and beyond the desires of specific individuals:

City Attorney: The City Council must decide [in zoning cases] for the public interest and not to the interest of an individual. . . . The Council must consider other matters—smoke, noise, fumes, etc.—as well as concentration [of population and land usage].

Applicant: [He listed the commercial businesses and highways in the area of the property in question.] I do not think that a beauty shop [the proposed use] will affect the concentration.

Council Member 1: We have to consider the safety of the persons coming in on a plane. This is a zoning change that we are asking you to go along with us. Until you do this, I am not going to go along with you.

123

. . . You're not going against me, but 200,000 people and all the visitors that come [into Austin].

These quotations indicate the necessity to impose collective standards even when they are contrary to individual volition. How, then, do the decision-makers legitimatize their performance in this respect?

It should first be noted that there is one important area of agreement among all the decision-makers with regard to one collective standard: each person maintains that in order to prevent economic monopolies within the city, zoning must not be implemented purposefully to favor established or anticipated business enterprises. Preferential treatment toward specific commercial interests, Austin's decision-makers insist, cannot justify approval or denial of zoning applications. While, as we have seen, certain decision-makers explicitly recognize economic competition in land use, they perceive this as a vested right resulting from determining conditions apart from individual ownership of property. For instance, a council member once commented that the City Council cannot apply "the zoning laws like a protective tariff for [the protection of investments in] the downtown district" of Austin. Another council member supported this contention by saying that "you cannot monopolize business through zoning."

Members of the Planning Commission, as a matter of value orientation, ignore the specific requests presented by both opponents and proponents of zoning applications. That is, there is a definite tendency on the part of the commission members to give little weight to verbal expressions made by participants who appear at public hearings. Replies to interview questions reveal this orientation. As one commissioner commented:

I am in favor of the property owner using his property as he wishes where it does not violate some clear and sound zoning principle. I am in favor of zoning as a principle but it should be applied with due understanding of individual rights. I have a strong belief in zoning property for its best use. When it [the best use] is not clear, I vote the individual's request. These items are the basis for my decisions:

124

1. I am well informed on property values here in Austin;
2. I carefully consider surrounding uses and future use;
3. I have been very successful in my own business undertakings.

I believe in zoning according to what is the best use under the circumstances regardless of the individuals concerned. . . . I am not *governed* by what the majority wants; I take it [the desires of the majority] into consideration, but my decision is not governed by it.

Another commission member said:

What the individual wants will not influence my vote. It's the highest and best use—best for the area.

Still a third member expressed his viewpoint on this subject:

Good planning is not harmful to the individual. . . . While we realize the individual's rights, we are not concerned about the individual. We are thinking about what is best for the future of Austin. One person might own a piece of property today and another tomorrow—but the city will stay. We decide on the best use of the land under the circumstances.

And, finally, a fourth commissioner firmly stated:

The [zoning] hearing doesn't affect me. It doesn't bother me at all. I vote the way I think it [the zoning] should be.

Each of these statements was made by those commission members who lean toward the economic value orientation. It can be seen from these remarks that the foremost social value justification lies in their economic orientation that "we zone land and not people." When land is to be zoned for its supposedly highest and best use in accordance with prevailing or anticipated economically determining conditions, there is no necessity to raise the question "Zoning for whom?" Desires of participating individuals receive little recognition, since members of the economic bloc advocate zoning according to "the best use of the land under the circumstances." Thus, they supplant our initial question—"Zoning for whom?"—with the question "Zoning for what?" The answer, they contend, lies in arriving at a decision that reflects those factors associated with the economic value orientation. Since conditions within the area under consideration dictate the use of any part of such area, volition on the part of participating individuals is negated in favor of the reflecting economic conditions.

125

The members of the economic bloc argue that when the benefits to the whole (derived by sustaining the *status quo* in land use) exceed the benefits to the part (which might be expected by a change in zoning), then the application is to be denied.

Protectionists on the Planning Commission maintain that the public-welfare concept requires a deliberate degree of imposition rather than merely reflecting economic conditions. A protectionist's reply to the question "In what instances can planning be detrimental to the individual?" reveals the contention that the public welfare must be an imposition:

> In the long-run basis, there is no harm. The detriment is in the owner's mind rather than actual, since there is some solution as to the best use for every piece of land although it may not be what the person wants. . . . Public welfare is most important. . . . [But] zoning must be consistent with the development in a neighborhood or trend of change. I am interested in maintaining stable neighborhoods. It is what zoning changes will do the neighborhood, not individual interests. . . . It is a matter of how the land should be used and the needs of the neighborhood.

At a public meeting of an organization unconnected with the formal zoning procedure, the same Planning Commission member insisted:

> . . . that although urbanization has been very rapid in Austin, people who have moved into the city are small-time people—rural people. They feel that any home is "my castle," "my neighborhood is my domain." They do not want large-scale planning. . . . There is the dominance of individual rights. . . . It is alright; it's a good philosophy. But it is not a healthy situation for a city of 200,000.

These quotations of a protectionist reveal the inclination to zone land for the purpose of fulfilling certain needs so as to preserve neighborhood developments. The viewpoint rejects the "highest and best use" contention and instead concentrates upon the creation of desirable land usage appropriate for stabilizing neighborhoods. While the protectionist quoted above stated that land is the subject matter in zoning, in actuality his concluding comments strongly indicate a preference to *impose* or *sustain* existing collective standards considered significant for a neighborhood atmosphere. Public welfare, for

126

protectionists, is a matter of imposing social norms for land use to accord with what is best for the neighborhood. Those members holding to the protective perspective reject the notion of reflection in favor of imposition. When land use complements neighborhood development, then the public interest is realized apart from individual aspirations as expressed by participating individuals.

As a matter of value orientation, then, we find both protectionists and those of the economic bloc rejecting the necessity to weigh desires of participating individuals. But apart from the specific justification contained in their respective social value orientations, members of the Planning Commission share other values to support the negation of individual aspirations. During an interview, a member of the Planning Commission explained his stance:

Commission Member: The desires of the neighborhood do not affect me. For two or three reasons: (1) they [the individuals residing in the neighborhood] are not informed on zoning conditions; (2) they see it through their own eyes; and (3) I don't think the adverse affect on them is as great as they think it will be.

Interviewer: Then what need is there for the open hearings?

Commission Member: To bring out all aspects of the problem and sometimes they [participating individuals] do bring out aspects that I have not thought of. They don't have any place there except as it bears on zoning laws and implications. How it [the zoning change] will affect them has no bearing.

Interviewer: How many cases are influenced by the information furnished by the public?

Commission Member: Not too many because a large number of cases are the same—about 15 to 20 per cent.

The exposure to extensive data by commission members prior to zoning hearings minimizes reliance upon the arguments of participating individuals as a source of information. For commission members have immediate access to official city reports prepared for each application, field trips are taken to observe the land in question, and private discussions occur among commission members as well as with relevant city officials. Moreover, actions taken upon previous zoning cases set precedences which sometimes bind members of the commission to a certain course of action. The fact that other applications have been denied or granted in the near vicinity of the area in question will sometimes influence the voting behavior of these decision-makers. As a commission member once stated: "I have always [consistently] opposed commercial development between Burnet Road and the Dallas Highway."

One final reason accounting for the minimization of evidence presented at public hearings is private conversation by participating individuals with commissioners. While the extent of this type of decision-formation cannot be accurately determined, nonetheless its influence is not so significant as one might speculate. That is, "politics" in zoning in the city of Austin does not deserve extensive emphasis as an explanatory factor in the decision-making process performed by commission members. For some members refuse to participate in such private conversations; others do so with the qualification that this is only another source for obtaining relevant information concerning a zoning application. Moreover, during the several private conversations in which this writer observed or participated, commission members simply reiterated their respective social value orientations toward zoning. As vested groups formed in the effort to influence zoning decisions, investigation of their pressuring techniques—such as letters to individual commission members, private conversations with members of pressure groups, and confidential data given to this writer—revealed arguments almost identical to those that are aired in open hearings before the Zoning Committee and City Council. The following is a typical case in point:

A property owner requested a change in zoning from "A" to "BB" in order to construct apartment units. Several persons appeared to express vigorous opposition to this zoning change before the Zoning Committee. This Committee, after the formal hearing, voted unanimously to grant the requested zoning change. Following adjournment, several members of the Zoning Committee discussed this particular case with the applicant. One member suggested that the applicant take the architectural

128

drawings of his proposed apartments and show these plans to several commission members who do not serve on the Zoning Committee. Then this commission member turned to the other and asked, "How do you feel on his application? Are you going to vote for it?" "Sure, I'll vote for it," replied the second commission member. Whereupon, the first commission member exclaimed: "Mr. ——— [the remaining commission member on the Zoning Committee who heard the application] I know will vote for it. So you have three votes there. *I just don't see how the request can be turned down when there is a 16-unit apartment located immediately behind this lot you own.*" [Emphasis supplied.]

From this conversation it is seen that although votes were committed to a zoning application, the commission members, whose comments are recorded here, did so for the same reason as when they approved the request as members of the Zoning Committee: the existing apartment units justify expansion. But though this applicant later spoke with several other commission members in private, his request was denied by the Planning Commission in a three-to-two vote (with one commissioner abstaining) on the grounds that the area was well developed with single-family residences. Later, the applicant withdrew his zoning-change request.

While it appears that such maneuvering most often remains in the bounds of the social value orientations espoused by commission members, *sub rosa* activity persists to a limited extent. Nonetheless, this writer maintains, after over four years of fieldwork in the community as well as through personal knowledge, that the influence of *sub rosa* activity is definitely a minor factor and plays a very small role in most decisions. While on occasion "politics" intervene in zoning decisions, there is no justification for stressing this aspect of the zoning process. The social value orientations presented in this chapter clearly dominate and, therefore, account for virtually all zoning decisions.

While the social value orientations of commission members apparently give little importance to expressions by participating individuals, in reality there are times when the commissioners seek to abate the outcries of property owners through protective measures. This is the procedure followed when a zoning change is granted for a piece of property attached to a well-developed residential area. In this event, the applicant will be required to accede to protective considerations by sealing off one land use from the other. This device is known as "screening." Most often the applicant must erect a sturdy and attractive fence, evergreen hedges, or both; or the Planning Commission will establish a "buffer zone" upon the applicant's property by maintaining a certain amount of the land under consideration that abuts a residential area as "A." In this manner the particular objections of protesting residential property owners receive a degree of consideration in zoning decisions.

Members of the City Council are somewhat ambivalent toward the incorporation of desires expressed by participating individuals into their value orientations. As elected representatives, they implicitly value democracy—the notion of going from individual desires to a collective representation—yet they also feel an obligation toward a public welfare concept that rises above the notion of democracy. As a result, there appear to be several possibilities for value-specificity in the viewpoints of opponents and proponents in the zoning decisions of council members.

First, when acting upon zoning applications in which no one appears in opposition to the requested change, the members definitely tend to approve the request. In one instance, a council member stated that "since there is no opposition, we might as well pass it [the zoning application]." On another occasion, a council member exclaimed that "no one appeared against it [the zoning application]. Why not grant it?"

A second social value in which participating individuals receive consideration by council members is apparent when certain council members reject a zoning application because they hold the opposition to be sufficiently serious to justify this. Sometimes the motivation for this course of action springs from political considerations, at other times from the sheer fact of neighborhood opposition to the zoning change. As one council member stated:

Council Member: I have some pretty fixed ideas on zoning. I weigh those ideas against the human element. It has been my policy that when at least 75 percent of the homeowners object violently, I go with the people. This is mostly wet and dry.

Interviewer: You mean beer and liquor cases?

Council Member: Yes. . . . In zonings, since I represent the people of Austin, if there is a great outcry by the people, I let this represent my opinion over planning. I represent people first and property second. Of course, there are times when there are outcries by a people but it is a fake. A person will come in with a petition of hundreds of names. This is sometimes a false outcry. . . . [But] you can't please all the people all the time. If you try to, you're a damn fool.

Several other comments by council members indicate the importance of the opposition in causing denial of a zoning application. One member said in discussing a zoning application:

[At one time] . . . a "C-2" [zoning classification] was requested [for the property we are now considering], but we [the City Council] turned it down because the neighbors opposed the zoning change.

And as another commented:

We sure are going to have a lot of people unhappy if we grant this zoning change.

A third social value for dealing with participating individuals is compromise. One council member purposefully seeks to resolve differences between participants through bargaining. He insists that "all we [council members] can do is to compromise without the sacrifice of principle." He contends quite often that "we [members of the City Council] run our government on the support of the governed." During one specific hearing he remarked:

We have many service men living there [in a subdivision near the area under consideration]. I have received letters and calls from them [in opposition to this proposed zoning change]. Now Bergstrom [Air Force Base] spends $30,000,000 a year out there [for property improvements] and we don't want to lose it. You [in opposition] won't get all you want; Mr. ———— [the applicant] will get most of what he wants, but not all. The art of being up here [as a member of the City Council] is to prevent clashes. We have no utopia in this world.

131

The compromise settlement was raised in another case involving a request for a change in zoning from "A" to "C." The Planning Commission recommended that part of the request remain "A" with the remainder of the request zoned "O." Individuals appearing in opposition to the zoning application favored this recommendation; the applicant hesitated. The following discussion took place before the City Council:

Council Member 1: Are you [the applicant] willing to compromise?

Applicant: We feel that the whole tract has to be developed. It [the Planning Commission's recommendation] is going to make it very difficult to do this. We will have some trouble in financing the construction if our zoning request is denied or modified. We believe that the whole thing must be zoned some type of commercial zoning. . . . [But] we will be willing to accept a "GR" on 41st Street and "O" on 40th Street.

Council Member 2: I think that is realistic.

Council Member 1: All that I know is to compromise without sacrificing principle.

(The council then approved a change in zoning from "A" to "O" for part of the property in question, and the remainder was zoned "GR.")

A fourth social value whereby participating individuals receive consideration is through direct contact with members of the City Council outside formal sessions. While there is no way to determine the extent of this practice, nonetheless one council member was particularly susceptible to this. Although he advocated the economic orientation toward zoning, his standard for passing upon zoning cases was usually expressed in this statement: "I can't see how that zoning change would hurt anybody." The writer was unable to arrange an interview with this council member, but the discussion relating to one effort to set an interview reveals an admitted ignorance of zoning by this council member. After the writer requested an interview, the following discussion ensued:

Council Member: How long will it take?

Interviewer: About an hour or an hour and a half.

132

Council Member: Hour or hour and a half! How can you talk about zoning for an hour and a half? I don't know a damn thing about zoning.

Lacking a knowledge of zoning, this council member tends to be swayed by personal appeals from participating individuals. In one particular instance, an applicant spoke with this councilman in private prior to the council hearing. The influence of this conversation is reflected in what was said by the council member when the case was acted upon by the City Council. He is designated as "Council Member 1":

Council Member 1: I made a trip over [the location of the land in question].

Council Member 2: I went there, too.

Council Member 1: They [the applicant] have a very nice place there. The neighbors in front and on the side are in favor [of the requested zoning change].

Council Member 3: We [members of the council] will take Mr. ————'s [Council Member 1] recommendation and grant it [the zoning request].

(The motion failed to carry by a three-to-two vote; the application was denied.)

Council Member 1: I'm sorry, fellow [speaking to the applicant]. I tried [to get this passed for you].

When the politically inclined council member has no immediate interest in the case as a result of direct contacts, or when he is not alarmed concerning the political effects a proposed zoning change might have upon the geographical area of the city with which he personally identifies, he simply follows the viewpoint of other members on the council. As he once stated in reply to a question by another member of the council inquiring how he would vote on an application before the council:

Whatever you boys [the members of the City Council] want. If you vote for it, I'll vote for it; if you vote against it, I'll vote against it.

Of course, there are instances when other members of the City Council appear to favor the applicant as an individual in contradiction to the councilman's general value orientation toward planning through zoning. However, favoritism of this sort is not characteristic of this body; it is most likely that the value orientations already presented in our discussion of the economic and protective perspectives—not politics—account for the outcome of an overwhelming number of zoning cases. Even applicants, when questioned on this subject during an interview, contended that they seldom spoke with council members concerning pending zoning applications. In reply to the question, "Did you contact any member of the City Council," several applicants stated:

INSTANCE 1:
Applicant: No. I don't think that it is proper procedure. I know each member of the City Council by first name. They are personal friends of mine and it would be taking undue advantage of them to do so. [This applicant's request was denied by the City Council.]

INSTANCE 2:
Applicant: As far as going to the Zoning Committee, people of the Planning Department, or the City Council, we have no point in doing that—unless new evidence comes up that might render a new decision on the request. [This applicant's request was denied by the City Council.]

Again, as with the Planning Commission, applicants, whenever they contact members of the City Council in private, seek to determine the extent of the opposition to their cases so as to prepare their arguments. Oftentimes, there is no deliberate attempt to obtain commitments from council members. Although fairly reliable sources informed this writer that there are instances when applicants could "count on" the votes of certain council members before final disposition of a zoning application, such prior approval is more likely to stem from the common economic value orientation possessed by councilmen and applicants toward zoning. Because the economic value orientation accounts for initiation of zoning applications on the part of applicants in most cases, and since the same orientation dominates the

134

council, it is only to be expected that applicants would feel that passage is certain before hearings are held, and on this basis specific votes can be "counted" prior to the formal hearing.

A fifth social value councilmen have in handling the desires of participating individuals is simply to eliminate the notion of considering these desires. This is the position assumed by those council members who insist upon rigorous application of the economic social value orientation when zoning land. By maintaining that zoning decisions should reflect what is considered to be "the highest and best use" for the land in question, there is no necessity for the economically oriented decision-makers to incorporate the desires of participating individuals. Zoning, according to the economic approach, simply reflects determining economic conditions that will warrant either change or maintenance of existing land usage. This viewpoint is apparent in the following accounts:

INSTANCE 1: A person applied for a zoning classification to permit the off-premise sale of beer in an existing bowling alley:

Council Member 1: You just can't win on zoning. I wish that the sale of beer were not made a zoning issue. But if the sale of beer is legal, I cannot deny a person the right to sell beer. It just doesn't hold for us to let one man out there [now in business within the general vicinity of the bowling alley to] sell beer just because he doesn't have the opposition that this request has.

Opponent 1: What is zoning for?

Council Member 1: The basic principle is to zone land for the highest and best use. I am going to have to vote for the land and not the people.

Council Member 2: You cannot ever decide it [the sale of intoxicating beverages] on a moral opinion. The vote in Austin is five to three for wet.

Opponent 2: When you vote, do you vote for the majority [opinion of the people in the area] out there?

Council Member 2: We can never do that—the change in the environment [determines the basis for approving zoning requests]. The majority can never determine—we have to look at it [the property in question]. We will, [however,] alter our votes in the proximity of an election.

135

INSTANCE 2: On occasion, the city attorney explains the legal aspects connected with zoning. He once stated in regard to collective representation:

If the wishes of the people in the area on a head count were the sole criterion for passing zoning, the zoning ordinance would be void.

INSTANCE 3: An applicant sought a change in zoning to allow the placement of a beauty shop in an existing single-family dwelling:

Council Member 1: This is a poor old lady [applicant] who wants to beautify hair. She took a poll and 11 out of 12 [of her immediate neighbors] favored the application.

Council Member 2: I thought we were supposed to support [the recommendation of] the Planning Commission. In the future, we should just take a poll of the neighborhood!

(The council then voted to grant the request by a four-to-one vote; Council Member 2—an economically oriented decision-maker —voted to deny.)

From these instances it is seen that zoning, in the view of certain councilmen, should not reflect the desires of participants; rather, zoning should accord with the economic value orientation. As one proponent of the economic position expressed himself in a discussion of an application to allow the construction of apartments in an existing single-family residential area: "We must all recognize that the highest and best use for Mr. ——— [the applicant] is apartments. But it [the use of the land for apartments] is not the highest and best use for the area." And during an interview, another council member maintained this same social value orientation:

Zoning is not a majority idea. It is as far as the whole City of Austin is concerned, but not as far as a particular neighborhood. A lot of the people who come up there [before the City Council in protest] think so. It's [the basis for zoning decisions] its [the land's] highest and best use.

A sixth and final social value for handling the desires of participating individuals is espoused by some members of the City Council who hold that applicants for zoning changes have a community re-

136

sponsibility, since higher property values oftentimes result from the city's own activities. Certain council members maintain that the city government furnishes services that make property valuable and, consequently, individual owners owe an obligation to the general welfare.

INSTANCE 1: The City Council held a hearing on a zoning application initiated by the city of Austin to prevent the erection of high signs and large buildings and to require certain setbacks from the city's newly erected auditorium. The city government desired to protect the appearance of the auditorium and to avoid congestion of buildings around it. The discussion on this matter demonstrates the point of view of some council members toward land evaluations that result from public endeavor:

Council Member 1: The City bought the 97 acres [surrounding the City Auditorium] to control the area to keep it beautiful. We have dug three [water] wells for air conditioning and for beautification. We have roads planned to make this part of town more valuable. It takes a long time. East Avenue is going to be widened with 60,000 cars per day. The dam [constructed by the federal government and located in the river from which flooding water once engulfed a large area of the land in question] has caused the present value of all this land. I can remember when spinach and cabbage were planted there along the river which was fertilized by the flooding water. Water used to go up as high as the Deaf School. All that area was undeveloped.

Don't question the motives; sound planning must be done. Government can exist only with consent of the governed. All that we were aiming at is to try to ameliorate against a few signs to prevent the view of the auditorium from being blocked. . . .

Opponent: I can't understand any reason for a 25-foot set-back, except taking care of the dreams of the planners. Just make a resolution to control the signs without wronging the other property owners. . . .

Council Member 1: You used to have nothing but spinach and corn on that land fertilized by the floods. Now the land has increased in value because of the dams [constructed by the federal and city governments] and the Lamar Street bridge that has made possible the development of residences in the western parts of the city which would not otherwise have been there. . . . We don't want to hurt your property in any way. When you come from the country into the city, you have regulations that you

137

did not have [while residing in the country]. I know of some things you do in the country which I cannot say before the people here in this room.

Council Member 2: If I were a property owner over there, I would view it from this point of view: it has happened in other towns without zoning that the area around an auditorium has become so congested that it isn't valuable for anything.

Opponent: I lost half the value of my filling station over there [near the auditorium] because of action taken by the City Council.

Council Member 1: What made the value of it? You found the [city] road was going to be over there, but you missed [in your calculations] by 30 feet.

INSTANCE 2: A large subdivider became involved in a vigorous defense of a zoning application. A lawyer represented the subdivider in the case before the council. The dispute centered upon the council's desire to prevent passage of the requested zoning change unless the applicant were willing to relinquish the navigation easement over the property. The applicant refused to yield. The council sought this type of agreement so as to protect egress and ingress to the city airport located near the property in question.

Council Member 1: We have to consider the safety of the persons coming in on a plane. This is a zoning change that we are asking you to go along with us. Until you do this, I am not going to go along with you.

Applicant's Attorney: The condition that you set will not enable us to make use of this property.

Council Member 1: It [the zoning] takes a give up, a pick up, and a take up. It [the zoning] takes reciprocal agreement. . . .

Council Member 2: Will this [demand for a navigation easement] impair the navigation rights?

Applicant's Attorney: Yes, it would.

Council Member 1: When we take the navigation rights, we'll have to pay.

Applicant's Attorney: But this [demand for a navigation easement] is giving up our navigation rights without pay.

Council Member 1: You are talking about a very small piece of property without any intrinsic worth.

138

Applicant's Attorney: That's right. But you will be taking the navigation rights.

Council Member 1: What value would . . . [the subdivider's] land be if Austin had not passed all the bond issues that furnished water, sewage, and lights?

Applicant's Attorney: It's been a help—I know that.

Council Member 1: All right! Doesn't he [the subdivider] owe something to the city? Of all people, there should be a reciprocal relation between him and the people of Austin. We can postpone it [the application], or we'll be kind enough to vote it down. We don't want to be harsh; we want to be reciprocal. Private enterprise must give up certain rights for the good of the whole.

(The final vote was postponed; later the application was denied because the applicant refused to yield the navigation easement.)

These two illustrations reflect the legitimacy of demanding compliance to welfare standards because of the benefits individuals derive from the general welfare. In these instances, among others, the general welfare justifies imposition upon the units composing the whole.

The preceding evidence, then, indicates a strain between individual desires and collective standards. Furthermore, there is no consistent method whereby decision-makers move from the wishes of those they represent to a collective decision; decision-makers rely upon a variety of social values. While recognizing the existence of strains between the requirements of the public welfare intrinsic within the zoning procedure and the desires of participating individuals, no consistent solution has been established to resolve this dilemma.

Decision-makers themselves are cognizant of the difficulty involved. The sole decision-maker advocating the notion of utilitarianism does so with full awareness that the alternative is social imposition in the form of a collective-welfare standard, with the consequential loss of individualism and the "spirit" of risk (through the speculation resulting from the randomness of ends). Other decision-makers openly admit the impossibility of pleasing participants: "You just can't win on zoning," lamented one council member. Or, as another

139

councilman commented: "We are not able to make friends consistently over zoning [decisions]." As a result, zoning becomes an imposition justified by: (1) reliance upon certain determining economic conditions established by the economic social value orientation as relevant; and (2) social valued-conceptualizations of what zoning must be achieved to provide for the public welfare.

There is also the value of democracy—the notion that the public has a direct bearing upon zoning through its voting power—which should be reflected in zoning decisions. On the other hand, there is the social value to promote the very objective zoning supposedly accomplishes—that is, to regulate land use in an orderly fashion so as to promote and sustain the public peace, health, safety, morals, and general welfare. Should full consideration be given to individualism, then the goal sought through zoning will be lost; should full consideration be given only to the aim sought through zoning, individualism will be lost. As one council member succinctly stated, "It's the desires of the people versus orderly development." Consequently, the decision-makers who ignore individual desires in their value orientations impose a collective welfare concept predicted upon economic conditions or in accordance with neighborhood utility and need. The alternative of individualism denies the feasibility of social planning itself, and results in unpredictability due to its randomness of ends.

Another fundamental factor accounting for the difficulty in reaching consensus concerning a collective-welfare standard among the decision-makers—even when a collective standard is imposed—stems from the endeavor to pass upon zoning in a cultural context that sanctions private ownership of property. While zoning can operate apart from consideration of property ownership, zoning itself is a normative system that determines the rights of land use associated with property. Thus, a major difficulty stems from the effort to regulate land use by imposing collective standards through zoning in a social situation that permits private ownership of property. Although property ownership itself involves normative systems, the social value still persists in our society that landownership includes the right of property use for the purpose of forwarding the exclusive welfare of property owners. The

140

difficulty of establishing a collective standard through zoning is created by the existence of a normative system that blends together property ownership and property rights. The problem is clear in the following illustration:

> *Commission Member 1:* . . . I don't think we should grant a change in zoning if the area in question is too small for the zoning the owner requests—even if it [the land in question] does border on a thoroughfare.

> *Commission Member 2:* I sympathize with Mr. ——— [Commission Member 1] that it [the land in question] should be larger in area. But I don't believe we should penalize this one man because he doesn't have the area.

> *Commission Member 3: His [the applicant's] property is being taken away from him* [if we deny him the request]. I don't believe we should deny him the right he already has. [Emphasis supplied.]

From the empirical data dealing with the individual-collective social value orientation, we can find no consistent method, in practice or in theory, for moving from individual desires to a collective decision. Theorists who recognize the impossibility in their formal treatments are simply ascribing to a social situation that exists in reality. In brief, the demands for the whole versus the desires of its parts remains an enigma in reality and in theory.

The Present-Future Time Value Orientation

Time is an intrinsic and essential element in the social value systems of the decision-makers. All the decision-makers, be they protectionists or advocates of economic values, rely upon a particular time conception to orient land-use activities in space. So important is time to the entire zoning process that it becomes an inseparable ingredient of the economic-protective value orientation. Even in discussing the *E-P* social value orientation, we made constant reference to time in the phrase "present and anticipated land-use activities."

Decision-makers sharing any element of the economic approach —in the form of *E, EP,* or *PE*—hold in common to some extent a particular social value conception of time; likewise, individuals pos-

141

sessing any element of the protective value orientation—in the form of *P, PE,* or *EP*—will have in common specific social values of time.[13] The decision-makers expressing either a *PE* or an *EP* combination fluctuate from a protective time orientation to an economic time orientation.

The empirical data employed in this section will deviate somewhat from the foregoing treatments. Instead of relying solely upon the view of Austin's decision-makers, we shall also examine the time values of participants. Because the time values of individuals appearing before the Zoning Committee and City Council as proponents of or opponents to zoning applications differ from those expressed by the decision-makers, a better understanding of the time values affecting the patterning of land usage over space can be ascertained.

All the decision-makers and participants, regardless of their particular value orientation, perceive time as a conception for placing events in the order of occurrence. Time, according to this shared aspect, does not place events as such; rather, the individual utilizes a time concept as a convenience to place events in the order of occurrence. In this manner, decision-makers and participants refer to what has occurred in the past, what is happening in the present, and what will occur in the future—but only to refer to events in proper sequence. The following comments demonstrate this:

INSTANCE 1:

Commission Member: I voted against it [the application] to be consistent with voting against the three other changes I have voted against in the area [under consideration].

INSTANCE 2:

Commission Member: Because at the time of the other [zoning] hearing we agreed that Harmon Street would be the barrier between the commercial and residents, I second the motion.

INSTANCE 3:

Opponent: All of us who are protesting [this zoning application] obtained our homes from Mr. ——— [the subdivider] at a time when the property was zoned "A" Residential. It [the subdivision in which the

142

speaker resides] was properly planned. It seems that if this [the land covered by the request] were going to develop into commercial [uses], it should have been zoned *before the residences developed.* . . . I am unable to satisfy myself why the zoning change was not made *prior* to this [request] so that the prospective owners [now residing in the subdivision] could know. [Emphasis supplied.]

In each instance a development or event is located along a time dimension. Past action—an event prior to existing ones—will sometimes become part of the actor's social value orientation that commits him to a present or future course of action. But in such cases, time per se is not conceptualized as a *determinant* of social action; rather, there is a social conceptualization of time that serves to express the sequence of events.

There are sufficient data showing the importance of time conceptions as social value orientations affecting zoning decisions. The following comments made by Austin's decision-makers demonstrate the relevancy of time as a social value expression affecting the patterning of land-use activities over space:

INSTANCE 1:

Commission Member: I voted against it [the zoning application] not because I thought it [the land in question] was improper for residential use, but it [the land in question] isn't quite ready for commercial use.

INSTANCE 2:

Commission Member: Those of us who went out there [to inspect the property in question] concluded that the area was not ready for this zoning [requested by the applicant]. Maybe some day it [the land in question] will be ready for it [the zoning requested], but not today.

INSTANCE 3:

Commission Member: I move that this application be denied. I think that it [the area covered by the request] is a residential area and should not be intruded upon by apartments at the present time.

INSTANCE 4:

Commission Member: It [the area requested for rezoning] is a spot zone; there is no question about that. [But] it is only a matter of time until the people [in the general vicinity] will come in [requesting zoning

143

changes for their property] and ask for apartments and offices. It is pioneering [to grant this zoning change now].

INSTANCE 5:

Council Member: This area [in question] used to be a very nice residential area. Some day it will be valued for commercial property.

INSTANCE 6:

Council Member: I think in time the value of your property will be more valuable than for its present use.

INSTANCE 7:

Council Member: Planning is the art of timing.

These remarks by different individuals reveal a reliance upon time conceptions in reaching decisions in the zoning process. What, then, are the time value orientations that make time a social value determinant in the zoning process?

In Austin's zoning process, the decision-makers do not hold to any sacred conceptions of time as this aspect has been developed in Chapter Three. That is, no member on either the Planning Commission or City Council relies upon social values that make time reversible and/or recoverable—ritual time—or considers that the mere passage of time must be accorded respect—tradition—in action upon zoning applications.[14] By failing to attribute a sacred quality to time, decision-makers thereby reject the notion of sacred space. For we have already noted, again in Chapter Three, that sacred space must contain a notion of sacred time as an intrinsic quality. That is, if space itself is sacred, a social conception of sacred time must prevail. It is because the decision-makers separate time from space that sacredness toward space can be irrelevant when they pass upon zoning applications.

This is not to say, however, that sacredness plays no part in the zoning process; indeed, this element intrudes throughout as an integral aspect of the social value systems. For those persons holding to the protective element maintain that some activities and events are sacred. For them, the most sacred activity is residential utilization of property. Residential use as the preferred land usage is not called into

144

question, since they believe it deserves the fullest protection possible through zoning. As one person who incorporates the protective element in making zoning decisions emphatically stated: "A residence is the most desirable thing. It's the most sacred thing and should be allowed under any zoning."

Members of the economic bloc reject the notion that land use is sacred in character; they challenge this contention by denying this aspect as a viable argument in zoning land. Still, there is a sacred facet to zoning for even those sustaining the economic value orientation: while land use itself is not sacred, the criteria for determining land use are sacred. Decision-makers holding to the economic value approach do not question the validity of their orientation; they insist that the economic conditions that apparently determine land use must not be jeopardized, but rather perpetuated and reflected in zoning.[15]

Because the economic-protective value orientation of the decision-makers excludes sacred time, then all time conceptions dealing with the past of the traditional and ritualistic sort must be rejected as valued criteria for deciding zoning applications. By placing time in the secular sphere, past time does not impinge upon zoning decisions; by eliminating past time, Austin's decision-makers express only present and future value orientations of time.

To give specificity to the present and future and to select from the means a zoning classification for accomplishing the end in zoning, the decision-makers create and sustain social value orientations. The following analysis seeks to present the varying time conceptions employed by Austin's decision-makers to demonstrate time as a social value orientation in the zoning process.

PRESENT-TIME CONCEPTIONS

The economically oriented protagonists value contemporary time as time at any moment in which *existing economically valued conditions* necessitate the granting or denying of land-use change. We have al-

145

ready seen that the conditions considered to be economically relevant are land usage (such as transportation routes, railroads, commercial enterprises, residence) and topography—insofar as these factors affect the economic return from investments. Such contemporary conditions prescribe for those persons holding to the economic orientation the zoning classification to be given to property. By utilizing cognitive data from existing economically determining conditions in applying its social value standard of zoning property for its highest and best economic yield, the economic bloc incorporates present time as an aspect of its value system. The following statements reflect this time orientation, coupled with the economic approach:

INSTANCE 1:

Commission Member: I make the substitute motion that we grant this request for the reason that the existing situation *has been present* and that the [automobile] count in front of the school *is* 15,000. . . . [Emphasis supplied.]

INSTANCE 2:

Commission Member: I move that this [request] be granted. It is a logical extension of an *existing* "C" zoning. [Emphasis supplied.]

INSTANCE 3:

Commission Member: I think I shall have to vote against it [the request for a "C-1" zoning to permit the sale of beer in an existing drive-in grocery] in view of the Commission's rule that we grant this ["C-1" zoning classification] only in a well-developed commercial area. There *is* no commercial development [in the vicinity]. [Emphasis supplied.]

INSTANCE 4:

Council Member: I look at this piece of property as an extension of [an existing] "O" Office [classification]. This property is not suitable for a residence. We can handle any future change. The character of the neighborhood *is* for an "O" Office. [Emphasis supplied.]

INSTANCE 5:

Council Member: Don't you [the opponent] think the ———— Road *is* increasing in traffic and changing the nature of [the land use in] the area? [Emphasis supplied.]

146

On the other hand, the protectionists value present time as any moment in which *existing protective-valued cognitive data* warrant granting or denying zoning applications. The existence or absence of certain desired attributes in accordance with the protective value orientation constitutes the desirable present for protectionists. Existing cognitive data that will promote or protect residential development and requirements, devoid of the economic effects of the profit motive, define the protectionists' present time conception. The following quotations illustrate the time element in connection with the protective value orientation:

INSTANCE 1:

Commission Member: I move that this request be denied for the following reasons: (1) the property [in question] *is* in a well-developed residential area and it [the requested zoning] is incompatible with the development in the area; and (2) there *is* no indicated need for commercial development in the area. [Emphasis supplied.]

INSTANCE 2:

Commission Member: The tendency of development out there [in the area under consideration] makes it [the actual land covered by the request] unfit for residents. I am in favor of making the change [in zoning]. But I think every consideration should be given to protect the people [living] out there.

Decision-makers holding to *EP* and *PE* social values tend to accept the present-time conceptions that blend with their dominant orientation. Those holding to an *EP* value generally prefer to orient in terms of the economic value of present time, but on occasions they will orient through the viewpoint of the protectionists. The exact reverse is practiced by those individuals holding to the *PE* combination—they prefer the *P* present-time conception and on occasions value the *E* present-time conception. Because illustrations for these two positions would be needlessly repetitious, we shall forego the presentation of examples.

In summary, present time is socially valued by both the economic bloc and the protectionists in terms of existing cognitive data

147

that sustain their respective value orientation toward zoning. Any land use that once occured is interpreted merely in terms of sequence. However, any land use to follow—that is in future time—is another important ingredient of the valued time orientation for each perspective.

FUTURE-TIME CONCEPTIONS

Comments such as the following indicate an awareness of the future and a degree of prediction as to what will occur on the part of Austin's decision-makers:

INSTANCE 1:

Commission Member: It [the area requested for rezoning] is a spot zone; there is no question about that. [But] it is *only a matter of time* until the people [in the general vicinity] will come in [requesting zoning changes] and ask for apartments and offices. It is pioneering [to grant this zoning change now]. [Emphasis supplied.]

INSTANCE 2:

Commission Member: I'm of the opinion that in the *future* . . . your property will be part of a community [shopping] center. [Emphasis supplied.]

INSTANCE 3:

Council Member: I think in time the value of your [the opponent's] property will be more valuable than for its present use.

INSTANCE 4:

Council Member: The past makes the present and the present makes the future.

How do the decision-makers conceive of the future? What are their conceptions of "what is to be" as opposed to "what is"? In what manner do the decision-makers endeavor to predict the future course of land-use development? To answer these questions, we must analyze the social value systems of the actors with regard to the matter of future-time orientation. While differences exist in terms of the economic-protective value orientations, it should be noted before considering dissimilarities that both approaches perceive future time as

148

a secular condition. Each perspective contends that time "yet to come" possesses regularity that makes future time absolute, everlasting, and inevitable. Time will take place; it cannot be regulated nor eliminated. On the other hand, pertinent value differences between the two perspectives exist, to which we shall now turn.

Those advocates of the economic orientation positively value the future as the time span that has *predictive reliability* for foretelling land usage. In dealing with future time, the economic position contends that it must be able to foretell patterns of land use; it is this span between the present and the time when nonexisting land use can be predicted to develop that constitutes the future for individuals arguing from the economic approach. Time is simply a dynamic force that initiates change in man's social activities over space; it is an inevitable development that dictates shifts in land use. Aging is synonymous with change. Time "yet to come," according to the economic value orientation of future-time conception, *will bring change as an inevitable process* that can be neither regulated nor eliminated. Because future time is an unalterable aging process, zoning must passively comply with this determinant condition of time. The following comments made by different decision-makers support these generalizations concerning the economic bloc's future-time social conception:

INSTANCE 1:

Council Member: An "A" Residential [area] *will go down* and *inevitably* apartment houses come in and improve the property. I don't think that this has occurred here yet [in the area we are now considering for rezoning]. *It will take place one of these days.* But it isn't [taking place] right now. [Emphasis supplied.]

INSTANCE 2:

Council Member: The days come when things move on. I wouldn't be surprised when the whole area [under consideration] becomes "C." . . . The day comes when residences will be otherwise.

INSTANCE 3:

Council Member: Change is going to come just as sure as I am sitting here.

149

INSTANCE 4:

Council Member: Right now, it [the land covered by the request] is not ready for it [the zoning change]; a few years hence it [the land in question] might be [proper for a rezoning]. This is my personal opinion; I might be wrong.

INSTANCE 5:

Council Member: I don't see any reason for all this talking. I'm the only one raising questions. But just to know everything is something. Things are changing every day.

INSTANCE 6:

Council Member: This area used to be a very nice residential area. Some day it will be valued for commercial property.

INSTANCE 7:

Commission Member: This area will be used for some form of business at some time in the future.

INSTANCE 8:

Commission Member: It will just be a matter of time before it [Bull Creek Road] will be widened.

In each instance decision-makers with an economic leaning implicitly or explicitly contend that changes occur simply because of an anticipated time.

But to what factors do members of the economic bloc attribute the necessity for change due to time? What standards do individuals holding to the economic value orientation employ in their efforts to predict future land-use developments?

The economic-value argument maintains that certain consequences *inevitably* flow from the operation of certain economic forces. Shifts in degree and in kind with respect to the economically determining conditions of contemporary land usage and topography bring about an automatic and, hence, predictable pattern of land-use development. It is only a matter of time before changes take place in the economically determining conditions, which then account for further changes in land use. This is the so-called "natural trend of de-

150

velopment" to which reference was made when we outlined the economic value orientation as a social value system in a preceding section of this chapter. The most predominant factor contributing to land-use change, according to the economic value approach, is the introduction of new traffic routes. Of course, as indicated by the following instances, the economic values associated with topography and prevailing land use also contribute to the notions of what is to take place in the future:

INSTANCE 1:

Opponent: Since 1931, those corner lots have been zoned "C." This Council is not responsible for this. But you will be responsible for setting up a chain reaction that will make the entire block business if this is granted.

Council Member: The only thing that will determine a chain reaction will be the economics. The character of 24th Street has changed over the years. If you had a lot there [owned property on this street], you wouldn't build a home on there now.

INSTANCE 2:

Council Member: The days come when things move on. I wouldn't be surprised when the whole area becomes "C." The residences along 24th Street are converting over to "C." The day comes when residences will be otherwise.

INSTANCE 3:

Council Member: A lot of people don't want to see Austin grow. They want to keep the city like it was in childhood. At one time I opposed one-way streets, but I have come around to support them. *There is a growth that is going to take place that we can't hold back.* Land that sold for $200 an acre during the depression has sold for $12,000 and would sell for more today. [Emphasis supplied.]

INSTANCE 4:

Council Member: The time may not be right now, but it [the existing residential street] is going to be one of the major thoroughfares of Austin when it is widened. It will be used very heavily for [traveling to] the airport.

151

INSTANCE 5:

Council Member: On 19th Street, the highest and best use will be commercial. The traffic [volume] has changed the nature of 19th Street over the last several years.

INSTANCE 6:

Commission Member: I'm of the opinion that in the future, as Austin grows, just as sure as ———— Road [a thoroughfare] is out there, your property will be part of a community [shopping] center. We have to have food stores to eat.

INSTANCE 7:

Commission Member: I make the substitute motion that we grant an "LR" [zoning]. I checked pretty carefully on that area. One of the principal objections of the people was that it [the change in zoning] would devaluate their land. But the fact that this is a natural area set apart from the other [areas used for residences] by a natural barrier, this objection does not hold. One of the other objections was that it [the proposed zoning change] would create a traffic hazard. But it is the residences that create traffic; business just takes advantage of it. This land [in question] is not suitable for residential use. I believe we must vote *for the long-run advantages.* [Emphasis supplied.]

INSTANCE 8:

Commission Member: Sooner or later we are going to have busi*ness here* [on the land in question]. Since this land is cut off by natural barriers, I believe it is suitable for business [use]. [Emphasis supplied.]

The predictive strength in foretelling future land uses rests, for the economic perspective, upon shifts in the cognitive data that the economically oriented persons value. Because these decision-makers perceive land use as "intrinsic" within certain determining conditions, all future land development "complies" with economic features. Zoning, therefore, must reflect this "natural trend," since "natural" consequences will ultimately yield "the highest and best use." Future time from an economic approach, then, is that span of time yet to be experienced that inevitably initiates a certain pattern of development in accordance with determining economic conditions.

Nonetheless, members of the economic bloc express statements

152

that demonstrate uncertainty of what development in land use will take place beyond the present and even beyond their social value of future time. Take such comments as the following:

INSTANCE 1:

Council Member: Things change beyond the comprehension of man.

INSTANCE 2:

Council Member: You can't tell, in this day of uncertainty, what is going to happen over the world.

INSTANCE 3:

Commission Member 1: It would be very unlikely that the ——— tract of land will be retail.

Commission Member 2: We have no way of knowing.

And one person who promotes the economic value orientation stated during an interview in reply to the question, "Do you feel there is an excessive amount of area zoned commercial in Austin?":

Too excessive. We should re-examine all "C"-zoned areas and re-zone "C" areas where it is clear that the property will not be used commercially or is not the best use for it. Of course, this does not supply an answer to future commercial use. We are without a means to prevent this; we have no way of knowing how to show too much "C" zoning.

Remarks such as these indicate uncertainty toward land-use developments on the part of the economically oriented decision-makers. To explain these expressions, in light of the previous generalization about the economic perspective's prediction of time, requires reliance upon another time conception employed only by individuals holding to the economic approach: the concept of "remote time."

Remote time is a social time conception, held by persons possessing the economic orientation, that refers to any point in time *beyond prediction.* While the economically oriented decision-makers recognize time as an "inevitable" process that "accounts" for change, nevertheless, they acknowledge that economic factors will permit prediction only to a certain extent. Thus all time beyond the point

153

yielding predictive reliability becomes the remote-time span. Any effort to foretell land use for the remote-time span is viewed simply as speculation.

There are at least two reasons for the existence of a remote-time social concept. First, if the economic viewpoint is to be successful in predicting future land-use patterns, there must be a minimum level of existing use in order to foretell what is to take place. That is, a minimum level of land-use development must first prevail before a definite and predictive trend can get underway from an economic perspective. But by recognizing that land-use developments can be expected to take place beyond the predictive quality of determining economic conditions, these decision-makers require the conception of remote time. Second, the tendency among decision-makers holding to the economic approach to stress the importance of private ownership of property prevents prediction. Because such persons perceive the initiation of land-use change as strictly within the domain of the property owner, the randomness of ends enters into the situation. Although Austin's economically oriented decision-makers, with one exception, acknowledge zoning to be an imposition of a collective welfare, nonetheless zoning classifications prescribe a range of land use permissible upon property. The economically oriented decision-makers maintain that the specific utilization of land is to be initiated in accordance with the utilitarian doctrine. Under this ideology of "free" enterprise, each person supposedly pursues economic interests that promote his own welfare as limited only by the market situation and zoning classifications. Within this framework, the sum of each individual effort to realize maximization of private interests yields the collective welfare. As an economic-protective oriented member of the council stated during an interview:

I believe in free enterprise. I think that supply and demand will cause such property to develop best in the long run. I do not believe that if a property does not develop [commercially after being zoned this classification] in three years that it should revert back to the residential [zoning]. I am a realist in planning. I believe in putting the land to its best use so that the property owners can live with it and the planners too.

154

The resulting utilitarian dilemma, with its randomness of ends, provides no predictive instrument for the economic value orientation to account thereby for certain decision-makers relying upon a remote-time conception.

Remote conception of time has an important bearing upon the planning efforts performed in accordance with the economic viewpoint. Because such individuals "have no way of knowing" what will take place in terms of land-use development, it becomes virtually impossible for the economic orientation to plan beyond the future-time conception. Although the economically oriented decision-makers recognize the "inevitability" of time and the changes time "initiates" as an independent variable, planning is a vain effort from the economic perspective in dealing with time beyond the future. For one cannot adequately plan when one does not know what is going to occur. Therefore, it is not surprising that persons who hold to the economic perspective refer to economic efforts beyond their future time as sheer speculation:

Protective Commission Member: This is one case where zoning will affect a lot of residential area.

Protective-Economic Commission Member: Since she [the applicant] doesn't have any [proposed] use, she is zoning for profit.

Economic Commission Member: It [the application] is speculative zoning.

Protective Commission Member: That [speculation] doesn't affect me [in my decision]. Commercial use is rather [permissively] extensive; any more restrictive zoning other than "C" would do.

(The motion to deny received unanimous support.)

Protective Commission Member: I move that we grant an "LR" on the basis that it [the land in question] adjoins an existing "C" use and that it [the land in question] is located on a street.

(The motion to grant an "LR" zoning received a unanimous vote.)

In this illustration, the members with an economic aspect in their value orientation—that is, *E, EP,* or *PE*—rejected the applicant's

155

request for "C" zoning in favor of an "LR" because the existing economically determining forces were not present to yield prediction for a "C" zoning classification. Asking for "C" required the application of remote time, accounting, then, for the charge of "speculation" in land use. Unwilling to move into a time conception that promises only the unknown, those decision-makers with an economic perspective rejected the "C" request. But the economic bloc accepted the motion to grant "LR" because the existing economic conditions permitted prediction of an "LR" trend. On the other hand, the above example shows the unwillingness of the pure protectionist to accept the economic contentions. Instead, the protectionist relied upon the value that the zoning classification closest to "A" Residential must be given in accordance with existing cognitive data to preserve residences or to meet the needs of residents.

During an interview, a commission member holding to the economic perspective proclaimed his value of remote time:

Use of land is what determines the price of land. Therefore, commercial zoning should not be granted for speculation purposes.

Thus, while the economically inclined decision-makers express full awareness of remote time, they nonetheless refuse to grant zoning changes if the proposed change must be placed within the remote time span.

The protective contention values the future as the time span *necessary for the implementation of nonexisting zoning classifications in terms of protective values toward zoning.* Protectionists orient their zoning to a future-time conception in terms of what zoning they anticipate should be accomplished in the way of bringing about desirable protective measures. The future is the time span *required* to realize nonexisting land usage that will accord with the protective social value orientation toward zoning. Thus, the protective perspective desires future time as a conception of time yet to come *during which* land-use change will be brought about *through zoning* in a manner complementary to protective values. The protective orientation, therefore,

156

denies that time *brings* change in land use, holding instead to the value that time is essential for accomplishing zoning changes in agreement with preservation or creation of residential use and needs.

The protectionists possess no anticipation of time beyond their future time orientation. Moreover, once land is zoned according to notions held by protectionists, there is a reorientation toward the future. As protective zoning comes into existence, it necessarily becomes part of the present that requires preservation from the zoning efforts of the economic orientation. Preservation itself orients individuals to perform in the present, not the future. Since the secular time orientation of protectionists, unlike ritualistic and traditional time conceptualizations, precludes the possibility of preserving what is to be, the future can only be anticipated. Time, therefore, once defined as essential by protectionists will be redefined as inevitable when land is zoned in compliance with protective values. Time is then reinterpreted as an insurmountable element in the present and as an inevitable future development. It is a time perceived as a regular phenomenon occurring regardless of human effort to regulate or eliminate it. During this secular passage of time in the form of the present, protectionists endeavor only to perpetuate existing land usage in accordance with protective values.

The future-time conception held by protectionists is most difficult to illustrate through empirical data. The conception advanced here is, rather, an abstraction that cannot be fully substantiated in the zoning data collected for this study. However, the following instance lends support to our generalizations concerning the protectionists' conception of what the future is to be:

Economic Commission Member: We build to the future and look to the future. Since it [the property in question] is adjacent to an existing commercial area, I move that we grant it [the zoning request under consideration] with a 25-foot buffer zone from the surrounding property.

Protective Commission Member: I would like to make a substitute motion that this [zoning] request be denied for the reason that it is an encroachment in an established "A" Residential area and that there is ample "C" land in the area.

157

The above protectively oriented commission member rejected the economic value and inserted the protective in a bid to interpret "what should be." In this effort to deny, there is at least an implicit desire that the future shall not yield a land use contrary to the protective value orientation of the present time. The reverse of this negative stance, then, would be a desire to preserve land use that is in keeping with protective values, and to allow only those zoning changes that sustain contemporary protective usage. The reason for the lack of explicit data resides in the fact that protectionists never expressed an awareness of a well-developed social value toward future time in their verbal statements.

In light of the foregoing discussion of the future-time orientations valued by the decision-makers, what is the relationship of time to zoning? What bearing do these respective future-time orientations have upon zoning decisions?

To begin with, we have already noted the impact of the remote-time conception upon zoning decisions made by the economic protagonists whereby such decision-makers reject zoning applications when the proposed use cannot be predicted in terms of determining conditions. Yet there is one other important point to note regarding the importance of future-time orientations for zoning decisions: those individuals advocating the economic value orientation maintain that zoning decisions *must reflect* time as a determinant of change; persons who hold to the protective notion contend that zoning *must determine* the future course of land development. Thus, the economic orientation does not perceive zoning as a predictive instrument; rather, zoning, according to this perspective, merely mirrors those economic factors that determine land use in the time yet to come. On the other hand, because the protectionists maintain as part of their value orientation that zoning must determine—not reflect—land valuations, they endeavor to make zoning itself a predictive device to foretell the course of land use over space.

Empirical data for this contention regarding the protective view-

158

point are lacking. However, the following statements uttered by economically oriented members distinctly indicate that they feel future zoning must comply with, hence reflect, time as a constantly changing determinant in land use:

INSTANCE 1:

Council Member: You are supposed to zone the land for the highest and best use. If the character of the land is changing, the zoning must change. All along the Interregional [Highway] was residential and everyone knows that it is not for residences now. Time has changed all this.

INSTANCE 2:

Council Member: Generally, the only way to protect yourself [from intruding uses] is to buy in on deed restrictions.

This latter comment acknowledges the tendency on the part of the economically oriented decision-makers to negate zoning as a social condition prescribing the future distribution of human activities over space; it encourages persons to rely upon deed restrictions rather than upon zoning as the instrument for preserving residential use in the time yet to come.

The creation of land-use districts through so-called "master plans" also demonstrates the bearing of time conceptions upon land use. For, essentially, a master plan is a normative scheme applied to sustain present land usages and to direct future patterning in land development. It is one of the major instruments for assuring a self-fulfilling prophecy. By adhering to the normative system of a master plan, both the economic and protective orientations define things as real, and therefore the consequences become part of reality.[16]

From the economic viewpoint, a master plan designates certain economic conditions: the placement of thoroughfares, streets, and railroad facilities; the designation of certain land uses as necessarily following from the presence or absence of transportation facilities; and designation of land uses in accordance with topography. Once a master plan requires these items through imposition, then land use must conform to such determinants. And insofar as the economically oriented decision-makers seek, in zoning matters, to make certain that land use actually adheres to such planning, a master plan becomes a predictive instrument. However, both the notion that zoning must reflect economic conditions rather than control them, and the belief in the utilitarian doctrine of private ownership, intervene to prevent reliable prediction. Because of these values held by the economically oriented individuals, the economic orientation calls for "flexibility" in all master plans. An absence of a minimum level of existing economic developments and the presence of random ends intrinsic to the theory of individualism prevent prediction to explain why the economic orientation requires that master plans be adaptable and responsive to change —change that, as we have seen, the economic approach views as intrinsic in the very passage of time. The following remarks indicate alarm—because of the economically oriented values on the part of some council members—toward master plans:

INSTANCE 1:

Council Member: Austin has always been a planned city. I think that any city ought to work toward a plan. We have always got to recognize that a plan for a city is like a plan for a home: it always requires remodeling. A plan must be used as a guide and not a hard, set rule.

INSTANCE 2:

Council Member: We have got to have a master plan that will allow for changes that take place within a city.

The protectionists tend to reject the argument that flexibility is an essential ingredient of master plans. Instead they want to assure the actualization of the master plan as a normative system in practice. A master plan is to be made a self-fulfilling prophecy simply through conformity to its contents as a normative system. The protectionists maintain that a master plan need not mirror economic conditions; the plan must be made an instrument of change itself rather than reflecting the type of change the economic approach claims takes place over time. By perceiving the master plan as a predictive device, then, the protectionists implement a self-fulfilling prophecy. They are able to

160

accomplish this because they have no concept of remote time. Furthermore, they contend that the "determining" conditions of the economic value orientation must be manipulated to comply with notions of protection.

It appears, then, that the very time orientations employed in planning influence the distribution of social activity over space insofar as zoning itself is effective. The economic perspective tends to advocate land use that reflects economically determining conditions, while the protectionists seek to promote residential utility and need in their future-time orientation. Indeed, the remote-time conception of the economic perspective causes decision-makers who lean toward this position to cling more closely to the present rather than engaging in speculative activities that would be necessary if they dealt with land-use development related to remote time. Because members of the economic bloc tend to conceive zoning in terms of a future-time conception restricted to predictive reliability, zoning as a normative system is restricted to the immediate future. There is, subsequently, a hesitancy to deal with an extended time span that they view as the remote future. This accounts for Austin's economically-oriented decision-makers' dismissing planning efforts that either ignore the remote-time conception altogether or attempt to control activities within remote time—as the protectionists continually do. This emphasis upon the present resulting from uncertainty toward the future (that is, of remote time) is apparent in these remarks made by a certain council member:

1. The past makes the present and the present makes the future.

2. On the path of progress are many skeletons. But we can't create any utopia.

As Eric Hoffer states, uncertainty towards the future causes individuals to hold fast to the present, while hope in the future induces individuals to seek utopia.[17]

Perhaps it is this difference between the two orientations that accounts for the absence of a time conceptualization emphasizing grati-

161

fication with respect to land-use control in Austin's zoning process. The data collected in this study indicate very little concern with this problem. It can be said with certainty that the decision-makers hold no distinct social value orientation in terms of immediate versus deferred gratification related to use of land. However, there was some degree of expression along this line, as suggested by the following statements made by several commission members:

INSTANCE 1:

Commission Member: I believe that we must plan for the long-run advantages.

INSTANCE 2:

Commission Member: I am opposed to strip zoning. In the long run business becomes so congested that a thoroughfare loses its efficiency and businesses themselves lose.

Although these expressions reveal a conception of the future in terms of gratification, there is no general social value orientation of this form of time by any decision-maker.

There is still another value orientation of future time in the zoning process in that some decision-makers reveal an inclination to interpret time as a cost item. Decision-makers usually express time in terms of cost when a delay in zoning might prevent the applicant from utilizing his land to achieve a certain revenue. This viewpoint of time as a cost factor is expressed only by those who espouse an economic orientation.

INSTANCE 1:

Commission Member: Delay costs money for subdividers—for example, interests on loans.

INSTANCE 2:

Protective-Economic Commission Member: I think a study should be made [of the entire area under consideration].

Economic Commission Member: I agree with you. But I don't see any reason for holding these people [the applicants] up for five months while the study is made.

162

The individuals constituting the audience appearing at public sessions of the Zoning Committee and City Council also express definite time orientations. In arguing for or against zoning applications, they employ all the conceptions of time already discussed with regard to the decision-makers. For example, applicants, like the economically oriented decision-makers, usually insist that time inevitably brings about change as an unalterable force to which zoning must accommodate:

INSTANCE 1:

Applicant: I know that when these people [in opposition] moved out there, their homes were out in the country. I know how they must feel. But as time goes, it [the land usage] changes from one thing to another.

INSTANCE 2:

Applicant: Times change. We have got to make way for progress.

However, there is, in addition, another orientation of time that certain participants utilize that does not constitute an element in the social value orientations of the decision-makers. For while the participants who advocate approval of zoning applications generally employ identical time conceptions composing the economic value orientation, only opponents of zoning changes make extensive use of sacred time. The latter do this in a determined attempt to prevent changes in land use. Such persons rely upon a traditional concept of sacred time: time is accorded respect and reverence in the sense that the mere passage of time legitimizes the *perpetuation* of existing social activities connected with land use. Traditional time is time made sacred because it is a form of time that circumscribes events to which individuals accord acknowledgment. The following comments made by persons testifying at public zoning hearings illustrate the interpretation of time in the sacred sense:

INSTANCE 1:

Opponent: Our neighborhood is unlike many others. We have our family roots for 40, 50, 60, and 70 years in this neighborhood. [He calls

163

the names of families living in the neighborhood corresponding to these numbers of years.] We have watched our family grow—others to come and go. Some have remodeled their homes, fences, made additions and improvements to their homes.

INSTANCE 2:

Opponent: Father bought here years ago. . . . He was an oil field worker working for $12 a week. Please remember that we have been born and raised here and let us remain living here.

INSTANCE 3:

Opponent: There have been two blocks out there we have been fighting for. I have lived there for 20 years. Let me keep that little place I have out there to sit on my porch and enjoy the sunshine and watch the cars go by.

INSTANCE 4:

Opponent: I was born and raised out in that community. It is one of the basic communities into which you can buy. It still is.

INSTANCE 5:

Opponent: I went out there in 1937. It is a family area, peaceful and quiet. I would like to see it remain such.

INSTANCE 6:

Opponent: This [proposed zoning] affects a fine old neighborhood with 100 homes and 500 people. I was just in one home 110 years old— fine enough for any governor. I bought my home to retire in. . . .

INSTANCE 7:

Opponent: We have lived in the area for 50 years. We have lived in the same house for 48 years.

INSTANCE 8:

Opponent: We have nine people opposed to this zoning change. They have been living in this neighborhood in the houses they own for up to 52 years.

Quotations such as these reveal an effort on the part of participants opposing zoning changes to employ tradition to buttress argumentation against zoning changes. There is in these remarks a denial

164

of the necessity for time to initiate change as claimed by the economic determinists. Instead, the regularity of time—perceived by the economic approach as a determining and inevitable force that makes for change—is a justification for perpetuating existing land-use activities. Thus, the same cognitive datum of regularity expressed in the several time conceptions is variously valued in Austin's zoning process as: (1) legitimatizing the *preservation of existing land uses* by the opposing participants; (2) an *inevitable force that causes change* by the economically oriented decision-makers; and (3) *necessary* for zoning in terms of certain social values possessed by the protectionists.

We also find participants maintaining that zoning is a predictive device. Unlike the economically oriented decision-makers, the opponents among the participants and, occasionally, the applicants for a zoning change contend that zoning must be treated as a predictive instrument. They argue that zoning itself must be *imposed* as a condition in order to determine the course of future land-use development. Expressions by several participants reflect this predictive aspect:

INSTANCE 1:

Applicant: We would like to have the commercial zoning because we want people who buy out there [in our establishing subdivision] to know what is going to happen. We don't want to wait until people buy their lots and then come in to ask for commercial zoning for this property. It will be a fair job to the public and to the people out there.

INSTANCE 2:

Opponent: We have been down here before [to speak in opposition to zoning changes]. We are very conscious of our area and what goes on. I am thankful for the zoning laws that protect us from noises, odors, and the protection [zoning brings] to our children. . . . [But] once that zoning is changed, no one will have control of what goes in there [on the property in question].

INSTANCE 3:

Opponent: All of us who are protesting this zoning change obtained our homes . . . at a time when the property [proposed for rezoning] was zoned "A" Residential. It [the subdivision in which he lives] was properly planned. It seems that if this [the property in question] were going to

165

develop into commercial, it should have been zoned before residences developed. Some of us as individuals were perhaps naive. . . . [But] I am unable to satisfy myself why the zoning change was not made prior to this request so that the perspective owners could know. There have been no changes in the area. If it is decreed that it is commercial property today, it should have been commercial when we bought our homes in this subdivision.

INSTANCE 4:

Opponent: They [the residents living in the vicinity of the property in question] purchased that property 30 years ago for residences. They have lived there all these years in residential security. They moved there so they could have peace and quiet.

INSTANCE 5:

Opponent: My over-all objection to this zoning application is that it is spot zoning. Once you lower a section in an area, the next person will want a little lower restriction [for his property abutting the land in question]. This will lead to a slum.

Such expressions call for zoning regulations that impose controls over land use so as to permit prediction rather than to reflect future conditions. The individuals holding to this value desire that zoning classifications be implemented so as to make certain that the future will be the same as the present. Through imposition, time is to be held constant; time is to become a regularity without initiating change; time is to be made sacred in the traditional sense.

But as individuals come to rely upon sacred notions in the form of a traditional time conception and the value that residential utilization and needs are not to be jeopardized, then zoning decisions contrary to protective arguments are interpreted by protectionistic opponents as the exercise of arbitrary power. Such individuals interpret undesirable zoning decisions as actions of overwhelming proportions that simply cannot be overcome by reliance upon sacred conceptions connected with the protective contention. The empirical data support the generalizations stated in Chapter 3 of this study that power must be devastating to individuals whose sacred notions fail to prevail; individuals appearing in opposition to zoning applications do, in fact,

166

react in terms of power conceptualization. A woman opponent, for example, wept before the City Council while expressing the futility of her efforts through sacred argumentation in the form of traditional time and residential activity: "My neighbors told me it wouldn't do any good to come up here [to oppose a zoning change before the City Council]." And an interviewee who resisted an application in vain repeatedly commented during the interview: "I will never go up to City Hall to oppose a zoning change again; it doesn't mean a thing."

In many such cases, these persons maintain that they would sell their homes and relocate. As one interviewee responded to the question, "What are your plans now that the zoning application you opposed has been granted?" said: "I am thinking about moving. If I can get my equity [$1,400] out of it [his home], I am going to move." Another interviewee remarked: "If I don't like the situation, I'll take the [financial] loss [in selling my home] and move." Moreover, there have been actual instances where people have moved after the granting of a zoning change they sought to prevent. As a woman testified before a Zoning Committee hearing:

We bought out there [in the subdivision in which we now live] so we could be in a residential area. I bought a house from Mr. ——— and the area went commercial and I had to sell out [several years ago]. I don't want the same thing happening to me again.

On the other hand, persons who vigorously opposed the proposed zoning change contend, when an application was rejected by the decision-makers, that *their efforts* to resist account for the decision-makers' decision. In such cases, the opponents maintain that the zoning rejection reflects their own determination to bring about protective utilization of land. In reply to the question "How do you explain the decision by the City Council?" one interviewee stated:

I think the City Council is an elected organization. That makes a difference. Therefore, they are more appreciative of preponderance opinion—the weight of public opinion. We had 142 names on a petition which is pretty great against one [the applicant]. . . . The City Council is more prone to think of what the people want rather than what vested interests want.

167

And one opponent said to another in a private conversation after the City Council refused to grant a zoning application:

Well, I am finally coming to the conclusion that we really have a democracy after all and that the Council listens to what we want.

Such evidence reflects social conceptualizations of power on the part of the participating individuals. The opponents whose sacred notions are challenged by the approval of a zoning change respond with the feeling of futility. However, opponents whose sacred notions are not placed in jeopardy because a zoning application was denied by the City Council react with a feeling of power accomplishment.

The above data also substantiate Durkheim's contention that social value orientations related to space fade in the absence of desirable external objects to symbolize sacred meanings.[18] For as sacred notions contained in protective arguments were rejected by the decision-makers in the granting of a zoning application, the opponents endeavored to relocate in physical and social surroundings complementary to their protective value orientations. But whenever zoning cases were denied by the decision-makers, opponents hesitated to entertain the notion of relocating. Opponents who maintained that zoning decisions reflect power counteracting efforts by applicants to initiate land-use change were confident that the *status quo* would prevail in the future, and therefore refrained from moving; they expect their protective social values toward space to be sustained through the zoning regulations allowing only land-use activities that symbolize protective notions.

In sum, then, we have now set forth the three dominant value sets that orient the decision-makers to the elements composing the social action approach to the study of human ecology. Through the employment of social values, Austin's decision-makers: (1) select a specific zoning classification from the available normative alternatives to achieve the given goal; (2) determine whether or not to conform to the social conditions; and (3) give specificity to cognitive data and

168

to the stated end. Consequently, at this point all the elements essential to the social action theory set forth in Chapter Three have been examined, tested, and unfalsified[19] through an analysis of Austin's zoning process. We now turn our attention to the remaining two hypotheses of our study.

Chapter Seven

VALUE CONTENTIONS
IN THE ZONING PROCESS

We have already emphasized that ecological materialists deliberately refrain from using social values as a variable in their analyses. Instead, ecological materialists argue for a "value-free" explanation in accounting for ecological phenomena. By stressing only the "objective," "physical" factors that "demand" man's compliance in adaptation to space—for example, environment, technology, organization, and population—ecological materialism offers a positivistic approach which denies the relevance of volition.

Although such advocates reject the importance of social values— and while *Hypothesis II* in this study clearly challenges the positivist's perspective—we can now carry our argument even further by demonstrating that materialistic ecology simply verbalizes a particular value system. This, stated in the form of our third hypothesis, is:

HYPOTHESIS III: The theoretical perspective of ecological materialism is a *value system* that prevails in American culture and, therefore, cannot be considered "value-free."

170

Current voluntarists do not treat materialistic ecology as a value system in their critical writings. Instead, these ecological theorists simply insist that the perspective advanced by materialistic ecologists cannot rest entirely upon a biotic premise in the form of impersonal competition. Indeed, Walter Firey, the advocate of voluntarism, does not explicitly recognize the materialists' position as a system of values. While he locates the materialistic orientation within the cultural system, Firey still labels the viewpoint of materialism an "interest" facet of "rational" adaptation to space:

Interests (rational adaptation) dominate the spatial adaptation of certain social systems but these interests themselves come indirectly from broader and larger cultural systems; hence they cannot be viewed as self-given ends [values].[1]

However, in a later chapter analyzing land use upon Beacon Hill, Firey, without generalizing, places one component of ecological materialism—geography—within the value system:

. . . geographical factors can influence land use only indirectly through the element of values.[2]

Another voluntarist, A. B. Hollingshead, maintains that the materialists' notion of competition cannot be interpreted as a subsocial process, but rather that "cultural values and usages are tools which regulate the competitive process."[3] And William Form calls for the total abandonment of materialistic ecology in favor of a social-structure approach to the study of ecological phenomena.[4]

So it is that voluntarists refrain from placing the materialistic position within a *value system* conceptualization. We introduce hypothesis III, therefore, to state that, insofar as ecological phenomena are socially relevant, the so-called "impersonal" forces the materialists associate with "competition" do not take place on the biotic level. For not only is the "competition" of which materialists speak "regulated by the prevailing institutions, beliefs, values, and usages of the society,"[5] as already noted by voluntarists, but the very explanation materialists so elaborately defend as "value-free" is in fact a value orientation existing within the American culture.[6]

The theoretical approach of ecological materialism reflects the "economic value orientation" advanced by certain decision-makers who take part in Austin's zoning process. Both groups perceive identical physical conditions as determining the forms of social organization in man's adaptation to space. That is, the ecological orientation presented by materialists is virtually identical to the value orientation of several decision-makers taking part in Austin's zoning process. The competitive process that ecological materialists contend takes place in accordance with efficiency is merely a reflection of the profit-motive orientation of some decision-makers in the zoning process and, more broadly, of many individuals in the American culture. The zoning data reveal that man's effort to accommodate to cost—a dominant feature of materialistic ecological theory—simply expresses a desire on the part of certain individuals to adjust in this manner. The facts of existing land usages and geographical conditions that ecological materialists label "impersonal" forces dictating the distribution of ecological phenomena are essential aspects of the economic value orientation to be found in the zoning process. And, finally, the notion of "functional organization"[7] in terms of an "ecological complex,"[8] as espoused by certain ecological materialists, restricts ecological investigation to those very aspects of social life considered to be the only relevant data by those persons in the community of Austin who advocate the economic value orientation in the zoning process.

"Impersonality" as a Social Value

Ecological materialists maintain that their data are "impersonal," that is, "external," to individuals. These theorists insist that even man's social organization passively adapts to impersonal demands arising out of competition as an "external" condition for survival apart from volition. This inclination to perceive only the impersonal within ecological developments is characteristic of all materialistic ecologists: traditional ecologists such as Burgess, Faris, and Hollingshead treat impersonality as a "biotic," "unconscious," and "competitive" force;

172

neoclassical materialists such as Hawley, Gibbs, Martin, Duncan, and Schnore maintain the notion of impersonality by rejecting social values and/or by their insistence to study only the "pattern of physical activity."

As late as 1945, we find Ernest W. Burgess arguing:

> Competition, or struggle, *without self-consciousness being involved,* is posited as the central factor in ecological processes.[9]

Robert Faris, an outspoken biotic materialist in ecological thought, interprets competition as an impersonal force:

> The ecological order, which emerges from a process of competition, *may be distinguished from the cultural order which is based on different processes,* even though these orders are never in actual occurrence completely independent. The coherence of the ecological order is based on relations of a symbiotic character, similar to the symbiosis that produces the elaborate and interdependent communities of animals and plants, in that it arises *automatically and unintentionally out of the struggle for survival.* The component elements cooperate without knowing it, or at least without having to know it.[10]

Hollingshead once maintained notions of determinism through impersonal competition:

> The competitive process operating through the human mechanism of economic organization acts as an *impersonal* agency which distributes individuals *territorially* into the different parts of the community. . . .[11]

In the words of Carl Dawson, author of the chapter devoted to ecology in a text co-authored with Warner Gettys:

> . . . the distributive process through which all human units are located as to positions and function is impersonal and almost completely unconscious.[12]

Amos Hawley rejects the notion of social values as a legitimate conceptualization to account for ecological phenomena:

> Ecologists are as fully aware of the force of habit and sentiment as anybody else. As a matter of fact, however, the issue of rationality versus irrationality does not concern us. Human ecology studies the structure of organized activity without respect to the motivations or attitudes of the acting agents. Its aim is to develop a description of the morphology or form of collective life under varying *external conditions.* With its prob-

173

lem stated in that manner the irrelevance of the psychological properties of individuals is self-evident.[13]

Jack Gibbs and Walter Martin insist:

> Underlying the subject matter of human ecology and serving as a connection between it and the variables included in the universe of inquiry, there is a mechanism that operates independently of cultural values and the individual motives of men; this mechanism is *selective survival,* the cornerstone of most ecological theory.[14]

And, finally, Otis Duncan and Leo Schnore contend:

> The ecologist is interested in the pattern of *observable physical activity* itself rather than the subjective expectations that individuals may entertain of their roles.[15]

Analysis of the sort expressed in these quotations can proceed, however, only if it can be shown that impersonality does not or cannot prevail as a social value. Yet, the zoning data collected for this study distinctly show that the economically oriented discision-makers hold to the value of impersonality as advanced by the deterministic ecological theorists. Certain members of Austin's Planning Commission and City Council express a *desire* to approach zoning as an *impersonal* matter:

INSTANCE 1:

Council Member: The basic principle is to zone land for the highest and best use. I am going to have to vote for the land and not the people.

INSTANCE 2:

Council Member: We zone land and not people.

INSTANCE 3:

City Attorney: Zoning has to do with the land usage regardless of whether there are any people on the land. It is not a question of individual Council members to consider personalities at all. The only way zoning laws can be contained is by zoning usage. . . .

INSTANCE 4:

Commission Member: We must remember that we are zoning the property. . . .

174

INSTANCE 5:

Commission Member: It has been the policy of this Planning Commission to zone the land and not the people.

INSTANCE 6:

Commission Member: What the individual wants will not influence my vote. It's the highest and best use—best for the area.

INSTANCE 7:

Commission Member: I believe in zoning according to what is the best use under the circumstances regardless of the individual concerned.

To zone "land" rather than "people" is identical to the insistence by ecological materialists that ecology is concerned only with "external conditions" rather than with "subjective expectations that individuals may entertain." The impersonal concept held by advocates of materialistic ecology is a social value expression that, as the zoning data reveal, exists in reality. Thus, the desire expressed by certain decision-makers to zone land according to physical conditions is not only a conscious effort—contrary to the notions of traditional ecologists—but it must also be equated with the stance taken by the neoclassical materialists who express the appropriateness of external conditioning factors to account for ecological phenomena.

"Efficiency" as a Social Value

Some ecological materialists contend that impersonal competition operates to further an "efficient" adaptation to space. They maintain that the distribution pattern of ecological phenomena must result from man's effort to minimize the cost of his locating within an environment. Traditional materialists such as Park, McKenzie, and Burgess in particular stress the facet of cost in their ecological writings. Neoclassical materialists at least implicitly forward the notion of efficiency in advocating the operation of the mechanism of "selective survival."

George Zipf maintains that activities are located such that "the sum of the products of all masses moved, when multiplied by the work-distance, will be a minimum."[16] Park insists that "competition tends to select for each special task the individual who is best suited to perform it."[17] Then, according to Burgess, when the biotic order brings about disorganization, there can be no condemnation "so far as disorganization points to reorganization, and makes for more *efficient* adjustment. . . ."[18]

Faris entertains the notion of efficiency as the major determinant accounting for human migration:

> The ecological migrations are the movements in the struggle for a *better place* in the *economic order*. People desert the less favorable regions when they find opportunities to better themselves in new places, and they move to more desirable places when they find themselves able to *support* themselves there.[19]

Hawley also argues for efficiency in the following quotations:

> In short, organization is an adaptive technique; adaptation may be its essential function. Thus organization may be taken to mean the relating of individuals to one another in such a way as to increase the efficiency of their actions. This is by no means a narrow or specialized definition. All human behavior manifests a tendency toward economy of effort through the dovetailing of activities and the development of division of labor. Even a type of activity so far removed from sustenance matters as sport displays this tendency.[20]

> The demands upon the component individuals tend to be precise and exacting; and only those with skills and abilities which contribute directly and most effectively to the particular function succeed in gaining a niche in the unit.[21]

Richard Ratcliff reasons:

> Despite numerous market imperfections and distortions, *natural economic forces* tend to create an urban pattern which is relatively *efficient* in its basic space relationships.[22]

> We recognize the pervasive power of the public interest in forming the urban structure through planning activities, zoning, and other land use controls. But good planning and sound zoning must be in harmony with the underlying economic and social forces which give cause for the city's existence. Thus well-founded zoning through city ordinance and natural zoning as a product of the economic competition of uses will produce a city structure basically the same.[23]

176

Although ecological materialists maintain efficiency through impersonal competition as a determining, subsocial force dictating man's adjustment to space, this contention cannot be defended in light of the existence of an identical orientation within the social value system of individuals holding to the economic value orientation in Austin's zoning process. For those persons advocating the economic value perspective insist that it is the conditions located in the "economic order" that prescribe the course of ecological development. They reason that man must efficiently utilize space because of the necessity to minimize costs involved in business activities. So Austin's economically oriented decision-makers zone land such that land use might conform to the value of efficiency in terms of cost considerations that they perceive as "intrinsic" in the utilization of space. The importance of cost is at least implicit in each of the following expressions made by the decision-makers who advanced the economic value orientation:

INSTANCE 1:

Council Member: If I were a property owner over there [in the area under consideration for a zoning change], I would view it [the proposed zoning change] from this point of view: it [the traffic congestion] has happened in other towns without zoning that the area around an auditorium has become so congested that it isn't valuable for anything.

INSTANCE 2:

Commission Member: Due to your dollar situation there [in this section of the city], there isn't any heavy residential [use] to go in there in blocks. We have to do the best we can [under the financial situation we face in zoning land]. [Emphasis supplied.]

INSTANCE 3:

Commission Member: . . . it is the banker, the businessman, and the real estate man that builds [*sic*] the city.

INSTANCE 4:

Commission Member: I would like to say that good planning takes into full consideration economic aspects of the situation. Planning and economics go hand in glove.

177

Because, as indicated by these remarks, the decision-makers orient the location of ecological phenomena over space in terms of efficiency, then efficiency itself cannot be said to be a subsocial, biotic, or "external" mechanism that operates apart from human volition. The zoning data reveal that man directs his efforts to locate within an environment with efficiency in terms of minimizing cost as one among several values accounting for the pattern of development in land use.

"Determining Forces" as Social Values

Not only do ecological materialists perceive competition in terms of efficiency as a paramount impersonal force explaining ecological phenomena; they also maintain that ecological shifts result from accommodations to alterations occurring in certain physical conditions. Man himself is only a passive creature manipulated by those forces of change that materialistic ecologists define as "external," "physical" conditions.

McKenzie succinctly stated the position of traditional materialism on this point when he wrote:

> The city may be likened to a great sieve which sifts and sorts its human elements and arranges them in space in accordance with their economic efficiency and their role in the life of the community. The physical structure of the city—its buildings, streets, and transportation systems—constitutes the mesh of the sieve, and competition among the human elements the dynamo which drives the machine.[24]

It is only too apparent from this written comment by a traditional materialist that man is simply a physical particle performing in limbo to the dictates of "economic efficiency" arising out of impersonal competition. Yet, neoclassical ecological materialists continue to press the traditionalists' claim that ecological phenomena flow out of the "physical structure of the city." Hawley states:

> The character of transportation is by all counts the most significant factor influencing the distribution of additions to the physical structure of the city. Most other influencing factors exert their effects indirectly

178

through affecting transportation. The network of streets establishes the major and subsidiary axes along which construction may occur. . . . Topographic features may necessitate departures from a symmetrical street pattern in which case building construction will be likewise affected.[25]

Hawley maintains that population characteristics, as external forces, reveal social change:

Demographic structure contains the possibilities and sets the limits of organized group life. Again, demographic changes, such as changes in the rates of birth, death, growth, and migration, have proved to be among the most cogent indicators of social change. There is irrefutable evidence in the shift of a population trend that a significant alteration has occured somewhere in the mode of [social] life of the aggregate.[26]

Duncan and Schnore also argue for the passive adaptation by man in accordance with changing, impersonal conditions:

Eschewing a formulation of his problem in terms of the individual or the culture trait, the ecologist takes the aggregate as his frame of reference and deliberately sets out to account for the forms that social organization assumes in response to varying demographic, technological, and environmental pressures. In this way, the ecologist seems to be contributing to the maintenance of a traditional sociological interest in explaining forms of organization and changes therein.[27]

In another publication Duncan, writing alone, contends social change, from an ecological perspective, to be a matter of spontaneous adaptation to shifts in determining physical conditions:

An ecological account of social change is attempted by referring to such instigating factors as environmental change (whether caused by man or by other agencies), changes in size and composition of population, introduction of new techniques, and shifts in the spatial disposition or organization of competing populations. The interdependence of factors in the adaptation of a population implies that change in any one of them will set up ramifying changes in the others.[28]

These comments echo the social value orientation of the decision-makers who espouse the economic perspective in Austin's zoning process. For it is the very contention of the decision-makers holding to the economic value orientation that shifts in land use occur because of shifting physical conditions in the form of population, transportation facilities, and geographical factors. As these circumstances alter, the economically oriented decision-makers reason, then so must man's social activities connected with land use conform to these shifting physical conditions. Like the ecological materialists, certain decision-makers believe that it is only appropriate that a functional relationship obtains between land usages which makes for efficient utilization of property in terms of the cost factor. Both groups rely upon the existence of traffic arteries, for example, as one important component justifying commercial development of property. The remarks of the several decision-makers who sustain the economic value orientation in Austin's zoning process support the above quotations expressing the viewpoint toward land-use change by ecological materialists:

INSTANCE 1:

Council Member: *The only thing* that will determine a chain reaction [in land use] will be *the economics.* The character of 24th Street has changed over the years. If you, [although an opponent to this zoning change,] had a lot there [on 24th Street], you wouldn't build a home on there now. [Emphasis supplied.]

INSTANCE 2:

Council Member: If you are going to stick with your adage of highest and best use, you will tend toward commercial use. This is the only way to upgrade a piece of property. This is not to say that we [decision-makers] ignore the needs of residences. I wouldn't think of taking an entirely residential area and turning it over to business. Zoning is nothing but progression anyway: starting from residences to duplexes, to apartments, to doctors' offices, to small businesses, and then to businesses.

INSTANCE 3:

Commission Member: When the City Council voted [funds] for a thoroughfare [to be located in the vicinity of the area under consideration], it [the proposed thoroughfare] destroyed whatever residential value it [the area covered by the application] might have had.

INSTANCE 4:

Commission Member: I make the substitute motion that we grant an "LR" [zoning]. I checked pretty carefully on that area. . . . But the

180

fact that this [area in question] is a natural area set apart from the other [surrounding area] by a *natural barrier,* this objection [by an opponent] does not hold. [Emphasis supplied.]

INSTANCE 5:

Commission Member: I move that the zoning request be granted. The nature of the terrain does not lend the land to residential development.

INSTANCE 6:

Council Member: The more people there is, the more activity there is—it increases the value of the property.

INSTANCE 7:

Council Member: Most all of you [of the opposition to the zoning request] will agree that the property on the highway is commercial for its highest and best use. We have to zone property for its highest and best use. The new shopping center [just constructed in the area] has changed the [nature of] the [entire] area.

INSTANCE 8:

Commission Member: That triangle [as the area we are considering for rezoning] is in transition [with respect to land use] *because of* its proximity to two major thoroughfares. Eventually all of it will be used for multi-family dwellings or business or both. [Emphasis supplied.]

INSTANCE 9:

Commission Member: With an 1,800 traffic count, it [the land bordering upon a street] is not suitable—I mean desirable—for residences.

INSTANCE 10:

Commission Member: Business is created by existing traffic; it does not create traffic.

INSTANCE 11:

Commission Member: I'm of the opinion that in the future, as Austin grows, just as sure as ——— Road [a thoroughfare] is out there, your property will be part of a community [shopping] center. We have to have food stores [in order] to eat.

It can be concluded on the basis of such comments as these that the social value system of several decision-makers corresponds to the

181

theoretical position put forward by ecological materialists with regard to the interpretation to be given to "objectified" features in the form of environment, transportation facilities, technology, and even population aggregation. Social change, for both groups, occurs from shifts in these elements as determinant factors demanding efficient conformity on the part of man's social organization so as to minimize the cost that is created by impersonal competition.

The two groupings also agree upon a social value orientation to be given to time as a determinant. For some ecological materialists and Austin's economically oriented decision-makers interpret the future as the time span having reliability for foretelling developments in land usage. We have already discussed this facet in the future-time orientation of Austin's decision-makers; the following quotations indicate the same inclination on the part of certain ecological materialists:

> Physical geography, natural advantages and disadvantages, including means of transportation, *determine in advance* the general outlines of the urban plan. As the city increases in population, the subtler influences of sympathy, rivalry, and economic necessity tend to control the distribution of population. Business and industry seek advantageous locations and draw around them certain portions of the population.[29]

> As indicated later on in this paper, ecological formations tend to develop in cyclic fashion. A period of time within which a given ecological formation develops and culminates is the time period for that particular formation. The length of these time periods may be ultimately measured and *predicted,* hence the inclusion of the temporal element in the definition [of ecology].[30]

These several quotations concerning time as taken from the writings of ecological materialists only duplicate the value system of Austin's economically oriented decision-makers toward a future time.[31] Indeed, since both groups depend upon identical forces to account for land-use change, prediction becomes a self-fulfilling prophecy. It is because the so-called "determining forces" are given meaning by some members in an urban community—through a value system within the culture—that ecological materialism can offer a

182

degree of prediction with regard to land utilization. If social values did not influence human behavior, then ecological materialism would lose whatever predictive strength it can claim.

Competition as a Social Process

On the basis of the evidence collected from Austin's zoning process, the ecological perspective of materialism has now been declared to be a social value system prevailing in the American culture. As such, competition is not to be considered a relevant ecological process in an impersonal sense—that is, a biotic, subsocial process. Thus, ecological materialists cannot continue to advocate even an analytical separation of data into ecological and cultural orders. The causal factors for ecological materialism are *social values* rather than automatic, unconscious, and value-free forces that account for the ecological processes conceptualized by materialistic ecologists. Indeed, the "impersonal" economic competition in terms of efficiency must itself compete with other value systems as an element of the *social* processes accounting for ecological phenomena. Stated in the form of a hypothesis:

HYPOTHESIS IV: The competition that affects ecological phenomena is a social process rather than a subsocial force.

It has already been argued in this study that individuals perceive physical cognitive data and interpret these in terms of a social value system. Therefore, the items ecological materialists label impersonal and determinative of things social are actually physical cognitive data that must be given interpretative significance by individuals through a social value system in order for "external" data to influence social organization. But identical objectified data receive different interpretations by the decision-makers: those individuals voicing the protective value orientation in Austin's zoning process attach a value system to identically perceived physical data that differs from the value sys-

183

tem of persons holding to economic notions. Consequently, we find both types of decision-makers (as well as participants) engaging in competition in an effort to direct the course of land-use activity in terms of their respective value orientations.

Social competition arises in the zoning process because all persons agree upon the notion of public welfare as the objective to be accomplished through zoning of land, but contention develops concerning the social value interpretations to be given to the mutual goal. Because individuals acknowledge a common purpose and agree to the zoning classifications as the means by which the goal is to be attained but fail to accord with respect to the value systems for giving interpretative significance to the end, we can speak of the existence of social competition in the zoning process. It is the varying meanings due to dissimilar social value systems that account for discord in land-use activities, rather than the impersonal competition advanced by the materialists.

The dominant value contention within the zoning process in the city of Austin takes place in the form of competition between the economic and the protective value orientations. The three possible combinations of social values under this form of competition are: (1) economic versus protective values; (2) economic versus economic values; and (3) protective versus protective values. The zoning data for Austin, however, reveal only the first two possibilities; participants and decision-makers compete with one another either in terms of economic values in opposition to protective ones, or in terms of one set of economic values in opposition to another.

Since the economic argument of certain decision-makers coincides with the perspective presented by materialistic ecology, then the very explanation advanced by materialists occurs in the zoning process as a social value system in competition with another, namely, the protective social value system. For particular individuals seek accommodation to those cognitive data they consider desirable in accordance with the economic framework of materialism. To the extent that the economically oriented persons succeed in seeing that zoning decisions

184

reflect their value orientation, then the theoretical perspective of ecological materialism becomes part of social reality—but as social, not subsocial, data.

Before presenting direct evidence to substantiate Hypothesis IV, it should be noted that most often applicants appearing before the various bodies passing upon zoning applications seek a zoning change to permit utilization of land so as to attain greater economic returns. Maintaining that land uses compete with one another, the applicant argues for a zoning classification to allow for the "highest and best use" for his property. Several instances show this value expression:

INSTANCE 1: A person applied for a change in zoning to permit the sale of beer for off-premise consumption. His attorney maintained:

The sole purpose of this application is for the purpose of the sale of beer off-premise. His [the applicant's] customers demand it. And as an individual proprietor, he [the applicant] must compete with the other food stores in the area. . . . We are not approaching this from a moral standpoint, but from a profit standpoint.

INSTANCE 2: The importance of zoning from an economic standpoint is seen in the comments made by the following applicant who sought a "C" zoning classification:

Applicant: If the land is developed for residences, I would get $1,-500 [by selling the land]; if it's used for commercial, I can get $15,000. I already have a drive-in grocery interested in this [property in question].

Commission Member 1: We can't make a zoning change [solely] on whether it is worth $1,500 or $15,000. We have to do it on zoning [principles].

Applicant: But then the tax department of the city will come along and tax the property [at a valuation of $15,000] for commercial uses. I'll keep coming back here before the Commission and ask for a change until I get it. I'll leave the land as it is until I do get this zoning.

Commission Member 2: That's one of the problems we are faced with. I make the substitute motion that we give this land a "GR" classification because the land is not suitable for residential development.

185

(The Planning Commission unanimously voted in favor of the motion to grant a "GR" classification.)

INSTANCE 3:   An applicant relied upon an existing thoroughfare to justify his economically valued claim for rezoning:

This property is not deed-restricted to residential development. We feel that some light commercial use could be very advantageous. I know that it is disagreeable to the person living next to it. I, too, would object. *But this [property] is along a thoroughfare and there is no other economical use for the land.* We don't know what use the land will be put. I want this to be clear to the neighbors. [Emphasis supplied.]

But while applicants, as indicated by these several illustrations, profess an economic motive to justify zoning reclassifications, opponents of zoning applications counter with both economic and protective arguments. This accounts for the presence of competition in the zoning process and the formulation of Hypothesis IV.

In order to sustain Hypothesis IV, six rather detailed case studies will be presented. The first four are designed to illustrate the value competition between economic and protective values; the remaining two cases reveal the value competition between economic and economic values. The most telling social values will be italicized in the following accounts.

ECONOMIC VALUES VERSUS PROTECTIVE VALUES[32]

The case studies presented below manifest discord between the economic and the protective desires within Austin's zoning process. While in some cases the economic element intrudes into the arguments expounded by opponents of zoning applications, the dominant concern expressed by the opposition is, nonetheless, the protection of existing residential usage:

Case 1:   An applicant, represented by an attorney, requested a change in zoning from "A" to "LR" for one section of the land in question and a "C-1" classification for the smaller of the two tracts to be considered. The applicant intended to erect a shopping center for retail purposes under the "LR" zoning and construct a drive-in grocery with the sale of beer for off-premise consumption under the "C-1" classification.

186

The attorney initiated his case by displaying a map of the area in question and the immediate vicinity. He noted: (1) the property in question bordered 326 feet upon Berkman Drive; (2) a gully used as a drainage ditch composed the rear boundary line that "separated" the attached property from the tract under consideration; and (3) the extensive amount of land zoned for business development in the surrounding area:

Attorney: We are requesting "LR" for the whole area, and a "C-1" for a very small tract on the north side on a 70 x 70 area for a 50 x 50 drive-in grocery. It will be for the sale of beer to go.

This tract will permit other businesses. The layout contemplates eight other businesses. We have a contract with the fence people for the construction of a cedar fence 25 feet inside our property line which will then be bordered with oleanders for every six feet. Everyone knows they [the oleanders] are evergreens of all colors.

There will be ample off-street parking for at least 50 cars.

In addition to the natural and artificial constructions, on the north end there is an easement for power lines. There will also be a cedar fence here and shrubbery.

It [the proposed uses] fits in with the idea of this fast-growing neighborhood with its local retail. *This area here is not suitable for residential development because of its heavy easement, the gully, and the street—* while being protected by very strict developments in the fencing and landscaping.

Opponent 1: We have been down here before to protest a change in zoning for this property. We are very conscious of our area and what goes on down there. *I am thankful for the zoning laws that protect us from noises, odors, and the protection [zoning regulations bring] to our children.* . . . We now have a petition of 632 names in opposition to the zoning.

There is a section across the street that is already "GR." The children must go up —— —— Street next to ——————— [a drive-in grocery store] to go to school and back home. So we give our children a good crack at the danger of traffic. There is also a tremendous shopping center being considered [just a slight distance from the one being proposed here]. I wonder why they [the applicant] can't go in with the one across the street or the one being built? Now our children will have another crack at the traffic. The streets are too narrow.

There is a clause in the deed that the property could not be sold for "LR."

The people feel that if this is approved they should go down to the city hall to get their taxes lowered, get street lights, and more police protection. . . . Once that zoning is changed, no one will have control of what goes in there.

Opponent 2: I got one son attending the elementary school. *We have a nice, quiet neighborhood.* I don't feel that I would be doing my son justice if I did not oppose this. I have been in law enforcement for ten years. I don't believe that there should be a sale of beer in this type of residential development. I have seen too many beer cans thrown across high fences. *If there is a filling station, I don't want to be awakened by the noise.*

Opponent 3: I have a perfect view of the commercial property they have proposed here tonight. They [the applicant] want to put the "C" zoning right in our back yard. I want to know about the up-keep of the fence. I want to know if they will keep their shrubbery as we keep our residences. If this is granted, we would probably have to move away. This would cause us to lose some of our [financial] investment.

We are young. If we just have the chance, we will develop something decent. If we have "C" Commercial in our backyards, we will not have this chance. . . .

Opponent 6: We have a six-foot fence in our backyard now. You could not put a fence any higher. But this does not cut off the view. . . .

Opponent 7: The damage of selling beer near Harris Elementary School will be more damaging than commercial development. . . .

Opponent 8: If this plan were to go through, new developments to the east would use the access streets. This would put a strain on the traffic facilities. When we bought here we inquired about the commercial property in the area and we were informed by reputable people that the area could not support commercial development.

Attorney: I do not represent cases unless it is sound zoning. I turn down as many cases as I accept. I do not consider zoning to be a personal problem. This is Town Hall where we voice our opinions. I believe in the use of land as the individual sees fit as long as it does no harm to others. The laws do not permit people living far away or close by to tell a person how he can and can't use his own land.

The state law does provide for consideration only of people living immediately in front and in back, not to the right or left. The City Ordinance has extended this around for 300 feet.

What is the highest and best use of the property as long as it does no greater harm to the surrounding property? This is what we are here to decide tonight.

The traffic is there. *It is not created by the developer. If there were no traffic there, we would not want to locate there. These people [the applicant] have been in business for a long time and have found there is enough traffic there to support the business.*

188

The courts are recognizing that these little shopping areas are for the needs of the neighborhood and should be within walking distance— not traveling distance. The concept of zoning has changed from separation of business from residence because of the traffic problem. Now we believe in dispersing business and residences throughout the city.

The question of selling beer is not a legal question; it is a zoning question.

You have no guarantee that your neighbor will keep up his lawn. These people [the applicant] are known for their up-keep and will make every effort to do so. Under the present plan, there is no provision for a filling station.

Case 2: The owners in this case possess a piece of property bordering an existing street in the process of being widened. The zoning requested by co-owners of the property covered by the application was for a change from "A" to "C" to permit the sale of the land as commercial property:

Applicant 1: I am one of the owners of the property. We presented our case in 1956 and in 1957. We are asking to be in harmony of the adjoining property. *The highway department has decided to widen East Seventh Street.*

Applicant 2: I'm also owner of the property on the corner. She [Applicant 1] is my sister. We would like to conform to the neighborhood. Behind us is a junk yard; to the east is the same zoning we are requesting.

Proponent 1: I'm in favor of this. Everything else is commercial. Why discriminate?

Proponent 2: In view of the fact that *there is going to be a highway* [*in front of the property in question*] *and this will not be favorable for residences,* I favor the request.

Opponent 1: My property adjoins this place. *Why does it* [*the zoning classification*] *have to be changed? Is there any law saying that land on the highway has to be changed?* The land along the Airport Boulevard is not commercial. Why make it commercial when it can be changed to another business classification [other than the requested "C"]? *They want to get rid of the land, but they must think about us who are left behind.* If it is granted commercial, then they [the applicants] will come back for a "C-1" to sell liquor. And we would have to fight them again.

We [Negroes] don't have any place to go. We are hemmed in on the south, north, and west. The only place we can go is east—out in underdeveloped areas where there is no electricity or sewer. *Where can we go to get peace and quiet?*

189

They [the applicants] just do this to make money. Money is the root of all evil. They have many more opportunities to make money that we [Negroes] don't have.

Opponent 2: There have been two blocks out there we have been fighting for. I have lived there for 20 years. *Let me keep that little place I have out there to sit on my porch and enjoy the sunshine and watch the cars go by.* We're still good friends [with the applicants]. *I fought with them to keep this residential when I moved there.*

Opponent 3: I helped them [the applicants] years ago to keep the area residential. If this is changed I would have to get out. We don't want this "C" to be there. We have commercial on Sixth Street behind us with a lot of noise. I am a citizen of Austin for almost 80 years. *I moved here [in this block] 50 years ago and I want to stay here....*

Opponent 4: *It's a fine neighborhood there. I would be glad not to see things disturbed there.* But if we have to, we have to accept it [the zoning change].

Applicant 1: The time we were against rezoning was when a Latin American wanted to put in a liquor store. The man who said that he didn't want things disturbed should note that there is a little furniture store on Eighth Street.

Case 3: A person applied for a zoning change from "A" to "BB" to construct apartment units. He and his attorney presented arguments in favor of the request before the City Council:

Applicant: We're requesting this change of zoning to permit us to build an apartment house on this property. It will be 16 or 22 units and *I think it will be very economical for this property.* I own the apartment house to the south [of the property in question]. If this zoning is granted, we will, of course, start [construction] on it as soon as possible.

Council Member 1: What is the size of your lot?

Applicant: 260 by 120 feet.

Council Member 2: One of the major objections is the lack of off-street parking and the congestion on the street.

Council Member 3: Is the corner lot zoned "C" now?

Applicant: All four corners are zoned "C."

Attorney: The total area is about 34,000 square feet. There will be about 1,100 square feet per apartment. According to the [city's] regulations, that area will permit 22 units.

190

We have here some plans [blueprints of the proposed apartments]. These are duplications of our apartments to the south. These were prepared by ———— [a local architectural firm]. The construction will be $200,000 or $11 per square foot.

Council Member 3: You will be fronting on Bonnie Road?

Attorney: That's true. We also have sectional maps of the area [showing land usage on the surrounding properties].

Council Member 3: What is your set-back on Bonnie Road?

Attorney: Thirty feet. This [area] map shows the uses. The general area to the north consists predominantly of single-family residences ranging from $8,000 to $13,500 per resident. The average age [for homes in this block] is from 15 to 18 years. There are two mixes of families in the area. There are 8 or 9 duplexes in the area. The block immediately to the east is mixed with one-and-two-family residences. The four corners are zoned commercial.

As we see it, *the area can be generally characterized as not an active area from the standpoint of residences.* It is mixed with one-and-two-family residences and influenced by commercial uses. *We submit this [our proposal] to be the highest and best use.*

We have prepared a designation on the map of the City of Austin showing the apartment houses of the sort we propose. Out on Enfield Road and the general vicinity, there are at least ten apartment houses of the kind we propose that have been constructed over the last ten years. *This shows a trend in the direction of apartments and it also shows a decided demand [for apartments].*

We have a list of the people living within 400 feet of this property [now before you for rezoning]. There are 30 individuals—counting husbands and wives as one and not counting Mr. ———— [the applicant]— and nine have protested [this zoning application]. This is only a third. The remaining two-thirds have filed no opposition.

This construction will improve the area rather than detracting from the values. The site is ideal for transient people.

Council Member 1: What will they [the apartment units] rent for?

Attorney: Between $90 and $110 per month. The location is a convenient distance from Lake Austin, the municipal golf course, and the school. *This is the highest and best use and will contribute the most from the point of the whole community if for no other reason than that it will increase the tax rolls.*

Some references were made about the fact that the tenants are transients and are of an unattractive sort [during the Zoning Committee hearing]. [The attorney then lists a number of persons and the length of time each person remained in the apartment house the applicant owns to the rear of the property in question.] I don't think those people can be classified as transient or unattractive. This apartment house will not attract the undesirables.

I have a letter from ———— [local real-estate agency]. [The attorney reads the letter, which states that the proposed use is the highest and best use for the property, and acknowledges a demand for apartments in the area.] I might add that Mr. ———— [the applicant] has already investigated the finances of the project. He will experience no difficulty in financing it. As a matter of fact, the present holder of the apartments he now owns will be happy to finance this [undertaking]. If the tenants were unattractive and the rent-collection poor, the person willing to finance these apartments we are proposing would not be interested.

The zoning change should be allowed. It will be to the interest of the community, it will not detract from the value of the area, a majority of the people in the area are not opposed, and it will increase the tax rolls.

Council Member 3: Are there any multi-unit apartments along Bonnie Road?

Attorney: Not in the immediate area, no.

Council Member 1: You say that there are only a third [of the people living within 400 feet of the property in question] opposing this?

Attorney: According to my computations. Mr. ———— is here who lives next door. He would like to say a few words.

Proponent: Sooner or later, any property is in a transition period from residential to some better use. In checking within the 400-foot area, there are few homes. *With the competition of new subdivisions, there is no need to prolong the transition period; you might as well speed it up.* We have a $22,100 home [in this block] and we have been thinking about [converting it to] apartments.

Opponent 1: This piece of property is about the same size of the area required for duplexes. This has been an improving community; it has been moving forward, not backward. The area has been changing. *But we bought our home as "A"-Residential.* The past Planning Commission agreed that Enfield Road would have "BB" zoning for apartments. But there has been nothing said about this area. This property [under consideration for rezoning] has been vacant since 1950. There has been no "for sale" sign until this [application] was brought up by the company

192

whose letter he [the applicant's attorney] read. It has not been sold because it is owned by the man who is now making this request.

He's [the applicant] proposing that the nine-foot alley now serving 16 units will have to serve these 22 he proposes. He can't take care of off-street parking unless he has one and one-half parking spaces for each apartment unit. This has been our experience out there.

We have finally gotten the ditch fixed and we are getting our street paved. *We are improving our community.*

There is not very much demand [for these proposed apartment units] if the number of apartments that are rented has anything to do with it [the demand]. There are vacancies there now [in the apartment house the applicant owns]. He [the applicant] has made the payments. But he has held the property vacant for ten years. He says there are no new houses. But he didn't point out the vacant lots. There are no vacant lots on which to build. But we have been living out there as a community.

As far as money is concerned—we are all interested in taxes—a man who appraises my house for loans states that if the area is zoned for "BB," all the houses in the 300-foot area would lose 25 per cent. I asked him what he meant by that and he said that while someone would pay me the price I ask, the money-men who loan will reduce the value 25 per cent. So if this is reduced by 25 per cent, then the tax roll will drop one-fourth.

He [the applicant] is asking the "BB" because that is the best way *he* can make money for the vacant land while the people who have been living out there for all these years will have to suffer 25 per cent in losses. If our "A"-Residential is going to be protected, it [the property in question] should not be changed to something else.

Mr. ——— [the applicant's attorney] put a list showing that nobody cares. But those of us who will have to face the "edifice" every morning have done a lot of thinking. We are not well versed as to how things should be done [in opposing zoning changes]. The Planning Commission discussed this [proposal] very carefully. It is composed of real estate men who know land value. The people who attended the Planning Commission meeting did not come here today because they feel that the City Council would follow their Planning Commission's decision and some of them couldn't get off of work to come here.

Council Member 3: You stated that there was not a "for sale" sign until this application came up?

Opponent 1: That's right.

Council Member 3: Now wouldn't you say that this land [under consideration] being behind an efficiency apartment will be more valuable than the lots on the street you own?

193

Opponent 1:   That's right. But we were there first.

Council Member 1:   Wouldn't you [the applicant] like to withdraw this request? If it's turned down you will have to wait another year before you can come back in with another request for this property.

Attorney: We would like for you [members of the City Council] to go out and see the property first before making your decision.

Council Member 1:   We don't think it is time [to grant this zoning change]; the area is not ready for that type of development [just yet].

Attorney: I would like to postpone a decision on this so that you can go look at the property. I would also like to talk with my client about it.

Council Member 1:   We are familiar with the area. We are ready to vote on the application now. You can go in the other room to discuss this with your client.

(The applicant and his attorney left the council room for private consultation, whereupon a council member explained the situation taking place to persons opposing the zoning application.)

Council Member 2:   We are letting him [the applicant] think about withdrawing his request so that he does not have to wait for a year to come back with another request. We do this so that if he wants another zoning classification other than for "BB" which might be given, he could come back in without waiting a full year.

An "A"-Residential [utilization] will go down and inevitably apartment houses come in and improve the property. I don't think that this has occurred here yet. It will take place one of these days. But it isn't right now.

Council Member 3:   *We must all recognize that the highest and best use for Mr. ——— [the applicant] is apartments. But it is not for the area.*

Opponent 2:   It is not a deteriorating neighborhood.

Opponent 3:   There have been two new houses in our block and seven in the next block over the last ten years. So it isn't going down.

(The applicant and his attorney return to the council room.)

Attorney: We will withdraw our request.

Council Member 1:   All right. We don't know what will be the course of human events. It's [the present state of affairs] just like Jell-O.

194

(The council voted unanimously to accept the withdrawal.)

Case 4: A person applied for a change in zoning from "A" to "B" for the purpose of erecting multi-unit apartment buildings on an undeveloped site. The immediately surrounding property contained only single-family dwellings. The request covered 9.7 acres:

Planning Director: The Planning Department has been working with Mr. ——— [the applicant] to subdivide the area into single houses and duplexes. This is difficult to do. For a tract that is as narrow as this one, there could be no road down the middle because the lots would then be too narrow.

Applicant: Everyone is familiar with the narrowness of this tract. Very earnestly we have attempted to work it out with single-family homes with the Federal Housing Authority. We in our organization are proud of our homes. We have in mind the garden-type of apartments with one-story level buildings. What we do create, we feel, will be the best use of the property.

We carried the plans of the Planning Department to the FHA for approval of homes built on this tract without a penalty. They said they would approve the homes but with a penalty. *You can't build a $14,000 home on an 80-foot lot.*

Commission Member 1: Should you go to the single-family dwelling, you wouldn't need a zoning change.

Applicant: But we certainly would like to build nice single-family dwellings. But we cannot because: *(1) the price of the land prevents this; (2) the type of development that is already there restricts the land to residences; and (3) the cost of placing homes on this property to fit in with the area would be prohibitive.*

We would not want to develop the land into low type of homes. That would tear down what we have already put up out there as the developers of the subdivision surrounding this property. We plan to put up attractive apartments. But we couldn't go to the expense of drawing-up the plans without first getting zoning approval.

What is the property suitable for? First, it is not suitable for a park. Second, it is not suitable for single-family homes. Third, we feel that it is suitable for multi-unit homes. Fourth, this tract could be cut up into six church sites or 12 church sites. But single-family units are out. If a developer built single-family homes, he would spend $500,000 without selling a house. We plan to put between 40 to 50 units on the property.

Proponent: I do architecture work for Mr. ——— [the applicant]. He asked me to tell that we want to erect apartment units yet with a resi-

195

dential atmosphere. People using these units have a right to privacy and quiet. Each apartment would have a patio; there will be pools and garden areas that will add to the area. We plan to build a street on the north of the property leaving a green belt. We will grow hedges to screen off the area. This would be much better than looking at a corn crop that they have there now. It would be less of a fire hazard. The character would be residential. I believe that the whole development can be blended into the area without destroying its residential area.

Proponent: We are trying to develop a very difficult piece of property. Many people here are fearful of the traffic hazard. But the plans have been drawn so there will be no danger from the traffic. It will be an asset to the community to have these apartment units. *We are not building to sell, but as an investment.* We are not trying to destroy any neighborhood.

Commission Member 1: All of you that are here in opposition to this zoning, please raise your hands. [About 140 persons respond.] Since there are so many here, is there a spokesman?

Opponent 1: By the show of hands you can see the interest we have. *We are proud of our area. We moved in with the understanding that the area was "A"-Residential.* I purchased my home on the belief that this land [now being considered for rezoning] would be kept "A"-Residential and would be developed in homes. My home borders on this property.

Mr. —— [the applicant] thinks that he could build his apartments that we could be proud of. That is his opinion. We do not think so. The history of this type of development will show that apartment areas deteriorate because the people are transients and will not take interest in the area. *The devaluation of property is not our major opposition. Most of the people are young couples with children. We want to see this area kept residential.*

Mr. —— [the applicant] said that he would keep it [the proposed apartment units] to a single floor. But I noticed that his application would allow for a 45-foot height.

I would like to show the interest Mr. —— [the applicant] has stirred up. There are 840 signatures on this petition opposing this zoning.

Another very serious factor: if this is changed to a "B," you are going to create another serious problem for our schools. The present population will saturate the school's 24 classrooms. If you multiply the number of apartments by two, there will be no place to put these children.

Opponent 2: *This is a matter of democracy.* The city has leaned over backward to solve this problem. This seems to be a case of the whole

196

against several people. We are married people who want to live in this residential area. His [the applicant's] gain will be our loss. I would favor a park here. I would like to make this as a personal request.

Opponent 3:   We have no objection to the erection of single-unit homes commensurate with the residences in the area. I am opposed to multi-unit apartments being constructed here.

Opponent 4:   We have done all we can as a one-family group to present our case to the City Council. We respectfully submit our plan to you that we don't want to be let down.

Planning Director: One point on this park that was suggested. As Director of Planning, I would not recommend it. It is not a proper location. Our interest is in the development of Bartholomew Park that is nearby. We will have a bond issue to support its development. This is not the ideal park site. I did not recommend it for a park. I don't want to get anybody's hopes up.

Opponent 5:   The matter of traffic on Cameron Road should be considered. The traffic is already a mess; with the multi-housing units, it would get worse. *It would become a great danger to our children.*

Opponent 6:   I have a firmer belief in zoning than I ever had. I believe that the zoning laws have been set up to protect the residential areas. *Residences are the most desirable use for land.* If a person seeks to do away with the zoning laws in the face of all this opposition, all our efforts have been foregone.

Opponent 6:   There is only one duplex in the area. I don't know how it got there. If the tract is properly subdivided [with consideration given] for the roads, I would not have any objection to duplexes. I would oppose Mr. ——— [the applicant] having a complete hold on its development.

Opponent 7:   The people on my street are opposed. We are against it for the logical reasons presented. *It is a matter of principle that these people [the applicant] keep to their word and develop the land for residences.*

Opponent 8:   I would like to know if Mr. ——— [the applicant] can ask for a change in zoning without stating his reasons as to what he is going to do with the land?

Commission Member 1:   We do not judge the specific use. The only thing we are interested in is the best use of the land and for the whole good of the community. That includes traffic circulation, schools, homes, and the surrounding land use. Anything that is under "B" can be used for

197

the land. If we think these uses [under the classification of "B"] are not suitable for the ground, we will not grant the zoning requested.

Opponent 9: You mentioned the land use as a factor. Do you consider safety a factor in deciding zoning cases?

Commission Member 1: We sure do.

Opponent 9: If you are not acquainted with the traffic hazards, I wish that you would come down and see for yourself.

Opponent 10: Let him [the applicant] built a house in the middle of this property and let him have a big yard in front and a big yard in back!

Opponent 11: Will we have the opportunity to appear before the City Council to veto this?

Commission Member 1: Yes.

Opponent 11: If this is denied, how long must he [the applicant] wait to ask for another permit?

Commission Member 1: One year.

Opponent 12: It is not only the people who live adjacent to this property who oppose this zoning change, but people on other streets. This is a community protest and not just the people on the street adjacent to this property.

Commission Member 1: Now that the opposition has had its say, we will let the applicant have his rebuttal.

Applicant: I can understand why they should oppose this zoning. If I lived there, I too would object. But several things should be noted.

First, there was never any promise by the property owner what this property would be developed into.

Second, the penalty from FHA would be severe. I have discussed the possibility of conventional loans from businesses in Austin and they felt that the 86-foot lots would be too small.

Third, the schools throughout Austin are crowded. This is an opportunity to take a piece of property and put it on the tax roll at a higher value.

Fourth, I and my associates have other property in the city. We would be glad to furnish a listing of our holdings to show the extent of our care we give to the property we own.

And last, we can build duplexes on the lots under the present zoning. But this would defeat our purposes. We wish to erect multi-housing units

198

that would be in accord with the area. We feel that this would be a greater favor than duplexes. This would be 80 units. There would not be many more units. But having duplexes would not coordinate with the area as it is now developed.

Commission Member 1: You said that the penalty would be severe. Suppose the people along the property [we are considering for rezoning] wanted to sell their homes and refinance them under FHA. How would this zoning change affect them?

Applicant: I asked if the multi-housing units we planned with screens, patios, etc., would these affect the surrounding values? The FHA didn't know. But we do know it would not be acceptable to FHA if it were an unorderly development. For homes of the caliber required by the present development in this area would need lots with a 130-foot depth. If there were some way to restrict the height of the apartments below 45 feet, I would go along with this.

Opponent 1: How much money would you have to pay for the penalty by FHA?

Applicant: We do not know because we could not go to the expense of drawing detailed plans and submit them to FHA. But every businessman knows that a severe penalty cannot be afforded by a builder.

These several cases disclose the competition that takes place in zoning in the form of one value system opposing another. Expressions of economic necessity for rezoning land were made by applicants; to overcome the economic argument, opponents propounded a value system that, while intertwined with economic arguments, nonetheless, stresses residential utility as the most desirable use for property.

It should be noted, particularly in Case 3, how applicants endeavor to placate the protectively oriented opposition by granting concessions in an effort to reduce the possibility of a drastic change in the character of land use from single-family residences to other uses. By offering to erect screening devices, plant shrubbery, design physical improvements in keeping with residential styling, plant "green strips," and so forth, the economically oriented applicant attempts to preserve residential attributes that the protectionists cherish so highly. This is the general procedure when an application covers property near a well-developed single-family residential area. The applicant

199

seldom extends such qualifications when the surrounding area to the property in question can be considered in transition from one use to another or if the proposed use is to be located in an area that can be considered a logical extension of an existing zoning.

ECONOMIC VERSUS ECONOMIC VALUES

Not all value contentions assume the form of economic desires challenging protective values. Another significant value contention involves discord between economic values. When this occurs, applicants maintain the necessity for rezoning on an economic basis, and the opposition counters with an economic orientation. The opponents seek to prevent personal economic losses by arguing against anticipated economic gains by the applicants.

Of course, even in the above four cases presented to demonstrate the economic versus protective value contentions, persons feared economic devaluation of their property and improvements if a zoning change were granted, and, therefore, economic factors intrude into their arguments. But the protective-minded person considers the possibility of an economic loss secondary to his desire to sustain residential utilization. The economically oriented, on the other hand, emphasizes financial loss in terms of the profit motive rather than in those of promoting protective considerations of residential utility when challenging zoning applications.

"Case Study 5" was selected to illustrate the economic opposition by adjacent property owners; "Case Study 6" demonstrates economic resistance to a zoning change by divergent vested interests within the city of Austin.

Case 5: A person applied for a change in zoning for a piece of property located next to an existing duplex rented as a source of income. The applicant requested the zoning change to allow for the placement of a used car lot. The comments by persons composing the opposition express both protective and economic values. However, the owner of the duplex located next to the property in question, in particular, stated economic values:

200

Applicant: I am the owner of this property we are trying to get re-zoned and I want to sell. It has to be rezoned for me to sell it.

Proponent 1: I intend to buy this property if this zoning change is made. There's plenty enough room there with the driveway there without obstructing traffic. I want to use it for a used car lot.

Planning Director: You propose this property for a used car lot. There will be no strip-downs?

Proponent 1: No.

Proponent 2: I am a real-estate broker in this contract. I am in favor. A lot adjoining this is already "C," and the rest of the block is "C" and residential. *It's too expensive land for any other use but "C."*

Opponent 1: The Rosewood Housing Project is right across the street with 1,200 to 1,500 kids. This [proposed use] will be a danger to them in crossing the street.

Opponent 2: I have been here [before the Zoning Committee] more than one time to oppose this zoning change. I think if this is granted it will become a danger to our children.

Opponent 3: We should keep our community residential to protect our children.

Opponent 4: I own the duplex just to the east of this property [under consideration]. Six years ago I bought that lot where I now have the duplex. I applied for "C" to let my tenant have a beauty shop. I was turned down by the City. After that I built a nice duplex. *I can assure you that it will not be of any benefit to me to have a used car lot next door to my duplex. It doesn't add anything to the land.*

Case 6: During the period of time covered by this study, one of the most controversial cases involved the rezoning of an existing, but undedicated, city park. Located on the most important highway artery through Austin, the city of Austin requested a change in zoning to a "GR" classification to permit utilization of the land for commercial purposes. Amounting to almost 36 acres, and known commonly as the "East 40" tract, the land was considered to be extremely valuable for extensive commercial development as a major shopping center.

The public arguments presented below fail to identify the actual composition of the opposition to the proposed zoning change. But financial support for circulating petitions was reported to have come from several existing shopping centers whose business activities would be negatively affected by a competitor on the "East 40" tract. Opposition also came from individuals who: (1) valued the land for park purposes; (2) owned

201

vacant commercial property in the general vicinity; and (3) feared the loss of a real-estate commission, since the amount would not be theirs, but the city's.

Because this zoning application involved a city park, citywide interest was manifested, accounting for the fact that the proponents included: (1) city officials; (2) members of the City Council; (3) a former state senator; (4) members of various city boards such as the Park Board and Planning Commission; (5) editorial writers of Austin's largest newspaper; and (6) other "interested" citizens such as representatives of the Chamber of Commerce.

The following account begins with a presentation of the hearing held before the Zoning Committee:

Planning Director: [This city official presented the "Zoning Change Staff Report," prepared for all cases by the Planning Department.]

Opponent 1: It looks like that every five years we have to come out with an "old Ironside" campaign. This tract of land has been used a lot—men driving golf balls, flying of airplanes, baseball, football, dog training. We have a lot of drag races out there.

I believe the city with very little expense can keep the strip. They [the city government] could fix it for a drag race—the soap box derby. There's a big demand for it. We'll need it worst than those people who are trying to bid on it. We have a girl school out there. I wonder how they will feel about this rezoning.

Opponent 2: There were some petitions circulated around. I was requested by the people who signed the petitions to present a fair picture. I would like to bring out that a great deal of traffic will be generated out there if this zoning is granted. Red River Street is not large enough to handle the problem. The neighborhood would be affected by the traffic problems generated due to commercial development of this property.

I understand there is a question of grade elevation on Interregional Highway because of the railroad. If the grade elevation goes into effect, it would have an affect upon the nature of the business that will go out there.

It is used by the recreation department to teach golf lessons.

Opponent 3: Does a person who lives in a residential area next to a business area have to pay higher taxes?

Commission Member 1: We are not in the taxing business, but the tax would not be increased unless the value of the land goes up.

Opponent 4: A sale price for this land of $1,000,000 is not good enough. This sum of money would just go elsewhere and we would never see it. We wouldn't know where the money goes. I have a petition in opposition to this change.

202

Commission Member 1: This is a zoning hearing. We do not want to hear about the sale of the property. We are here to study the case for the best use of the ground.

Opponent 5: My main question is about the traffic problem. You get a 60-foot right-of-way on Red River Street and a 40-foot street on 41st Street. Park Boulevard has a 30-foot pavement. This street arrangement is bad on the commercial land and bad on the residential property. This is because 80 per cent of your traffic goes west.

If this tract of land goes commercial, it may not increase your tax. But it will increase your insurance rate because of the traffic.

Commission Member 1: I think you brought out a good point. We give serious consideration to traffic circulation. This Commission is trying to look ahead for the city. Years ago when land was cheap we could buy the property for 75-foot streets. But now we got [*sic*] it and we got to do the best we can.

Opponent 5: All that does is that it puts a heavier load to the owner of the property in the area.

Opponent 6: I want to object to this rezoning application because I own some property right across the street. *I could sell my home maybe 50 cents on the dollar after the community center is put in.* I don't think any member on this board would want to have a shopping center across from his home.

The city paid $60–$70–$80,000 to get the best planners into this city to design a master plan. These professional planners recommended against the rezoning of this land for business. It's just like a doctor: asking them what the trouble is and then not paying any attention to the experts.

That property is used every day. If the recreation department wanted to, it could use it more. *I think that the city has a moral obligation not to hurt any property owner in an action the city government might take.* And the city government will definitely hurt the property owners in this case. When I moved out there and the property across the street was a park, I never heard of a city selling its parks for a real estate deal. *It will hurt the value of the residential area out there.* I don't believe that the city should morally sell any of its property when it is going to hurt the property owners.

If there were only three or four people opposing the change rather than a house full we have here, it would not be morally right for the Zoning Committee to zone this land.

Opponent 7: If the city paid a great deal of money to obtain advice as to what should be done with this tract, I cannot see how the city can go against the recommendation of the professional planners. The city will need these breathing spaces later on.

Opponent 8: It seems to me we are putting on all the defense. We have no offensive to show why there should be rezoning. We have many reasons why it should not be rezoned—open spaces, recreation, no need for further business development. There is no real need for commercial property with Delwood Shopping Center there. It would seem like to me that there is no need to have more business in the area.

Opponent 9: Five years ago the Northwest Civic Club opposed this. That park is being used now for unorganized play. We need it. That's a high class neighborhood out there and we need this park. As far away as I am living from this property, the neighborhood all around me is opposed to this zoning application.

Attorney [representative for the Catholic Academy located in the area]: We are faced with an open door. The City Ordinance provides for 37 uses under "GR"—many of the uses being undesirable for the Academy out there such as repair shops, open-air theaters, skating rinks, public stables, court trailers. Since we have not been presented with any plan for a particular use, it would harm the interest of my client. If you did throw this wide open, then unquestionably you are going to create a traffic hazard in the area—for the children going to school and to the play area. You would have to widen Red River Street at a financial burden to the adjoining property owners.

Opponent 10: I am an old timer in this city. I have been wrangling with the Planning Commission ever since Mr. ———— [a former city manager of Austin] came into office. He tried to keep my packing house for shipping spinach out of the city; he wanted the land to be used for residences.

I have studied this area intensely. A few years ago the Safeway Stores tried to buy this same tract of land. We had petitions opposing it. Everyone out at the north end of town is opposing this rezoning.

One of the things the Planning Commission talks to me about is to zone land along the line for its use possibility. The idea was not to zone stuff and let it lie idle. I made an intensive study of the area. Safeway Stores bought 14 acres from me in the area. They have been trying very hard to develop a community center. But they can't get tenants. ———— Store has 500 feet. The city keeps raising the taxes so that he now pays $500 a year on this. *But the owners of business property in the area are all afraid of the big interests coming in.* [This person then lists other business interests located in the vicinity, particularly noting the several vacant pieces of property scattered about which he owns or which his son owns.] *To my certain belief, there is not the slightest reason to open up the 40 acres to business which will prevent the businesses in the area from making a go of it. Some big corporation will come in and hurt all the business in the whole area that is already out there.*

204

The will of the people is against you. You will decrease the value of all business within two miles of this property if you rezone these 40 acres.

Planning Director: Let me state that there is a possibility of more than $500,000 in this property. But the property has to be zoned before it could be put up for sale.

Commission Member 2: Mr. Chairman, I would like to ask those who are opposed to this zoning application to please raise their hands. [About 45 persons respond.] In view of the number of people interested in this case, I would like to make the motion that we discuss the case for a decision rather than waiting for the hearings on all cases.

Commission Member 1: I am of the opinion that we have a lot to say. There are other people here for eight other cases.

Commission Member 3: Let's go on with the other hearings.

(The motion to vote upon a decision died for lack of a second. After a public hearing for each case was held, the Zoning Committee then discussed this application.)

Commission Member 2: I want to make one or two observations to clear-up the previous recommendation of the Planning Commission to sell the property. I joined in the recommendation to sell the property to get additional park property with the funds we obtained from the sale of this property. *But, as a real estate man, I do not now see how a large tract of land like this could be developed into business in that area. I am a little reluctant to recommend a [zoning] change for speculation.*

Commission Member 1: Whatever decision we make, we make it both as a member of the Planning Commission and as a citizen of Austin. This is something we have to take every consideration of every citizen in Austin, not just those around the area. I think we need to take into consideration the traffic circulation.

Commission Member 2: That's one of the exact points I would like to bring out.

Commission Member 4: University Junior High is scheduled to be closed in the next several years. Wouldn't this be a good location for a school?

Planning Director: I don't think the schools have shown any great interest.

Commission Member 3: I have been told that that piece of property is not needed for recreational purposes. *That property it too expensive to be used for park purposes.* On the other hand, I would not favor this re-

205

zoning unless the city is willing to provide the necessary widths for widening of the streets in the area.

Commission Member 2: In actuality, if that property is worth three quarters of a million dollars, the buyer will be willing to state the use of the land for condition to sale.

Commission Member 3: I think the property is going to have to be used commercially, and I think the city should restrict its use.

Commission Member 2: Over 70 per cent of the property that is zoned commercial in the city is not used for business. I think it is better to have the person applying for zoning changes to say what he will use the property for and say how much he would pay for the tract, and then zone the land.

Commission Member 1: Can our recommendation carry with it that certain uses be carried in the deed?

Planning Director: Yes. But the city goverment would like to see any deed restriction in a separate motion apart from the zoning. . . .

Commission Member 2: I move that the application be denied for these reasons: (1) there is insufficient access to this large tract and *the zoning will not make it a paying deal;* (2) the rezoning of this land will overload the existing streets; and (3) the three-block depth of this tract goes too far into residences.

(The motion to deny was upheld by a three to two vote. A week later, the Planning Commission met to conduct an open hearing. The following discussion took place.)

Commission Member 1: The thing that this Planning Commission is considering is the recommendation of the Zoning Committee and the city's request for a change in zoning from "A" to "GR." The matter of whether this property should be sold is up to the City Council. . . .

Commission Member 2: What is the recommendation of the Planning Department?

Planning Director: We do not have a recommendation with respect to how the land should be zoned. But if the property is zoned, then we have some comments as to how it should be zoned. . . .

Commission Member 3: The question came up about Red River and other streets before the Zoning Committee. I am of the opinion there would be more traffic on these streets if the zoning is granted. But would

206

it be more if there were businesses or more if there were apartments upon this property?

Planning Director: It would cause twice as much if it were developed with business.

Commission Member 3: It would be like this concerning traffic at the auditorium or baseball games. It would be stretched out over the day here, however.

Commission Member 2: Would there be any difference in the value that the city would get if it were not zoned for business and apartments?

Planning Director: I would say yes; but I am no appraiser.

Commission Member 4: I would like to ask Mr. ———— [the City Attorney] one point. Can the city take bids without the zoning?

City Attorney: It might could be done. As I have advised the city, however, it should not be done. It would raise a legal question.

Commission Member 4: That would be the opposite way the Planning Commission customarily expects.

City Attorney: I have advised that this [bidding] could not be done and [then] the land put up on sale to the highest bidder. Zoning is then offered as a condition as a basis for transaction. *And the city has no zoning for sale.*

Commission Member 1: I don't think that has any bearing on proper zoning. What kind of conditions are necessary for the sale of the land is a matter of private contract and not zoning.

City Attorney: That's right. But the people of the city are more protected by the city being the owner than by the private individual having ownership of this property. . . .

Commission Member 5: It is my understanding that an offer has been made for $800,000 when this land is offered for sale. It will be higher. *I don't think that the city is in a financial position to hold 36 acres worth $1,000,000 for park purposes.* Now if this zoning is granted, certain streets must be widened in the area at the city's expense. *The cost of the piece of property is so great that the price will assure high class improvements.*

Commission Member 4: *Do you recognize that that $800,000 [the expected sum from the sale of the property] is not pure profit for the city?* There will be the cost of utilities, widening, and paving.

Commission Member 1: We cannot consider the price in making zoning decisions. We must consider zoning of the land.

Commission Member 5: I cannot separate in my mind the sale price and the zoning. If the piece of land were worth only $100,000, I would be against this zoning.

Commission Member 1: I know it's hard to keep that figure out of your mind. But we are zoning the land. . . .

Commission Member 3: It has been the policy of the Planning Commission to get larger tracts developed and not scattered out for businesses. There are few places for large shopping areas than on this 36 acres. . . .

Commission Member 1: The tendency to zone for business along thoroughfares is wrong—that's strip zoning. *Eventually it [strip-zoned areas] becomes so congested that it lowers the value of the economic investments in the area.* The ultimate experience is that the property will not be fit for business. I agree that this should be used for business with some protection given to the people in the area. It isn't possible to have a business area which is not in contact with some residences.

Commission Member 2: The tendency of development out there makes it unfit for residences. I am in favor of making the change. But I think every consideration should be given to protect the people out there.

(The Zoning Committee's motion to deny the request was rejected by a seven-to-two vote. Therefore, the Planning Commission recommended that the change in zoning for these 36 acres be granted from "A" to "GR." But after this vote, the Planning Commission set forth recommendations for consideration by the City Council as part of the zoning recommendation. The Planning Commission suggested control concerning street widths, setback requirements for improvements upon the property, and regulations concerning signs.)

(The final zoning hearing was held before the City Council in an open and public session. Again, strong opposition to the zoning was expressed:)

Council Member 1: We will hear the people. Is there anyone representing the people [opponents to the proposed zoning change]? [No one responds.] Is there anyone in the area opposed to this zoning change? [About 15 hands are raised.]
This hearing is purely on the matter of zoning and not a matter of sale of the property. We will hear only the zoning arguments.

208

Competition as a Social Process

Opponent 1: Here are some points I would like to make:
1. Most of the streets bounding this property are residential streets. Widening would not help these streets. Putting a "GR" zoning on this land will put more traffic than the streets can hold. It will be a danger to the children.
2. *People who own property in the area deserve to be protected from a loss in [economic] value. Zoning is meant to protect the public and not destroy property values. That is the city's justification for zoning as I see it.*
3. *There is enough zoning for business development out there for the next 25 years.*
4. If this zoning change is granted, it would create a cancer in a neighborhood that has been very stable. *It will downgrade the [economic] value of the property which could lead to the creation of a slum.*

Council Member 1: Once before when we were deciding where to locate the city auditorium you came before us and suggested that it be placed on this property rather than downtown. That would have brought a lot of people out there. *But we are passing on zoning and not the sale of the land—just like a private piece of property.* Your presentation is very fine.

Opponent 2: I would not go on record as against something, but for something. Gentlemen, I wish that you would give consideration for some other use to this land. This is a cosmopolitan city. *It is growing and we may not have the money to buy land so close to the center of the city.* This could be used for park purposes. *Would we not gain more profits to sell this land two years from now for $1,000,000?* The radio commentators have stated the sale as if the decision to sell were a foregone conclusion. I hope that the decision of the sale has not been made.

Council Member 1: The city has looked forward to the future. The city probably has more property for its size than any city in the United States. [He then names the numerous parks, golf courses, airport, land owned by the city upon which Bergstrom Air Force Base is located, etc.] Cities don't generally look ahead. . . .
We are not going into the virtue of the land being sold or not sold. But long before, if the city had not bought this property, it would have been in apartments and businesses. It would have been in the hands of private enterprise, on the tax roll, and it would be a thriving business center.

Opponent 3: I don't think anybody is more interested than I due to the fact that I am right across from the property. . . . If my lot were vacant, I would probably profit. *But I have a $16,500 house on it. It would probably be worth $12,000 after this zoning is given.*

209

I had to get off of work to attend this hearing. If this hearing had been held in the evening, we would have had more people down here in opposition. We are in a middle class neighborhood which finds it hard to get off their jobs to come down here to protest. Also, there hasn't been enough time to organize opposition to this application.

I think the decision to grant or deny this request should be governed by the people within the 200 feet of this property and not the city as a whole. If the zoning laws mean anything, this property is being zoned for these 200 people and not the city. The majority of the people in the 200-foot area are against this zoning; I don't see how the city can vote against them. Morally, I don't see how it can be done.

When the city does sell land that it owns—not private enterprise—I think it is morally wrong for the city to sell for a profit even if one person opposes the sale. If it just hurts one person, there is a moral obligation to keep it as a park.

Council Member 1: It is claimed that the heart of the City of Austin is here. But I say that the heart that pumps the blood is Sixth and Congress. . . .

Council Member 2: It was mentioned that the zoning law doesn't mean anything. *But a person's right to use his land for the highest and best use—even in the face of the opposition—the zoning law will get this done.*

Opponent 3: But not when there is so much opposition?

City Attorney: If the wishes of the people in the area on a head count were the sole criterion for passing zoning, the Zoning Ordinance would be void. . . .

Opponent 5: As a person in the real estate business, it has been my experience that when a piece of property is next to commercial property, it will not get a loan from the FHA. This is the reason I oppose this zoning change.

Opponent 6: I am interested because I live there in the area. I am also interested in this zoning because I have an investment in my home. I am thinking that if something happened to me and should my wife want to sell my home, she could not get a FHA loan.

Council Member 1: I never heard of that before.

Opponent 6: I would like to suggest that the City Council consider the Master Plan and what its affects would be before making this decision.

Council Member 1: Maybe we should have put the auditorium out there—I don't know. . . . I have always stated that if the people of the

210

city were to vote on taxes, the taxes would be voted down. . . . The City of Austin always had a plan. We can't let the people vote on every zoning case. We make people mad up here. We want to hear you; but at the same time I want to answer you as matters come up. We just have to take it; do it; and take the consequences. Whatever business goes in there—and this is purely hypothetical—you will be fully protected by set-back requirements. . . .

Opponent 7: The thing that disturbes me is our junior high schools. It seems a shame to me that the city will sell the property for commercial purposes when the city could use it for schools. My reason is very selfish— we have children in the area.

Council Member 1: I won't answer this. It's on the advisability of sale.

Opponent 8: I notice that the Council is addressing itself to the general interest, so I present myself as part of that general interest. The issue is commercial versus park—and this is a general interest.

Council Member 1: Would you state your name and your occupation?

Opponent 8: I am ———, a newspaperman. . . .

Council Member 1: Okay, ——— and ——— [the names of councilmen], never attack a newspaperman for what he says. You [Opponent 8] are talking on free speech and not as a person within the 200-foot area. We always let people come before us if they like.

Opponent 8: As I understand it, this area is used to a certain extent for park purposes. It is an open, green area.

The city is not altogether a business area, super stores, and expressways. As much as we value Sixth and Congress, none of us would want to live there.

I find that one of the frustrating things about living in a city is to go to a quiet place. It is difficult to get children in a car. One of the most important things for a city is the green places near at hand.

The stresses of urban life seem to be sufficiently important for the City Council to consider seriously what they do with this area. I don't think it is easy to put a price tag on quiet areas and parks. I don't know what the dollar value is for tired people to go very quickly to quiet places. You are now choosing between a park and parking places. . . .

How far must we go from our homes in the city to green places where our children can go and where we can think? Conservation has had a long history in this country.

211

All I have to say is this—and I am appearing as a citizen. In my opinion, this issue is important enough, the 36 acres are important enough, to call an election. We need places to go for peace of mind.

Council Member 1: If you want tranquillity or peace, don't serve on the City Council. I am going to be activated by what I think is best for the city. We do try to see ahead. Of course, we have the other side, too. As Mr. ———— [an extensive property-holder residing in the city] says: "First find the right-of-way then buy it."

Opponent 9: I have in mind your [Council Member 1's] statement that we are not considering the sale of this land. But I find it hard to keep this out of my mind. We do not zone for fun. You have in mind the zoning of this property for sale at a profit.

The city has nothing to lose by delaying the sale. *The more the city grows, the more [economic] value that piece of ground will have for commercial use.* Whatever its value, it will probably double in value in three of four years—more than off-setting the taxes it will get over this period of time. The city buys land for city use and not for sale. . . . The city buys land for public use—just for that—that it needs it and not for a good sale. . . . There has been the argument for tax value. But we don't need to sell land for tax purposes. . . .

Council Member 1: Is there anyone else here in opposition to this zoning change? Since there is no one else opposing this who wishes to be heard, we'll hear from those who favor this application.

Proponent 1 [a large subdivider residing in the city]: We should sell the property and put it on the tax roll.

Council Member 1: The more people there is, the more activity there is—it increases the value of the property.

Proponent 2 [Chairman of the City's Planning Commission]: I am appearing here this morning as Chairman of the Planning Commission. At the Zoning Committee meeting, there were three members who voted against this request and two for this change. Two of the people who voted against the application had been on the Planning Commission only several months. They conscientiously changed their votes at the Planning Commission meeting. It is not unusual to change votes [during zoning hearings] before the Planning Commission.

The Planning Commission tried to look at this matter impartially as citizens of Austin. We try to look at the matter from what is the best use of the property and for the welfare of the city. And sometimes that decision is contrary to the views of the people who live in the 200-foot area—that is, what they think will be harmful to them.

212

We did recommend that the property be sold. We are as interested in having green belts in the city as anybody. But there are 52 acres dedicated for park purposes next to this land that have a creek, trees, and land that is more suitable for a green belt than the 36 acres we are now considering for zoning. *I think this land should be sold and the city use the money for the purchase of other developments. Larger areas and better areas could be bought with this money. And this is the reason for the Planning Commission's decision.*

Council Member 2: I'm looking at this zoning like any other zoning. I have always said we zone land and not people. The nature of the land has been changed by the highway [that is now there]. I move that we pass this request.

Council Member 3: I second the motion.

Council Member 4: In view of the fact that there is no need for this land in the area [for park purposes] . . . , there is no other usage for the property but "GR."

(The motion to grant was carried by a four-to-zero vote with one council member abstaining owing to personal reasons.)

Dispersed throughout cases numbered five and six are instances of economic values competing against economic values. Vested interest of the economic sort, for example, flourished as the city of Austin endeavored to rezone the property under consideration from a residential classification to a commercial zoning. At later hearings called by the City Council for the purpose of selling the "East 40" tract, identical pressure groups coalesced in opposition to the anticipated sale. Local newspapers carried advertisements appealing to the citizenry to sign petitions being circulated by a group known as the "Committee to Save the Hancock 'East Forty.' " On the other hand, the newspaper, as a matter of policy, printed articles advocating the sale. The issue partook of competition between the desire of the city of Austin to obtain a maximum sale price and the desire of certain private interests to prevent the sale so as to avoid the loss of a playground area and/or the possibility of the development of a shopping center upon the property to create business competition for existing business establishments. But the council's position to sell the property

213

prevailed when eventually the 36 acres were sold for $800,000 at a public hearing to a national retail outlet.

Throughout the hearing on zoning, however, the City Council and certain Planning Commission members made special efforts to refrain from any arguments concerning the actual profit-making motive underlying the city's effort to rezone the property. For these members maintain that the competition must focus upon contention between *land uses:* business development as opposed to park utilization. In so-doing, members of the City Council and several persons on the Planning Commission refused to consider competition between property owners: private ownership versus the City of Austin.

Conclusions

The fundamental argument within contemporary ecological theory is a dispute concerning the role of social values. Materialists, particularly neoclassical ecologists, *explicitly* reject social values as ecologically relevant; they refuse to incorporate social values as an aspect of ecological theory. On the other hand, voluntarists, in attempting to reformulate materialistic ecological thought, perceive social forces controlling or "regulating" the ecological materialists' explanatory factors, or they interpret the materialistic argument as a "rational" orientation that man employs in adapting to space.

The social action theory developed in this study differs from previous evaluations of ecological materialism by placing the argument of impersonality within a value system. The evidence gathered for this study of the zoning process in the city of Austin, Texas, supports this contention; this writer did not uncover evidence that would refute the hypothesis. The zoning data demonstrate that certain individuals regulate the distribution of social activities over space through the same frame of reference that materialistic ecologists use to explain ecological phenomena. To the extent that individuals, in locating over space, conform to the viewpoint espoused by the materialistic ecologists, then the materialistic approach is in fact enthnocentric. Material-

214

istic ecology merely reflects a particular social value system and, therefore, cannot methodologically view social values as a dispensable feature of ecological theory.

Austin's zoning data, furthermore, indicate that competition, from an ecological perspective—rather than existing as a subsocial, biotic process—takes the form of contention between social value systems. Competition is not merely regulated by the "prevailing social institutions," as certain ecological voluntarists would argue, but occurs when different social value systems operate within a framework composed of normative conditions such as legal strictures. Social competition arises when individuals share the goal of public welfare to be accomplished through zoning but disagree concerning the social value system to be employed in the attainment of this end.

The value competitions presented in this chapter do not, however, cover all value disputes; others take place in the zoning process. Some decision-makers and participants desire, for example, to have the planning director perform solely as a fact finder on the cognitive level; several other persons taking part in the zoning process insist upon specific recommendations from the planning director; and still other decision-makers desire to see the director's role as an aggressive force exerting a decisive impact upon zoning decisions. Value competition also arises concerning the organizational procedure for processing zoning applications. But these and other value disputes— while significant from an ecological perspective—remain out of bounds for this study. Instead, specific instances of value competition were selected for the testing of Hypotheses III and IV as presented in this chapter.

It is because the economic value orientation dominates the zoning process in the city of Austin that ecological materialism can be sustained to a limited extent. The causal factors advocated in the materialistic perspective indirectly contribute to an ecological explanation, since materialism prevails in the form of a social value system that makes possible a self-fulfilling prophecy in terms of the economic value orientation. Consequently, ecological materialists are left with the impression that their approach can be substantiated by reliance

215

upon statistical facts concerning population, technology, social organization, and environment.[33] However, statistical manipulations to obtain so-called "objective" verification of materialistic ecology cannot correctly be accomplished without full awareness that value systems underlie *all* ecologically significant phenomena. As Emile Durkheim states: ". . . even the most impersonal and the most anonymous are nothing else than objectified sentiments."[34]

In no way, however, should the present study be interpreted as setting forth ecological materialism as an "explicit" and "conscious" process rather than a "natural," "impersonal," or "unconscious" account as certain materialists are most likely to claim; ecological phenomena do not take shape in accordance with impersonal competition as an automatic biotic or physical process unknown to the affected individuals.[35] The ecological subject matter as defined by traditional (that is, biotic) materialists is, sociologically speaking, nonexistent; the ecological subject matter advanced by both traditional and neoclassical materialists is methodologically unsound.[36] *Indeed, it is the materialistic ecological theorist himself—not his subject matter—who is most unconscious of the real ecological variables accounting for ecological phenomena.* Materialists are completely unaware of the fact that they merely espouse a particular social value system that appears to dominate land-use development in our society at the present time. It is because the materialistic values are currently so dominant in American society that zoning is a reflective rather than an independent social force for controlling urban land use.

Since the explanation offered by ecological materialists simply echoes an existing value system in the zoning process, it follows that the "rational interest" under which Firey places ecological materialism must also be classified as a social value orientation. The disputes over land use do not revolve, as Firey claims in his ecological analysis,[37] about rational forces versus sentiments. The organized data in the present study require that the "rationalism" Firey associates with ecological materialism be reinterpreted as an economic value system.

Moreover, the debates between the two schools of ecological thought—materialism and voluntarism—are similar to the value com-

216

petition in the zoning process investigated in this study. Just as the decision-makers and participants taking part in the zoning process in the city of Austin argue in terms of whether zoning should reflect economically relevant conditions or regulate land use in accordance with protective notions, so, too, ecologists assume a stance on one side or the other. For instance, the following comment made by one decision-maker whose value orientation is predominantly protective in nature reveals the impersonal notion advanced by the economically oriented decision-makers—and implicitly the materialistic ecologist—in contradistinction to the idea of the value imposition advocated by protectionists—and implicitly the voluntarist ecologist:

> Some members on the Planning Commission sit up in a pious way and say, "We zone land and not people." Now who in the hell owns land? People! I like people, not the land. . . . They [the economically oriented decision-makers] zone land, not the person. But many people have only one piece of property and it is *personal* to them.

Or, as another economic/materialistic-protective/voluntaristic expression, a decision-maker said: "I represent people and not land."

Remarks such as these portray the value competition that exists in both ecological theory and reality: a debate between the notion that land usage reflects economic conditions and the notion that utility is a matter of value imposition. Moreover, when ecological materialists refuse to recognize the importance of social values in their ecological explanations, they hold to the same social value as the economically oriented decision-makers connected with Austin's zoning process: the distribution of activities over space are to mirror economically relevant conditions rather than social values other than the economic.

In conclusion to this chapter, it must be stressed that Hypothesis IV, as stated in this chapter, does not declare that value contentions must take place in the form of competition. Value conflicts or cooperation could also reasonably be expected to occur within social life and to affect the distribution of ecological phenomena. But "pure" cooperation and value conflict were absent in the zoning activities as performed in the community of Austin, Texas.

217

Chapter Eight

CONCLUSIONS

At a time when various governmental units in American society are increasingly faced with the necessity to plan so as to control land-use patternings in our expanding metropolitan existence, we ironically find a concurrent growth of materialistic determinism that denies the necessity of human volition in constructing land-use theories.[1] Indeed, there is no existing land-use theory from a sociological perspective that encompasses the full implication of human volition contained in the planning efforts designed to direct utilization of space so characteristic of an industrial society such as our own.

Only a handful of ecologists, as noted in Chapter 3, accord recognition to the importance of social action in presenting land-use theories. We called such writers "voluntarists" because of the priority they give to human volition. A second group, presented in Chapter 2 as "materialists," candidly eliminates all aspects of social life that would give the slightest indication of willful social acts designed to affect land usages. These latter writers espouse a rigorous approach that makes social action preordained; to them, man is merely a passive entity that lacks a sense of direction concerning its own behavioral characteristics and must, therefore, comply with either biotic or physical determinants.

Voluntarists, on the other hand, argue for the necessity to investigate the nature of social organization from either a social structure or a value perspective. They deny the relevance of biotic ecological orientations, and instead call for a sociological analysis of ecological developments. Still, certain shortcomings prevail within the perspective of contemporary voluntaristic writings: (1) voluntarists have not yet evaluated the renewed interest in the impersonal notions of determinism as set forth by the neoclassical materialists; (2) voluntarists do not place materialistic ecological orientations within a value system; and (3) voluntarists fail to note the social limits to human volition even while recognizing the exertion of purposeful action through social conceptualizations.

In an effort to offer a systematic orientation to overcome the shortcomings within the framework of voluntarism versus materialism, we argue in Chapter Three for the merits of a specific social action theory for the study of human ecology. According to the social action theory contained in this study, man locates over space for the attainment of a goal through the selection, with consideration given to social conditions, of a norm from the norms that constitute the means. In performing in this manner, man perceives relevant cognitive data. But because the goal, means, social conditions, and cognitive data require specificity for social action to take place, actors must rely upon value systems.

The social action theory to human ecology, as developed here, deals not only with the element of volition in juxtaposition to the materialistic perspective but also, unlike current voluntarists and materialists, with specific social factors that inhibit the exercise of volition. The extent to which choice can be exserted from the perspective of our theory is affected by two conceptualizations: (1) the nature of a social goal and (2) the presence of social conditions. The

219

former is an inherent restriction to complete control within social action; the latter is a component of social action created and sustained within a social system and, therefore, susceptible to violation by the human agent.

The presence of a goal is not a matter of choice; a goal can only be assumed, that is, interpreted as a given. Individuals cannot, contrary to contemporary social action theorists, employ social values *to select from ends*. Whenever actors confront the possibility of choosing, they do so only in order to accomplish a future state of affairs, that is, an end. It is not within the limits of logic for writers to argue that individuals choose from ends to attain an end. As individuals face alternatives, such items serve as the means to accomplish an end. It is impossible to avoid the fact that as individuals perceive normative alternatives with the possibility of choice, they do so "in order to" accomplish an objective. Otherwise, as is sometimes the case, should individuals perform "as if" a goal—*qua* goal—can be chosen, social disorganization can be expected to occur, since there will be an inevitable absence of the orientation toward a future state of affairs so essential to semblances of continuity in social action.

It would appear, at first glance, that the absence of selection toward the goal would negate exertion of volition—that man apparently cannot control social events—and social action therefore becomes deterministic even within a conceptual frame of reference in juxtaposition to the materialistic framework. Even the empirical zoning data seem to give credulity to conceptual determinism not only because the goal in Austin's zoning process is contained in the Zoning Ordinance but also because the means prevails within the Zoning Ordinance in the form of zoning classifications.

But the absence of volition with respect to the existence of both the end and the means does not completely account for all the factors inhibiting full expression of social action. For in addition, zoning data show the presence of social conditions—that is, norms for the attainment of an end that exclude the presence of alternative considerations. Social conditions are, by definition, designed to restrict hu-

220

man behavior within certain limits so that the given goal might be accomplished. *Conditions do not necessarily prevent the accomplishment of a goal.* In Austin's zoning process we found that social conditions—for example, legal strictures eliminating such considerations as spot zoning and zoning classifications that would restrict the location of religious buildings; and the Planning Commission's own standards for passing upon the "C-1" and "C-2" zoning applications— were established so as to increase the probability that the social welfare objective would be accomplished within certain bounds. Thus, social conditions exclude courses of action that are considered undesirable for the accomplishment of a given end. It is this aspect of social reality that creates the individual-collective dilemma presented in this study as a social value orientation in the zoning process. Conformity takes place by actors considering social conditions appropriate through the use of value systems; nonconformity indicates an expression of self-volition to account for the discord between private desires and collective requirements in the form of social conditions.[2] The failure for social behavior to comply to social conditions establishes a social control situation.[3]

So it is that social conditions represent an effort to inhibit expression of full volition in the human group. But unlike the conception of an end, social conditions are not inherently restrictive of choice within our social action scheme; instead, they are social data within a society that set forth a range of permissiveness.

Thus, the constructs of an end, means, and social condition, as well as materialistic determinism, furnish no analytical allowance for volition. Nor can we turn to cognitive data for locating the place of choice. For this latter construct simply refers to conceptualized criteria defining social and/or physical objects and their properties. Where, then, does volition preside in our specific social action theory? How can individuals exert expression in the form of permissiveness rather than submissiveness within the cultural realm of data?

The concept of social values is required to establish permissiveness within the social action theory. For it is through the employment

221

of values that choice can be exercised as individuals engage in social action. Only by relating social values to the end, means, social conditions, and cognitive data does it become possible to comprehend a possibility of human volition that (1) counters the arguments of positivistic-materialistic determinists and (2) can be exercised irrespective of the fact that man cannot select the goal to which he orients his behavior.

1. Values are relevant for volition with respect to the end only to the extent that an end lacks concreteness. As the end becomes vague and ill-defined, then tolerance is maximized; the range of permissiveness narrows as an end is made definite in what it contains. Individuals, when confronted with an amorphous goal, must employ social values to give specificity to the goal. In this manner, they may compete in terms of the value systems that might be utilized to give specificity to a vaguely stated goal. Such was certainly the case in Austin's zoning process wherein the goal of public welfare lacked conciseness. The decision-makers, therefore, employed a variety of social value orientations to give concreteness to the given end and engaged in competition because they possessed dissimilar values while agreeing upon the goal. In this manner, permissiveness enters into social action with respect to an end that must be taken as a given. Contemporary social action theorists ignore the sociological significance of what is equivalent to an amorphous goal—namely, so-called "ultimate ends." The social action theory presented in this study reveals a sociological justification for the presence of "ultimate ends," namely: social tolerance is inversely proportionate to clarity of the end. As an objective becomes more concrete in its very pronouncement, permissiveness fades; an indefinite goal presents the necessity for interpretation by individuals thereby to allow for the possibility of volition within the cultural order of data.

2. Social values prevail if choice is to be exercised by actors in selecting from the means. Individuals must at least implicitly rely upon values to select a norm from the alternative ones that compose the means. Thus, volition again exists in social action with respect to

222

the means. In Austin's zoning process we found that the decision-makers apparently chose a specific zoning classification from alternatives—that is, means—in terms of three dominant social value orientations: the economic-protective; the collective-individual; and the present-future.

3. In the selection from the means, individuals face social conditions; the range of alternatives that constitute the means will be affected by social conditions. As social conditions become more concise in their pronouncements, the range of volition narrows. But, as discussed in presenting Hypothesis II, the mere presence of normative conditions does not infer that human behavior automatically conforms to the content of social conditions.[4] Individuals abide in accordance with social conditions depending upon their values. The decision-makers in Austin's zoning process failed, in some cases, to perform by the requirements of social conditions. Certain ones, for example, approved zoning applications with the full knowledge that spot zoning would result, although forbidden to do so by the stipulations of legal normative conditions. Conformity or nonconformity occurred as social conditions were in accord with the respective social values of each decision-maker. Thus, actors express permissiveness when confronting social conditions by utilizing value systems to give specificity to social conditions in terms of conformity or nonconformity.

4. Finally, value systems must be utilized to give interpretative significance to cognitive data. The mere perception of data does not account for all aspects of social action; it is merely one ingredient—a matter of cognition. Further significance must be given for cognitive data to become integrated into social action. Through implementation of values, individuals give specificity to cognitive data. And we found this to have taken place in our case study: Austin's decision-makers attached worth to cognitive data through their respective social value orientations.

The crucial factor for volition, then, is the relationship between social values with the other elements that compose our social action

223

scheme. Voluntarists do not appreciate the full significance of this relationship; materialists and positivists deny the possibility altogether by rejecting the conception of social values.

These generalizations concerning the expression of volition are of particular importance not only to scholars but also to planners, city officials, and laymen. Such individuals must become aware that they engage in activities wherein their problems do not stem from the absence of a goal but from the necessity to clarify the social values involved in their efforts and to resolve the value competition that takes place. Specifically, the discords center upon the value orientations discussed in Chapters Five and Six: economic versus protective values; collective versus individual values; and present-time versus future-time values. Here, then, are some of the most prominent dilemmas facing those interested in directing the course of land use within our cities. We must come to realize that our problem is not one of selecting an objective, but rather that there is the necessity to resolve the value disputes that occur concerning the regulation of land use. It is not unreasonable to state that there is a general consensus that land use must be directed to advance the public welfare objective through zoning; disagreement centers upon the social values to be employed in order that our cities of tomorrow may continue as a way of life.

Yet, zoning itself as it is implemented by the decision-makers in the city of Austin is merely a negative control in the regulation of land use. While zoning does affect the patterning of land use, as the empirical data collected for this study reveal, this is only incidental in Austin's zoning process. It is precisely because Austin's decision-makers perform in an efficient manner that zoning cannot be the positive force that certain writers would prefer.[5] The indecisiveness of zoning can be traced directly to the economic value orientation that dominates Austin's zoning process. According to the economic notion, zoning classifications must reflect certain economic conditions in terms of the profit motive, which, as we have seen, contains effici-

224

ency as a primary consideration. Zoning can never become an *independent determining factor* for controlling land use whenever the economic orientation dominates owing to the randomness of ends and the remote time conception intrinsic within the economic contention.

In conclusion, this presentation not only argues for a cultural approach to the study of ecological phenomena; it also offers what appear to be the dominant features of a zoning process. We have seen not only the fallacies contained in certain ecological theories in light of the zoning data collected for this study, and have therefore constructed an alternative ecological perspective, but also that the social value orientations of the decision-makers revealed the very essence of zoning activities. To be sure, social values other than those espoused by the decision-makers and participants in the zoning process in Austin, Texas, may prove of greater importance in the zoning activities performed in other cities. Additional ecological studies must be undertaken in this respect. Nonetheless, the data taken from the zoning process in Austin, Texas, as related to contemporary ecological theories indicate that ecologists who advocate a physical or biological frame of reference fail to achieve a sociological understanding of ecological phenomena. And in light of our empirical findings, this writer now offers what is intended to be a systematic approach to the study of ecological phenomena from a specific social action theory within the framework of the cultural perspective.

NOTES

Chapter One

1. The most noteworthy exception is Houston, Texas, which has no zoning ordinance.

2. See, for example, Herbert Blumer, "What Is Wrong with Social Theory?" *American Sociological Review,* Vol. 19 (February, 1954), pp. 3–10; Daniel Katz, "Field Studies," in Leon Festinger and Daniel Katz (eds.), *Research Methods in the Behavioral Science* (New York: Holt, Rinehart & Winston, 1953), p. 74; Robert K. Merton, *Social Theory and Social Structure* (rev. ed.; New York: The Free Press, 1957), p. 12; William Foote Whyte, *Street-Corner Society* (Chicago: University of Chicago Press, 1955), p. 280.

3. The terms "ecology" and "human ecology" will be used interchangeably in this study.

4. A formal definition of these terms and the relationships between them are discussed in Chapter Three.

Chapter Two

1. The choice of the term "materialism" is a suggestion of Gideon Sjoberg, who in private conversations with me stressed the materialistic inclinations in ecological thought.

2. Robert E. Park, *Human Communities: The City and Human Ecology* (New York: The Free Press, 1952), pp. 14 and 148.

3. R. D. McKenzie, "The Field and Problems of Demography, Human Geography, and Human Ecology," in L. L. Bernard (ed.), *The Fields and Methods of Sociology* (New York: Farrar and Rinehart, 1934), pp. 58–59.

4. C. A. Dawson, "The Sources and Methods of Human Ecology," in Bernard, *op. cit.*, p. 286.

5. J. W. Bews, *Human Ecology* (London: Oxford University Press, 1935), pp. 14 and 284.

6. James A. Quinn, *Human Ecology* (Englewood Cliffs, N.J.: Prentice-Hall, Inc., 1950), p. 3.

7. Ernest W. Burgess, "Can Neighborhood Work Have a Scientific Basis?" in Robert E. Park, Ernest W. Burgess, and Roderick D. McKenzie (eds.), *The City* (Chicago: University of Chicago Press, 1925), p. 64.

8. C. A. Dawson and Warner E. Gettys, *An Introduction to Sociology* (New York: Ronald Press, 1929), p. 246. Emphasis supplied.

9. R. D. McKenzie, "The Ecological Approach to the Study of the Human Community," in Park, Burgess, and McKenzie, *op. cit.*, p. 64.

10. Park, *op. cit.*, p. 147.

11. *Ibid.*, pp. 147–148.

12. *Ibid.*, pp. 151–152.

13. Robert Murray Haig, "Towards an Understanding of the Metropolis," *Quarterly Journal of Economics*, Vol. 40 (May, 1926), pp. 420–424.

14. Park, *op. cit.*, p. 154.

15. *Ibid.*

16. McKenzie, *op. cit.*, p. 75.

17. Park, *op. cit.*, p. 161.

18. *Ibid.*, p. 156.

19. *Ibid.*, p. 158.

20. *Ibid.*, p. 156. Emphasis supplied.

21. McKenzie, *op. cit.*, p. 65.

22. A. B. Hollingshead, "Human Ecology and Human Society," *Ecological Monographs*, Vol. 10 (July, 1940), p. 360

23. Robert E. L. Faris, "Ecological Factors in Human Behavior," in *Personality and the Behavior Disorder* (New York: Ronald Press, 1944), p. 736. Emphasis supplied.

24. See Donald J. Bogue, "Needed Urban Research," in Donald J. Bogue (ed.), *Needed Urban and Metropolitan Research* (Oxford: Scripps Foundation Studies in Population Distribution, No. 7, 1953), pp. 38 ff.; and Jesse Walter Dees, *Urban Sociology and the Emerging Atomic Megalopolis* (Ann Arbor: Ann Arbor Publishers, 1950), p. 327.

25. Amos Hawley, *Human Ecology* (New York: Ronald Press Co., 1950), pp. 67 and 179.

26. Otis Dudley Duncan and Leo F. Schnore, "Cultural, Behavioral, and Ecological Perspectives in the Study of Social Organization," *American Journal of Sociology*, Vol. 65 (September, 1955), pp. 135–136. See also Otis Dudley Duncan, "Human Ecology and Population Studies," in Philip M. Hauser and Otis Dudley Duncan (eds.), *The Study of Population* (Chicago: University of Chicago Press, 1959), p. 683.

27. Jack P. Gibbs and Walter T. Martin, "Toward a Theoretical System of Human Ecology," *Pacific Sociological Review*, Vol. 2 (Spring, 1959), p. 33.

28. For purposes of our summary and analysis of the writings by the neoclassical materialists, we shall equate "sustenance activities" and "social organization."

29. Duncan, *op. cit.*, p. 709.

30. *Ibid.*, p. 683.

31. Duncan and Schnore, *op. cit.*, pp. 132–149.

32. Gibbs and Martin, *op. cit.*, pp. 29–36.

33. *Ibid.*, p. 30.

34. *Ibid.*, p. 33.

35. Jack P. Gibbs and Walter T. Martin, "Urbanization and Natural Resourses: A Study in Organizational Ecology," *American Sociological Review,* Vol. 23 (June, 1958), p. 276. Emphasis supplied.

36. Hawley, *op. cit.,* p. 178.

37. *Ibid.,* p. 180.

38. *Ibid.,* pp. 66–67. Emphasis supplied.

39. *Ibid.,* p. 264. Emphasis supplied.

40. *Ibid.,* p. 264.

41. Ernest M. Fisher and Robert M. Fisher, *Urban Real Estate* (New York: Holt, Rinehart & Winston, 1954), pp. 325–326.

42. Duncan, *op. cit.,* p. 682.

43. Hawley, *Human Ecology, op. cit.,* p. v.

44. Duncan, *op. cit.,* p. 683.

45. Duncan and Schnore, *op. cit.,* p. 138.

46. Hawley, *Human Ecology, op. cit.,* p. 73. Emphasis supplied.

47. Gibbs and Martin, "Toward a Theoretical System of Human Ecology," *op. cit.,* p. 35.

48. Duncan, *op. cit.,* pp. 682–683.

49. *Ibid.,* pp. 683–684.

50. It is this writer's interpretation that the neoclassical materialist is inclined to treat items of technology—such as automobiles, highways, buildings, machinery—as actual physical substances.

51. Duncan, *op. cit.,* p. 683.

52. Duncan and Schnore, *op. cit.,* p. 137. Emphasis supplied.

53. Pitirim A. Sorokin, *Sociocultural Causality, Space, Time* (Durham: Duke University Press, 1943), p. 61.

54. Stuart Chase, *The Proper Study of Mankind* (New York: Harper, 1948), p. 21.

55. Sorokin, *op. cit.,* p. 74.

56. Hawley, *Human Ecology, op. cit.,* p. 179. Emphasis supplied.

57. Duncan and Schnore, *op. cit.,* p. 144. Emphasis supplied.

229

58.   Sorokin, *op. cit.*, pp. 53–54. Emphasis supplied.

59.   Otis Dudley Duncan, "From Social System to Ecosystem," *Sociological Inquiry*, XXXI (Spring, 1961), pp. 140–149.

60.   Leo F. Schnore, "Social Problems in the Underdeveloped Areas: An Ecological View," *Social Problems*, VIII (Winter, 1961), pp. 182–201.

61.   *Ibid.*, p. 191. Emphasis in the original.

62.   Ecological studies by other neoclassical writers also contain this fixation notion. See, for example, Gibbs and Martin, "Urbanization and Natural Resources: A Study in Organizational Ecology," *op. cit.*

Chapter Three

1.   Milla Aissa Alihan, *Social Ecology* (New York: Columbia University Press, 1938).

2.   Warner E. Gettys, "Human Ecology and Social Theory," *Social Forces*, Vol. 18 (May, 1940), pp. 469–476.

3.   Walter Firey, *Land Use in Central Boston* (Cambridge: Harvard University Press, 1947).

4.   *Ibid.*, p. 3.

5.   *Ibid.*, p. 34.

6.   A. B. Hollingshead, "A Re-Examination of Ecological Theory," *Sociology and Social Research*, Vol. 31 (January–February, 1947), pp. 194–204. Since the publication of this article stating his voluntaristic orientation to the study of ecology, Hollingshead has altered his voluntaristic orientation and now apparently argues for a merger of both materialism and voluntarism in examining ecological data. See A. B. Hollingshead, "Community Research: Development and Present Conditions," *American Sociological Review*, Vol. 13 (April, 1948), pp. 136–146.

7.   William H. Form, "The Place of Social Structure in the Determination of Land Use: Some Implications for a Theory of Urban Ecology," *Social Forces*, Vol. 32 (May, 1954), pp. 317–323.

8.   Christen Jonassen, "Cultural Variables in the Ecology of an Ethnic Group," *American Sociological Review*, Vol. 19 (February, 1954), p. 41.

9. Hiram J. Friedsam, "The Time Factor in Social Ecology," unpublished M.A. Thesis (Austin: University of Texas, 1940), p. 55.

10. Julian H. Steward, *A Theory of Culture Change* (Urbana: University of Illinois Press, 1955), p. 32. Emphasis supplied.

11. *Ibid.*, p. 40. Emphasis supplied.

12. Sidney Willhelm and Gideon Sjoberg, "Economic vs. Protective Values in Urban Land Use Change," *American Journal of Economics and Sociology*, Vol. 19 (January, 1960), pp. 151–160. See also Gideon Sjoberg, *The Preindustrial City* (New York: The Free Press, 1960), Chap. IV.

13. Amos Hawley, *Human Ecology* (New York: Ronald Press, 1950), p. 35. See also Nels Anderson and Eduard C. Lindeman, *Urban Sociology* (New York: Alfred A. Knopf, 1928), p. 36.

14. Firey, *op. cit.*, p. 324.

15. Leslie A. White, *The Science of Culture* (New York: Farrar, Straus, 1949), pp. 22–39; Kingsley Davis, *Human Society* (New York: Macmillan, 1950), p. 34; Karl Mannheim, *Essays on the Sociology of Culture* (London: Routledge & Kegan Paul, Ltd., 1956), pp. 64 ff.

16. See Florian Znaniecki, *The Cultural Sciences* (Urbana: University of Illinois Press, 1952).

17. "Meaning is always the same to the person who is indicating the meaning as it is to the person who responds to it; otherwise it is not [social] meaning; it must have a universality to the meaningful." Stanley Taylor, *Conceptions of Institutions and the Theory of Knowledge* (New York: Bookman Associates, 1956), p. 111.

18. C. Daryll Forde, *Habitat, Economy and Society* (London: Methuen, 1949), p. 463.

19. *Ibid.*, p. 464. Emphasis supplied.

20. *Ibid.* Emphasis supplied.

21. See, for example, James H. S. Bossard, "Ecological Areas and Marriage Rates," *American Journal of Sociology*, Vol. 44 (July, 1938), pp. 70–85; John A. Clausen and Melvin L. Kohn, "The Ecological Approach in Social Psychiatry," *American Journal of Sociology*, Vol. 60 (September, 1954), pp. 140–149; Robert E. L. Faris and H. Warren Dunham, *Mental Disorders in Urban Areas* (Chicago: University of Chicago Press, 1939); Clifford R. Shaw, *Delinquency Areas* (Chicago: University of Chicago Press, 1929); Erle F. Young and Elsa Longmoor, "Ecological

Interrelationships of Juvenile Delinquency, Dependency and Population Mobility: A Cartographic Analysis of Data from Long Beach, California," *American Journal of Sociology*, Vol. 41 (March, 1936), pp. 598–610.

22. "The system of concepts which supports the life of a society is found only in the minds of the persons who make up that society. However, these ideas as pointed out above, are not subjective impressions. They are concepts, universals, objective ideas which like the language and logic have an independence of any single mind." Taylor, *op. cit.*, p. 105.

23. The following materialistic ecologists, among others, make this charge against the voluntaristic perspective: Hawley, *op. cit.*, p. 179; Jack P. Gibbs and Walter T. Martin, "Toward a Theoretical System of Human Ecology," *Pacific Sociological Review*, Vol. 2 (Spring, 1959), p. 33; and Leo F. Schnore and Otis Dudley Duncan, "Short Version of Paper Read at the 1958 Meetings of the American Sociological Society" (Seattle, Wash.), unpublished manuscript.

24. "The disjunct, isolated, miscellaneous impressions of individuals through comparison cease to be subjectivities, and at length a system is formed in which objectivity arises. Insofar as impressions cannot be compared or communicated they cannot be knowledge. Such impressions are without meaning, and hence, valueless for a society." Taylor, *op. cit.*, p. 104.

25. "It should be kept in mind also that the conceptual system has its numerous concealed categories—that is, concepts not explicitly present in the consciousness of a given individual, but nevertheless, carried by the society." *Ibid.*, p. 107.

26. White, *op. cit.*, p. 78.

27. Znaniecki, *op. cit.*, pp. 132 and 138.

28. Firey, *op. cit.*, p. 324.

29. Malcolm M. Willey, "The Validity of the Culture Concept," *American Journal of Sociology*, Vol. 35 (September, 1929), p. 205.

30. See Talcott Parsons, *The Structure of Social Action* (New York: The Free Press, 1949), pp. 44 ff and 77 ff; and Talcott Parsons and Edward A. Shils, "Values, Motives, and Systems of Action," in *Toward a General Theory of Action* (Cambridge: Harvard University Press, 1954), pp. 53 ff. However, it must be noted that the specific social action theory presented in this study departs from Parsons' social action approach by not accepting Parsons' definition of certain terms. For purposes

232

of this study, Parsons' viewpoint has been altered somewhat and the meanings of his terms—particularly "means" and "conditions"—modified so as to place the social action framework entirely within the cultural perspective.

31. Parsons, *The Structure of Social Action, op. cit.,* p. 44. The word "anticipated" is used in contradistinction to a "resulting" state of affairs. See Kingsley Davis, *Human Society* (New York: Macmillan, 1950), p. 124.

32. The terms "nondesirable" and "nonappropriate" refer to indifference on the part of actors. This definition is based on the one offered by Gideon Sjoberg and Leonard D. Cain, "Negative Values and Social Action," *Alpha Kappa Deltan,* Vol. 29 (Winter, 1959), p. 63.

33. The means *allows* actors to select the normative course of action to be followed in order to attain a given goal; a social condition *prescribes* a normative course for action so as to accomplish a given goal and therefore allows actors only the possibility *to conform or not to conform* with the requirements it contains. The means establishes a legitimate normative choice situation for actors; a social condition demands that actors abide by a certain normative course of action for the attainment of a given end to create thereby the situation for social control when conformity to a social condition is not forthcoming on the part of the individual.

34. Sorokin, *op. cit.;* Parsons, *op. cit.;* Émile Durkheim, *The Elementary Forms of the Religious Life,* translated by Joseph Ward Swain (New York: The Free Press, 1954); Firey, *op. cit.;* Znaniecki, *op. cit.;* and Taylor, *op. cit.*

35. Sorokin, *op. cit.,* p. 128.

36. Florian Znaniecki, *The Method of Sociology* (New York: Rinehart, 1934).

37. *Supra,* p. 36.

38. Sorokin, *op. cit.,* p. 148.

39. *Ibid.,* p. 187.

40. Mircea Eliade, *The Sacred and the Profane,* translated by Willard R. Trask (New York: Harcourt, Brace, 1959), p. 22.

41. Durkheim, *op. cit.,* p. 11.

42. Erich W. Zimmermann, *World Resources and Industries* (rev. ed.; New York: Harper, 1951), Chap. 1.

43. Eliade, *op. cit.*, p. 23.

44. Sorokin and Merton, "Social Time," *American Journal of Sociology,* Vol. 42 (March, 1937), p. 619.

45. Charles P. Loomis claims, contrary to the viewpoint expressed here, that time is a physical condition to which social action must conform. See Charles P. Loomis, *Social Systems: Essays on Their Persistence and Change* (New York: Van Nostrand, 1960), p. 38.

46. Eliade, *op. cit.*, p. 68.

47. Walter Firey, "Sentiment and Symbolism as Ecological Variables," *American Sociological Review,* Vol. 10 (April, 1945), pp. 140 ff.

48. Durkheim, *op. cit.;* pp. 230–231.

49. R. D. McKenzie, "The Scope of Human Ecology," in Ernest W. Burgess (ed.), *The Urban Community* (Chicago: University of Chicago Press, 1926), p. 170.

50. Hawley, *op. cit.*, p. 237.

51. Amos Hawley, "The Approach of Human Ecology to Urban Areal Research," *Scientific Monthly,* Vol. 73 (July, 1951), p. 48.

52. Hawley, *Human Ecology,* p. 235. Emphasis supplied.

53. Firey, "Sentiment and Symbolism as Ecological Variables," *op. cit.*, p. 140.

54. Firey, *Land Use in Central Boston, op. cit.*, p. 324.

55. John L. Landgraf, *Land-Use in the Ramah Area of New Mexico* (Cambridge: The Museum, 1954), p. 25.

56. Hawley, *Human Ecology, op. cit.*, p. 314.

57. *Ibid.*, p. 288.

58. Sorokin, *op. cit.*

59. Jonassen, *op. cit.*

Chapter Four

1. Zoning Ordinance of the City of Austin, Texas, April, 1931, Section 1, p. 3.

2. See Chapter Three for a discussion of the means-end approach as developed for use in this study.

3. Zoning Ordinance of the City of Austin, Texas, November, 1954.

4. *Ibid.*, p. 41.

5. For a discussion of the role of external considerations from a ecological perspective, see Gideon Sjoberg, "Urban Community Theory and Research: A Partial Evaluation," *American Journal of Economics and Sociology,* Vol. 14 (January, 1955), pp. 199–206.

6. Zoning applications requesting a "Special Permit" zoning classification and so-called "areal zoning" were omitted from consideration in this survey.

Chapter Five

1. Talcott Parsons, *The Structure of Social Action* (New York: The Free Press, 1949), p. 251.

2. See Chapter Three for a discussion of these terms.

3. See, for example, Otis Dudley Duncan, "From Social System to Ecosystem," *Sociological Inquiry,* Vol. XXXI (Spring, 1961), pp. 140–149.

4. Clyde Kluckhohn and others, "Values and Value-Orientations in the Theory of Action," in Talcott Parsons and Edward A. Shils, *Toward a General Theory of Action* (Cambridge: Harvard University Press, 1954), p. 395.

5. See also Kingsley Davis, *Human Society* (New York: Macmillan, 1950), p. 124, who writes: ". . . ends are *chosen*. They are chosen with reference to *values* in the first place." And Charles P. Loomis implies selection from ends: "Norms influence the range of goal choices. . . ." See Charles P. Loomis, *Social Systems: Essays on Their Persistence and Change* (New York: Van Nostrand, 1960), p. 16.

Chapter Six

1. Clyde Kluckhohn and others, "Values and Value-Orientations in the Theory of Action," in Talcott Parsons and Edward A. Shils (eds.),

Toward a General Theory of Action (Cambridge: Harvard University Press, 1954), pp. 409–412.

2. Amos Hawley, *Human Ecology* (New York: Ronald Press, 1950), p. 66.

3. Otis Dudley Duncan and Leo F. Schnore, "Cultural, Behavioral, and Ecological Perspectives in the Study of Social Organization," *American Journal of Sociology,* Vol. 65 (September, 1959), p. 142.

4. Talcott Parsons, *The Structure of Social Action* (New York: The Free Press, 1949), p. 64.

5. Talcott Parsons, *The Social System* (New York: The Free Press, 1951), pp. 60–61.

6. Christen Jonassen, "Cultural Variables in the Ecology of an Ethnic Group," *American Sociological Review,* Vol. 19 (February, 1954), p. 10.

7. Walter Firey, *Land Use in Central Boston* (Cambridge: Harvard University Press, 1947), pp. 17 ff.

8. Parsons, *The Structure of Social Action, op. cit.,* p. 64.

9. *Ibid.,* p. 64.

10. *Ibid.*

11. Kenneth J. Arrow, *Social Choice and Individual Values* (New York: John Wiley, 1951).

12. *Ibid.,* pp. 29–31.

13. The reader is referred to p. 95 in this chapter to ascertain the meaning of the initials used here.

14. The reader is referred to Chapter Three, where a general discussion of sacred and secular time conceptions appears.

15. ". . . concepts expressing themselves in economic activity might be sufficiently ultimate in some societies to be viewed as sacred." Stanley Taylor, *Conceptions of Institutions and the Theory of Knowledge* (New York: Bookman Associates, 1956), p. 109.

16. The notion of the "self-fulfilling prophecy" is developed in Robert K. Merton, *Social Theory and Social Structure* (rev. and enl. ed.; New York: The Free Press, 1957), pp. 422–423.

17. Eric Hoffer, *The True Believer* (New York: Harper, 1951) pp. 57 ff.

18. Émile Durkheim, *The Elementary Forms of the Religious Life,* translated by Joseph Ward Swain (New York: The Free Press, 1954), pp. 230–231.

19. For the notion of "unfalsified" rather than "verified" hypotheses, see Karl R. Popper, *The Logic of Scientific Discovery* (New York: Basic Books, 1959).

Chapter Seven

1. Walter Firey, *Land Use in Central Boston* (Cambridge: Harvard University Press, 1947), p. 34.

2. *Ibid.,* p. 90.

3. A. B. Hollingshead, "A Re-Examination of Ecological Theory," *Sociology and Social Research,* Vol. 31 (January–February, 1947), p. 198.

4. William H. Form, "The Place of Social Structure in the Determination of Land Use: Some Implications for a Theory of Urban Ecology," *Social Forces,* Vol. 32 (May, 1954), pp. 317–323.

5. Hollingshead, *op. cit.,* p. 197.

6. Sidney Willhelm and Gideon Sjoberg, "Economic vs. Protective Values in Urban Land Use Change," *American Journal of Economics and Sociology,* Vol. 19 (January, 1960), pp. 151–160. The theoretical perspective developed in this study is not contained in this article but is instead my own.

7. Otis Dudley Duncan and Leo F. Schnore, "Cultural, Behavioral, and Ecological Perspectives in the Study of Social Organization," *American Journal of Sociology,* Vol. 65 (September, 1959), p. 145.

8. Otis Dudley Duncan, "Human Ecology and Population Studies," in Philip M. Hauser and Otis Dudley Duncan (eds.), *The Study of Population* (Chicago: University of Chicago Press, 1959), pp. 683–684.

9. Ernest W. Burgess, "The Ernest W. Burgess Appraisal," in Howard W. Odum, *American Sociology* (New York: Longmans, Green, 1951), p. 353. Emphasis supplied.

10. Robert E. L. Faris, "Ecological Factors in Human Behavior," in J. McVicker Hunt (ed.), *Personality and the Behavior Disorder* (New York: Ronald Press, 1944), p. 736. Emphasis supplied.

237

11. A. B. Hollingshead, "Human Ecology and Human Society," *Ecological Monographs,* Vol. 10 (July, 1940), p. 360. Emphasis supplied.

12. Carl A. Dawson and Warner E. Gettys, *An Introduction to Sociology* (New York: Ronald Press, 1929), p. 220.

13. Amos Hawley, *Human Ecology* (New York: Ronald Press, 1950), p. 179. Emphasis supplied.

14. Jack P. Gibbs and Walter T. Martin, "Toward a Theoretical System of Human Ecology," *Pacific Sociological Review,* Vol. 2 (Spring, 1959), p. 33.

15. Duncan and Schnore, *op. cit.,* p. 137. Emphasis supplied.

16. George Kingsley Zipf, *Human Behavior and the Principle of Least Effort* (Reading, Mass.: Addison-Wesley, 1949), p. 350.

17. Robert E. Park, "The City: Suggestions for the Investigation of Human Behavior in the Urban Environment," in *The City* (Chicago: University of Chicago Press, 1925), p. 12.

18. Ernest W. Burgess, "The Growth of the City: An Introduction to a Research Project," in *The City, op. cit.,* p. 54. Emphasis supplied.

19. Faris, *op. cit.,* p. 737. Emphasis supplied.

20. Hawley, *op. cit.,* p. 178.

21. *Ibid.,* p. 215.

22. Richard U. Ratcliff, "Efficiency and the Location of Urban Activities," in Robert Moore Fisher (ed.), *The Metropolis in Modern Life* (New York: Doubleday, 1955), p. 128. Emphasis supplied.

23. Richard U. Ratcliff, *Real Estate Analysis* (New York: McGraw-Hill, 1961), p. 36.

24. R. D. McKenzie, *The Metropolitan Community* (New York: McGraw-Hill, 1933), p. 245.

25. Hawley, *op. cit.,* p. 385.

26. *Ibid.,* pp. 78–79.

27. Duncan and Schnore, *op. cit.,* p. 144.

28. Duncan, *op. cit.,* p. 683.

29. Park, *op. cit.,* pp. 5–6. Emphasis supplied.

238

30. R. D. McKenzie, "The Ecological Approach to the Study of the Human Community," in *The City, op. cit.,* footnote 2, p. 63. Emphasis supplied.

31. For a presentation of the time orientation espoused by the economically oriented decision-makers, see Chapter Six.

32. Willhelm and Sjoberg, *op. cit.*

33. See, for example, Duncan, *op. cit.,* pp. 678–716; Otis Dudley Duncan, "Population Distribution and Community Structure," *Cold Spring Harbor Symposia on Quantitative Biology,* Vol. 22 (1957), pp. 357–371; Jack P. Gibbs and Walter T. Martin, "Urbanization and Natural Resources: A Study in Organizational Ecology," *American Sociological Review,* Vol. 23 (June, 1958), pp. 266–277; and Eshref Shevky and Marilyn Williams, *The Social Areas of Los Angeles* (Berkeley and Los Angeles: University of California Press, 1949).

34. Émile Durkheim, *The Elementary Forms of the Religious Life,* translated by Joseph Ward Swain (New York: Macmillan, 1915), p. 419.

35. For example, Ernest W. Burgess maintains that ecologists should abstract "impersonal" data from "city life": "To be methodologically sound, urban research [as the study of impersonal competition] should abstract the ecological from the total phenomena of city life and deal with it separately." See Ernest W. Burgess, "The Ecology and Social Psychology of the City," in Donald J. Bogue (ed.), *Needed Urban and Metropolitan Research* (Oxford: Scripps Foundation Studies in Population Distribution, No. 7, 1953), p. 80. Our intention in this chapter, however, is not to make the materialists' orientation "explicit"; instead, this writer maintains that no materialistic ecological orientation can be "abstracted" as an "impersonal" framework since none exists except as a social value approach.

36. For a discussion of the methodological shortcomings in ecological materialism, see Chapter Two, pp. 22 ff.

37. Firey, *op. cit.,* p. 34.

Chapter Eight

1. A resurgence of materialistic determinism is reflected in the position argued by the geographer, Griffith Taylor: ". . . many scientists are coming to the conclusion that it is *the variation in the environment* which is the most potent factor of all in influencing human evolution, whether

biological or social." See Griffith Taylor, *Environment, Race and Migration* (Chicago: University of Chicago Press, 1946), p. 4.

2. This statement is assuming that actors have an awareness of social conditions. Nonconformity, from the perspective of a social group, can also occur because individuals may be unaware of normative requirements.

3. An analysis of social control from the social action theory offered in this study does not require special analytical constructs. See George Homans, *The Human Group* (New York: Harcourt, Brace, 1950), pp. 288 ff., for a justification of this contention.

4. See Chapter Five.

5. For example, Louis Justement, *New Cities for Old* (New York: McGraw-Hill, 1946), p. 29.

INDEX

241

DATE DUE

DEC 17 '70	MAR 12, '81		
JAN 28 '71			
FEB 19 '71			
NOV 21 '73			
FEB 16 '75			
OCT 23 '75			
NOV 9 '75			
MAY 13 '80			
APR 23 '80			
FEB 10 '81			
JAN 25 '81			
FEB 27 '81			
GAYLORD			PRINTED IN U.S.A.